THE
PAGAN
BOOK
OF THE
DEAD

Praise for Claude Lecouteux

"Lecouteux is a genius. I have been gratefully following his research—which provides information I have never found in other locations—for years."

MAJA D'AOUST, WHITE WITCH OF L.A.,
ASTROLOGER, COUNSELOR, AND
AUTHOR OF *FAMILIARS IN WITCHCRAFT*
AND *THE OCCULT I CHING*

"There is no other author alive who so thoroughly examines the subject as Claude Lecouteux."

REBECCA ELSON, PUBLISHER/WRITER OF
THE MAGICAL BUFFET WEBSITE

"Claude Lecouteux is the most versatile and wide-ranging of the scholars of the medieval imagination, and any book of his is a treat."

RONALD HUTTON, PROFESSOR OF HISTORY AT THE
UNIVERSITY OF BRISTOL, ENGLAND, AND
AUTHOR OF *WITCHES, DRUIDS AND KING ARTHUR*

THE
PAGAN
BOOK
OF THE
DEAD

Ancestral Visions
of the Afterlife and
Other Worlds

CLAUDE LECOUTEUX

Translated by Jon E. Graham

Inner Traditions
Rochester, Vermont

Inner Traditions
One Park Street
Rochester, Vermont 05767
www.InnerTraditions.com

Text stock is SFI certified

Originally published in French under the title *La mort, l'au-delà, et les autres mondes* by Éditions Imago, 7 rue Suger, 75006, Paris
First U.S. edition published in 2020 by Inner Traditions

Cataloging-in-Publication Data for this title is available from the Library of Congress

ISBN 978-1-64411-047-8 (print)
ISBN 978-1-64411-048-5 (ebook)

Printed and bound in the United States by Lake Book Manufacturing, Inc. The text stock is SFI certified. The Sustainable Forestry Initiative® program promotes sustainable forest management.

10 9 8 7 6 5 4 3 2 1

Text design and layout by Debbie Glogover
This book was typeset in Garamond Premier Pro with Civane and Gill Sans MT Pro used as display fonts.

CONTENTS

"In the Midst of Life We Are in Death"

The cruel goddess Death is one of the major preoccupations of the living, even if we scarcely enjoy talking about her. She is omnipresent, and each and every one of us will have to pay the toll that nature demands of us, sooner or later. In French literary works, death has been given various different names such as Trépas, ("Demise"), Faucheuse ("Grim Reaper"), and Camarde ("The One with a Flat Nose").* Death has been depicted with a scythe, a bow, a spear, and a violin made from a single bone. Death is also portrayed as a skeleton digging its own grave, a hollow-eyed specter, or a hooded figure. Death is typically represented as female in the lands where romance languages are spoken and as male in the Germanic-speaking regions. Emmanuel Lévinas notes:

> Death is not of this world. It is always a scandal, and in this sense, always transcendent with respect to the world. . . . We can understand corruption, transformation, and dissolution. We can grasp that forms move on but that something survives. Death cuts through all that; it is inconceivable and resistant to thought, and yet it remains indisputable and undeniable.[1]

---

*[Because a human skull lacks a protruding nose. Literary names in English for death include the Grim Reaper, Azrael (the Angel of Death), the Pale Rider, and so forth. —Ed.]

1

The dictionary carries a plethora of verbs to denote the action of death: *depart, decease, disappear, expire, perish, pass away, succumb, die,* and even the informal phrase *to snuff it,* which is suggestive of the old myth of life being consumed like a candle. In the ancient Greek legend of Meleager, the Fates (Moirai) predicted that his destiny would be linked to that of an ember burning in the fireplace. If the ember was entirely consumed, the child would die. In chapter 11 of the Old Norse *Nornagests þáttr* (Tale of Norna-Gest), written in thirteenth-century Norway, one of the Norns presiding over the birth of the hero becomes angry and says: "Therefore, I shape it that he shall not live longer than that candle burns—the one lighted beside the boy!"[2]

In addition to the verbs, there are many expressions for describing death: "leave the stage," "draw one's last breath," "give up the ghost," and "cease to exist," as well as other more folksy idioms like "kick the bucket," "buy the farm," "push up daisies," "bite the dust," "feed the daffodils," "hand in one's dinner pail," "croak," "cash in one's chips," and so forth. Keeping in mind the role played by words as instruments of thought, it is easy to see the importance of death in all civilizations. Attempts to escape what has been growing inside of us since birth has led to the invention of the Fountain of Youth, which Alexander the Great went off in search of, and ambrosia, the nectar of the gods that allegedly confers immortality. The medieval legend of Virgil the Enchanter tells us that he attempted an experiment intended to rejuvenate him. He asked his disciple to dismember his body and salt the pieces, then place them in the bottom of a barrel, on top of which he would set a lamp in such a way that its oil would drip inside the barrel day and night. Virgil should have resurrected after nine days of this treatment, but an unforeseen circumstance aborted the rejuvenation process. The greedy Acheron, the great recruiter of shades, never relinquishes his prey and, as Rabelais uttered in his last words: "Bring down the curtain, the farce is played out."

In the Middle Ages it was thought possible to understand names theologically as exhibiting the truths of the faith. Medieval etymology is a discipline, which, by being uncompromisingly literal, seeks to rediscover the true meaning of a word and its original definition, because the name unveils the nature of the thing. It is a form of thought.³ Isidore of Seville (d. 636) analyzed the Latin word for death (*mors*) and saw it as derived from "bite" (*mors-*)* because "the first man introduced death into this world by biting into the apple of the tree of life."⁴ This folk etymology enjoyed considerable popularity, and traces of it can be found throughout the entire Middle Ages. In the fifteenth century, for example, a poem titled *Le Mors de la pomme* (The Bite of the Apple) is directly inspired by it:⁵

> *La mort suis, Dieu m'a ordonnee*
> *Pour ce qu'Adam la pomme mort*
> *Sentence divine est donnée*
> *Tous les humains morront de mort* (ll. 85–88)

> [Death ensues, as God has ordered
> Because Adam bit the apple
> Divine sentence has been passed down
> All humans die of death's bite]

However, in volume VIII (11, 51) of his *Etymologiae*, Isidore also tells us that "death" [*mort*] comes from "Mars" (*a Marte dicitur*). . . .

Mors certa, hora incerta—while death is certain, the hour in which it will arrive is not. Sudden death was the form most dreaded by Christians, as this meant there was no time for repentance or last rites, and the religious literature of the Middle Ages reflects the *memento mori*, a reminder that we are all mortal and should be giving constant thought to our salvation. In the ninth century, Notker the Stammerer's *Liber Hymnorum* opens with a Gregorian antiphon, one line of which would go on to enjoy considerable usage throughout the Western world: *Media vita in morte sumus*, "In the midst of life we are in death." The fear of the fate awaiting the individual in the afterlife inspired the production of numerous poems advocating the rejection of this world

---

*[The Latin verb *mordere*, "to bite," has the past participle *morsus*, "bitten," which is also the source of the noun *morsus*, "bite." The related English word is *morsel*: a "little bite." —*Ed.*]

(*contemptus mundi*), this vale of tears in which the devil lays his snares. In the mid-thirteenth century, Hugh of Miramar, a Carthusian monk in Montrieux in the Var region of France, expressed it perfectly in his *De hominis miseria, mundi et inferni contempt* (On the Misery of Mankind, Contempt for the World, and [Contempt] for Hell).[6]

This same time was witness to the development of pamphlets titled *The Art of Dying Well*, which were illustrated with remarkably expressive woodcuts.[7] In them we see, among other things, Saint Michael weighing souls (psychostasia), demons at the bedsides of the dying, and devils carrying off the souls of sinners. Warnings are everywhere in the frescoes, the exempla, and the literature. For example, the tale of *The Three Living and the Three Dead* includes this terrible phrase spoken from the latter to the former: "You are what we once were; you will be what we are" (*quod fuimus estis, quod sumus vos eritis*).

In the churches, the *danses macabres* that depict a skeleton dragging behind it the representatives of the three orders of society anchored the presence of death in people's minds. This dance was foreshadowed in the earlier *Vision of Thurkill*, in which a parade passes by featuring a priest, a knight, a judge, a thief, peasants, a merchant, a miller. In a later period, the same message was expressed on sundials with mottos such as *Omnes vulnerant, ultima necat* ("All hours wound, the last one kills"), *Dies nostri quasi umbra super terram et nulla est mora* ("Our days on the earth are as a shadow, and there is none abiding"), or even *Ut flos vita perit* ("Like a flower, life perishes"),[8] which reminds each of us that the flow of time brings us closer to the end, an idea that also shows up in the writings of Montaigne: "All our days travel toward death, the last one reaches it."[9]

The memory of time's inexorable nature is also evident in one of Bossuet's funeral orations:

> Their years [of men] pass in succession like waves; they never stop flowing until finally, after some have made a bit more noise and traveled through a few more countries than others, they are all commingled together in an abyss in which it is no longer possible to recognize kings or princes or any of the other qualities that distinguish men.[10]

For those who know how to interpret them, there are many signs that herald death. To simplify matters a bit, we may say that everything which was unusual, disturbing, or distressing was interpreted as an "intersign" (*intersigne*),* depending on the circumstances.

On the other hand, in the Middle Ages we have the physical signs: someone destined to die soon is "marked," and this notion takes various forms. In the chansons de geste and courtly romances, a red cross appears on the clothing of the warrior who engages in his last battle. In Iceland there is an adjective, *veigr*, which indicates, without providing any further detail, that the individual so designated is imminently doomed to die.

In a German tale, Death has this to say:

Now, my godchild, you are going to receive my baptismal gift. You will be the best of doctors thanks to the medicinal herb that I am giving you now. Pay close attention to what I have to tell you: every time that you are summoned to see a patient, you will see me. If I am standing close to his head, you can be assured that he will recover his health and you can give him a little of this herb. If he is destined to perish, I will be by his feet.[11]

Hugo von Trimberg (ca. 1230–1313) recorded a story that remained extremely popular from the Middle Ages up to the eighteenth century, and echoes of which can be heard in Jean de La Fontaine's "Death and the Dying Man":

One night a woman gave birth to a child. Her husband had a visitor, whom he asked to be the godfather to the newborn child, adding: "Tell me your name so that I may be able to recognize you in the crowd."

---

*[The term *intersigne* refers to a "sign," in the form of an unusual and unforeseen event, which serves as a premonition or portent "announcing" a death. These intersigns usually appear to someone other than the person who will die, such as a friend or relative. The term gained currency through the studies of death legends in Brittany by folklorist Anatole Le Braz (1859–1926). —*Ed.*]

"I am Death," the other person responded, "and I bring many fears with me, both day and night."

"Oh, take pity on me and allow me to live a long life."

"I promise you that, my dear companion. Before I come to get you, rest assured that I shall send you messages." With these words, Death departed.

The man lived for a long time, a time of many harvests, then he fell ill. Death then appeared before him and said: "Let us be off, companion, I have come to take you."

"Oh! You did not keep your promise!"

"Think back!" Death replied. "One day you felt a stitch in your side and you thought to yourself: 'Alas, what could this be?' That was my first messenger. When your ears began to ring, your eyes to tear up, and your vision drew darker, those were two other messengers. When you had a toothache, when coughing racked you more severely than usual, and your memory became unreliable, I had sent you three. When you began walking more slowly, your skin became wrinkled, your voice became hoarse, and your beard turned gray, I was sending you four more. Don't you see, my friend, that I have kept my word. Let God take care of your soul by releasing it from your body."

And the good man died.[12]

The physicians of classical antiquity and the Middle Ages came up with methods for determining whether a patient would die or not; one of these methods is uroscopy. We have the following prescription, for example, from the thirteenth century: "If you wish to know whether a man will die or not, collect some of his urine in a container and have a woman who is nursing a male child pour some of her milk into it. If you see the milk float, the patient shall die; if it mixes with the urine, he can be cured."[13] There are other even stranger methods, such as this one: "Take some lard and smear it on the soles of his feet, then toss the lard to a dog. If the animal eats it, the patient will recover; if not, he will die."[14] And then there are more comical ones like the following: "Place some nettle root in a urine pot and have the patient piss on it. Cover

Uroscopy, Oxford ms. DeRicci NLM 78, fol. 42v
(thirteenth century).

the urine pot, set it in a secret place overnight, and in the morning, if the urine is white, he will die, and if it is green, he will be cured."[15]

The main lesson of the ancient texts is that death announces itself fairly often by phenomena that are interpreted in conformance with oral traditions and local beliefs. I am using the word "belief" here in the sense of an indemonstrable idea or fact that is accepted as true.

As we mentioned, phenomena of this sort are known as intersigns. While the collection of these has been most fruitful in Brittany, as is shown by Anatole Le Braz's work in the late nineteenth century[16] and another much more recent book by Bernard Rio,[17] it is important to note that every country, every province, has its own intersigns. In ancient times, the illiterate had their own system for deciphering the world, one that was based on analogies "that provided a hidden meaning to any reality or phenomenon of the world."[18] This is how night birds (such as owls) and even diurnal birds (crows, ravens) are often seen as messengers of death. The Grim Reaper therefore appears as a living being, and perhaps even a benevolent entity, since he takes the trouble to give a warning. But who is he warning? It is rarely the future deceased, and more often the latter's friends and family—but the Grim Reaper's omens are irrevocable, his law is absolute, and no one can escape his verdict.

All of this is evidence of not only the fear that death inspires, but also the resolve of human individuals not to accept that life will stop when death arrives. Folk wisdom does acknowledge that "when you are dead it is for a long time," which is repeated by Molière in his play *Dépit amoreux* (Love's Bitterness; act V, scene III). And then we have La Rochefoucauld's observation from around 1650 that "the sun and death cannot be stared at directly."

Intersigns and tradition are the starting point for all speculations, and God only knows just how many there are! From the adepts of spiritualism who offer explanations of OBEs (out-of-body experiences) and NDEs (near-death experiences),[19] to those who vouch for "trans-communication," there are many seeking to pierce the mysterious veil. And are we not living in a time where genetic research is dangling the hope for a longer life span before our eyes? This is a strange resurgence of the Fountain of Youth and the elixir of eternal youth that pushes back the frontiers of death; to do anything else but die! But it is not the demise itself that agitates people's minds, as much as the question of what comes afterward. This explains the belief in revenants who, when they appear before us, must answer the question: "What is it like after you die?" In the texts collected by Leander Petzold, the response is unvaryingly: "Nothing is at all what I imagined it would be."[20]

Let us clarify an important point from the outset. The *afterlife* is a world beyond the grave that, in folk traditions, can be reached in a dream, a trance, or bodily. The *otherworld* is a world that is different from ours, located in a vague "elsewhere," where time passes in a different manner and which is inhabited by fantastic or supernatural beings such as fairies or dwarfs, for example. In short, the afterlife and the otherworld overlap with one another, and the terms are quite often employed synonymously. But they also happen to differ and, as we shall see, they are sometimes adjacent to one another, with the otherworld forming a kind of antechamber to the afterlife.

More than one researcher has tackled the subject of the afterlife and of journeys to the otherworld, and I will cite the most pertinent of these studies in my own investigation.[21] Wilhelm Brousset was one of the first to take a serious interest in this topic. In a long 1901 article titled "Die Himmelsreise der Seele" (The Soul's Journey to Heaven) he approached the representations of the afterlife in various religions, and the trance, as an anticipation of the flight of the soul into the sky following death. In 1945 August Rüegg published his study of *Die Jenseitsvorstellungen vor Dante* (The Representations of the Beyond before Dante). He began with the primitive notions, and then looked at the Greek philosophers before analyzing a number of medieval visions. Several years later in the United States, Howard Rollin Patch's study *The Other World According to Descriptions in Medieval Literature* was published in 1950. After looking at Eastern and Greek mythologies, he examined Celtic and Germanic culture, and then turned his attention toward the visions and voyages to paradise. In 1981 Peter Dinzelbacher published his reworked thesis on *Vision und Visionsliteratur im Mittelalter* (Vision and Visionary Literature in the Middle Ages). In it he draws up a list of all the texts, classifies them, reviews the geography of the sites, and notes the encounters the visionary experienced in the afterlife and the influence this extraordinary experience had on his life.

In 1984 Ioan P. Couliano brought out his book *Expériences de l'extase* (Experiences of Ecstasy), in which he examines the ascension of the soul (psychonody), incubation, catalepsis, and the bridge of judgment in the medieval apocalyses.

In 1985 Jacqueline Amat published her study *Songes et visions, l'au-delà dans la literature latine tardive* (Song and Visions: The Afterlife in Late Latin Literature), in which she retraces the history of visions of the afterlife found in dream accounts from the second to sixth century. In 1994 Claude Carozzi published *Le Voyage de l'âme dans l'au-delà d'après la literature latine (Ve–XIIIe siècle)* (The Journey of the Soul in the Afterlife in Latin Literature of the Fifth to Eighth Century), which analyzes the relationships between the living and the dead, and looks at a number of the visions leading a person to the discovery of purgatory, hell, and paradise.[22]

The most suggestive book would be that of Carlo Donà, *Per le vie dell'altro mondo: L'animale guida e il mito del viaggio* (On the

Paths of the Other World: The Animal Guide and the Myth of the Voyage).[23] Examining all the functions of the animal that serves as a guide into another world and analyzing its position on the border of this world, Donà takes into account not only medieval texts but also Indo-European and Asiatic literature, as well as folktales. This multi-disciplinary investigation is the most extensive study to date in an area that is close to our own.

None of these extremely well-documented and fine overviews are concerned with what later became of the visions, or what impact they have had on post-medieval mentalities. An initial attempt to fill this gap has been made by Natacha Romasson-Fertin with her (unfortunately still unpublished) dissertation and, subsequently, by Vincent Gaston in his dissertation, and by Laurent Guyénot with his fine book *La Mort féerique* (The Fairy Death), published in 2011.

Natacha Romasson-Fertin examines *L'Autre Monde et des figures dans les "Contes de l'enfance et du foyer" des frères Grimm et les "Contes populaires" d'A. N. Afanassiev* (The Otherworld and Its Figures in the Fairy Tales of the Brothers Grimm and the Folktales of A. N. Afanasyev). She explores the depiction of the otherworld, the beings who are encountered there, then moves on to specific locations—subterranean, earthly, underwater, or aerial worlds—before concluding her study with an analysis of the functions and meanings of journeys in these particular places.

In 2005 Vincent Gaston defended his dissertation on *L'Initiation et l'au-delà: Le conte et la decouverte de l'autre monde* (Initiation and the Beyond: The Tale and the Discovery of the Other World).[24] His study is based on a corpus of fifty-four texts, twenty-four of which are variants of story type AT 471 (The bridge to the other world). His analysis is divided into three parts: (1) "Religious Marvels" (visions, exempla, hagiographic legends); (2) "The Figures of the Beyond" (guides, ferrymen, etc.); and (3) "The Stages of Realization" (rites and other elements that play a role in the process of initiation). In all its varied forms, the beyond is a place of revelation and of being chosen.

In *La Mort féerique,* Laurent Guyénot provides an anthropological study of the marvelous by studying the folk traditions that come to

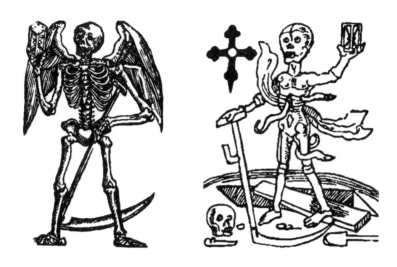

Human skeletons with scythes
were a common symbol of the Grim Reaper.

the surface in the novels and romances of the Middle Ages. He shows that the medieval fairyland is "a mytho-poetic discourse about the afterlife. This is why it opens such a unique window onto the secular imaginary realm of death." I cannot help but agree with his conclusions, and his analysis has the great merit of offering us a new way to read our ancient texts.

We will first study the legacy of classical antiquity, of mythology, and of religions, and then we shall discuss its impact on the literature of revelations. Next, we will look at what the chivalric romances owe to the latter, and we will venture out upon the paths of the otherworld, also taking into account the travelers' tales from this ineffable region that have come down to us through folktales and folk songs. We will conclude by comparing these journeys into the afterlife and into the otherworld with experiences of imminent death (NDE).

ONE

ACCOUNTS OF JOURNEYS INTO THE BEYOND FROM CLASSICAL ANTIQUITY

Long before the present era, numerous writers and philosophers provided accounts of journeys into the otherworld. One of the oldest is that of Odysseus in the *Odyssey* that Homer wrote around the end of the eighth century BCE.[1] Plato (circa 427–348 BCE) also provides an account with his story of Er, the native of Pamphylios, which to a certain extent represents the archetype of the medieval visions:

> Er, the son of Armenius, [was] a Pamphylian by birth. He was slain in battle, and ten days afterwards, when the bodies of the dead were taken up already in a state of corruption, his body was found unaffected by decay, and carried away home to be buried. And on the twelfth day, as he was lying on the funeral pyre, he returned to life and told them what he had seen in the other world. He said that when his soul left the body he went on a journey with a great company, and that they came to a mysterious place at which there were two openings in the earth; they were near together, and over against them were two other openings in the heaven above. In the intermediate space there were judges seated, who commanded the just, after they had given judgment on them and had bound their sentences in front of them, to ascend by the heavenly way on the right hand;

and in like manner the unjust were bidden by them to descend by the lower way on the left hand; these also bore the symbols of their deeds, but fastened on their backs.

And he had no idea how his mind had come back into his body:

But in what manner or by what means he returned to the body he could not say; only, in the morning, awaking suddenly, he found himself lying on the pyre.[2]

The Greek historian and moralist Plutarch (46–120 CE) left us two little-known accounts of visions that are precursors to those of the Middle Ages because of the many motifs they share in common. In one of them, Timarchus makes his way to the cave that is sacred to Trophonius so he can obtain an oracle there:

[Timarchus] descended into the crypt of Trophonius, first performing the rites that are customary at the oracle. He remained underground two nights and a day, and most people had already given up hope, and his family was lamenting him for dead, when he came up in the morning with a radiant countenance. He did obeisance to the god, and as soon as he had escaped the crowd, began to tell us of many wonders seen and heard. He said that on descending into the oracular crypt his first experience was of profound darkness; next, after a prayer, he lay a long time not clearly aware whether he was awake or dreaming. It did seem to him, however, that at the same moment he heard a crash and was struck on the head and that the sutures parted and released his soul. As it withdrew and mingled joyfully with air that was translucent and pure, it felt in the first place that now, after long being cramped, it had again found relief, and was growing larger than before, spreading out like a sail; and next that it faintly caught the whir of something revolving overhead with a pleasant sound. When he lifted his eyes the earth was nowhere to be seen; but he saw islands illuminated by one another with soft fire, taking on now one colour, now another, like a dye, as the light kept varying with their mutations. They appeared countless in number and huge in size, and though not all equal, yet all alike round; and he fancied that their circular movement made a musical whirling in the aether, for the gentleness of the sound resulting from the harmony of all the separate sounds corresponded to the evenness of their motion. In their midst lay spread a sea or lake, through whose blue transparency the colours passed in their migrations; and of the islands a few sailed out in a channel and crossed the current, while many others were carried along with it, the sea itself drifting around, as it were, smoothly and evenly in a circle. In places it was very deep, mainly toward the south, but elsewhere there were faint shoals and shallows; and in many parts it overflowed and again receded, never extending very far. Some of it was of the pure hue of the high seas, while elsewhere the colour was not unmixed, but turbid and like that of a pool. As they crested the surge the islands came back, without, however, returning to their point of departure or completing a circle; but with each new circuit they advanced slightly beyond the old, describing a single spiral in their revolution. The sea containing these was inclined at an angle of somewhat less than eight parts of the whole toward the midmost and largest portion of the surrounding envelope, as he made out; and it had two openings receiving rivers of fire empty-ing into it across from one another, so that it was forced far back, boiling, and its blue colour was turned to white. All this he viewed with enjoyment of the spectacle. But looking down he saw a great abyss, round, as though a sphere had been cut away; most terrible and deep it was, and filled with a mass of darkness that did not remain at rest, but was agitated and often welled up. From it could be heard innumerable roars and groans of animals, the wailing of innumerable babes, the mingled lamentations of men and women, and noise and uproar of every kind, coming faintly from far down in the depths, all of which startled him not a little.

After an interval someone he did not see addressed him: "Timarchus what would you have me explain?"

"Everything," he answered; "for what is here that is not marvellous?"

"Nay," the voice replied, "in the higher regions we others have but little part, as they belong to gods; but you may, if you wish, inquire into the portion of Persephonê, administered by ourselves; it is one of the four, and marked off by the course of the Styx."

"What is the Styx?" he asked. "It is the path to Hades," came the answer; "it passes across from you here, cleaving the light with its vertex; it extends upward, as you see, from Hades below, and where in its revolution it also touches the world of light, it bounds the last region of all. Four principles there are of all things: the first is of life, the second of motion, the third of birth, and the last of decay; the first is linked to the second by Unity at the invisible, the second to the third by Mind at the sun, and the third to the fourth by Nature at the moon. A Fate, daughter of Necessity, holds the keys and presides over each link: over the first Atropos, over the second Clotho, and over the link at the moon Lachesis. The turning point of birth is at the moon. For while the rest of the islands belong to the gods, the moon belongs to terrestrial daemons and avoids the Styx by passing slightly above it; it is caught, however, once in a hundred and seventy-seven secondary measures. As the Styx draws near the souls cry out in terror, for many slip off and are carried away by Hades; others, whose cessation of birth falls out at the proper moment, swim up from below and are rescued by the Moon, the foul and unclean excepted. These the Moon, with lightning and a terrible roar, forbids to approach, and bewailing their lot they fall away and are borne downward again to another birth, as you see."

"But I see nothing," said Timarchus; "only many stars trembling about the abyss, others sinking into it, and others again shooting up from below."

"Then without knowing it," the being replied, "you see the daemons themselves. I will explain: every soul partakes of understanding; none is irrational or unintelligent. But the portion of the soul that mingles with flesh and passions suffers alteration and becomes in the pleasures and pains it undergoes irrational. Not every soul mingles to the same extent: some sink entirely into the body, and becoming disordered throughout, are during their life wholly distracted by passions; others mingle in part, but leave outside what is purest in them. This is not dragged in with the rest, but is like a buoy attached to the top, floating on the surface in contact with the man's head, while he is as it were submerged in the depths; and it supports as much of the soul, which is held upright about it, as is obedient and not overpowered by the passions. Now the part carried submerged in the body is called the soul, whereas the part left free from corruption is called by the multitude the understanding, who take it to be within themselves, as they take reflected objects to be in the mirrors that reflect them; but those who conceive the matter rightly call it a daemon, as being external. Thus, Timarchus," the voice pursued, "in the stars that are apparently extinguished, you must understand that you see the souls that sink entirely into the body; in the stars that are lighted again, as it were, and reappear from below, you must understand that you see the souls that float back from the body after death, shaking off a sort of dimness and darkness as one might shake off mud; while the stars that move about on high are the daemons of men said to 'possess understanding.' See whether you can make out in each the manner of its linkage and union with the soul."

Hearing this, he attended more carefully and saw that the stars bobbed about, some more, some less, like the corks we observe riding on the sea to mark nets; a few described a confused and uneven spiral, like spindles as they twist the thread, and were unable to reduce their movement to a straight and steady course. The voice explained that the daemons whose motion was straight and ordered had souls which good nurture and training had made submissive to the rein, and whose irrational part was not unduly hard-mouthed and restive; whereas those which were constantly deviating in all directions from a straight course in an uneven and confused motion, as though jerked about on a tether, were contending with a character refractory and unruly from lack of training, at one moment prevailing over it and wheeling to the right, at another yielding to their passions and dragged along by their errors, only to resist them later and oppose them with force. For, exerting a contrary pull on the tie, which is like a bridle inserted into the irrational part of the soul, the daemon applies what is called remorse to the errors, and shame for all lawless and wilful pleasures—remorse and shame being really the painful blow inflicted from this source upon the soul as it is curbed by its controlling and ruling part—until from such chastening the soul, like a docile animal, becomes obedient and accustomed to the reins, needing no painful blows, but rendered keenly responsive to its daemon by signals and signs. "These souls indeed," the voice pursued, "are brought to their duty and made firm in it late and gradually; but from those other souls, which from their very beginning and birth are docile to the rein and obedient to their daemon, comes the race of diviners and of men inspired. Among such souls you have doubtless heard of that of Hermodorus of Clazomenae—how night and day it used to leave his body entirely and travel far and wide, returning after it had met with and witnessed many things said and done in remote places, until his wife betrayed him and his enemies found his body at home untenanted by his soul and burned it. The story as thus told is indeed not true: his soul did not leave his body, but gave its daemon free play by always yielding to it and slackening the tie, permitting it to move about and roam at will, so that the daemon could see and hear much that passed in the world outside and return with the report. The men who destroyed his body as he slept are still atoning for the deed in Tartarus. Of these matters," the voice said, "You will have better knowledge, young man, in the third month from now; for the present, depart."

When the voice ceased Timarchus desired to turn (he said) and see who the speaker was. But once more he felt a sharp pain in his head, as though it had been violently compressed, and he lost all recognition and awareness of what was going on about him; but he presently recovered and saw that he was lying in the crypt of Trophonius near the entrance, at the very spot where he had first laid himself down.[3]

The second vision recounted by Plutarch is that of Thespesius who "by a decree of the gods" was given the privilege of leaving his body "with the weighty part of his soul" while the rest of it "remained there like an anchor." For three days he explored the astral dwelling place where the souls of the dead came and went. He found himself projected to a spot between the earth and the moon "after having traveled in the blink of an eye a space that appeared prodigiously spacious; yet so gently and without the least deviation, that he seemed to be borne upon the rays of the light as upon wings" he was suddenly abandoned by the force that was holding him up. He came to a halt at the edge of a large, deep abyss (χάσμα μέγα καὶ κάτω διῆκον), the Lethe, which is here a kind of chimney that opens in the solid vault of the sky and plunges toward earth. Thespesius soon squandered his entire inheritance. Reduced to poverty, he sought to enrich himself through less than honest vocations.

> But the greatest blow to his good name was a response conveyed to him from the oracle of Amphilochus. He had sent (it appears) to ask the god whether the remainder of his life would be better spent. The god answered that he would do better when he died.
>
> In a sense this actually happened to him not long after. He had fallen from a height and struck his neck, and although there had been no wound, but only a concussion, he died away. On the third day, at the very time of his funeral, he revived. Soon recovering his strength and senses, he instituted a change in his way of life that could hardly be believed; for the Cilicians know of no one in those times more honest in his engagements, more pious toward heaven, or more grievous to his enemies and faithful to his friends; so that all who met him longed to hear the reason for the difference, supposing nothing ordinary could have caused so great a reformation in character. Such indeed was the case, as appears from the story as told by himself to Protogenes and other worthy friends.
>
> He said that when his intelligence was driven from his body, the change made him feel as a pilot might at first on being flung into the depths of the sea; his next impression was that he had risen somewhat and was breathing with his whole being and seeing on all sides, his soul having opened wide as if it were a single eye. But nothing that he saw was familiar except the stars, which appeared very

great in size and at vast distances apart, sending forth a marvellously coloured radiance possessed of a certain cohesion, so that his soul, riding smoothly in the light like a ship on a calm sea, could move easily and rapidly in all directions.

Passing over most of the spectacle, he said that as the souls of those who die came up from below they made a flamelike bubble as the air was displaced, and then, as the bubble gently burst, came forth, human in form, but slight in bulk, and moving with dissimilar motions. Some leapt forth with amazing lightness and darted about aloft in a straight line, while others, like spindles, revolved upon themselves and at the same time swung now downward, now upward, moving in a complex and disordered spiral that barely grew steady after a very long time.

Most of the souls indeed he failed to recognize, but seeing two or three of his acquaintance, he endeavoured to join them and speak to them. These, however, would not hear him and were not in their right mind, but in their frenzy and panic avoiding all sight and contact, they at first strayed about singly; later, meeting many others in the same condition, they clung to them and moved about indistinguishably in all manner of aimless motions and uttered inarticulate sounds, mingled with outcries as of lamentation and terror. Other souls, above, in a pure region of the ambient, were joyful in aspect and out of friendliness often approached one another, but shunned the other, tumultuous souls, indicating their distaste, he said, by contracting into themselves, but their delight and welcome by expansion and diffusion.

Here, he said, he recognized one soul, that of a kinsman, though not distinctly, as he was but a child when the kinsman died; but it drew near and said: "Greetings, Thespesius." He was taken aback and said he was not Thespesius but Aridaeus. "You were that before," was the reply, "but henceforth you are Thespesius. For you must further know you are not dead, but through a divine dispensation are present here in your intelligence, having left the rest of your soul, like an anchor, behind in your body. Now and hereafter know it by this token: the souls of the dead neither cast a shadow nor blink their eyes." At this Thespesius, by an effort of thought, became more collected, and looking steadily, saw a certain faint and shadowy line floating along with him, while the rest were enveloped all around with light and translucent within, although not all to the same degree. But some were like the full moon at her clearest, shining evenly with a single smooth and unbroken hue; others were shot through with scales, as it were, or faint bruises; others quite mottled and odd in appearance, covered with black tattoo-marks, like speckled vipers; and still others bore the faded traces of what looked like scratches.

Thespesius' kinsman—nothing need keep us from thus referring to a man's soul—proceeded to explain. Adrasteia, he said, daughter of Necessity and Zeus, is the supreme requiter; all crimes are under her cognizance, and none of the wicked is so high or low as to escape her either by force or by stealth. There are three others, and each is warden and executioner of a different punishment: those who are punished at once in the body and through it are dealt with by swift Poinê in a comparatively gentle manner that passes over many of the faults requiring purgation; those whose viciousness is harder to heal are delivered up to Dikê by their daemon after death; while those past all healing, when rejected by Dikê, are pursued by the third and fiercest of the ministers of Adrasteia, Erinys, as they stray about and scatter in flight, who makes away with them, each after a different fashion, but all piteously and cruelly, imprisoning them in the Nameless and Unseen.

"Of the other forms of chastisement," he said, "that visited in life by Poinê resembles those in use among the barbarians; for as in Persia the cloaks and head-dresses of the sufferers are plucked and scourged as the tearful owners beg for mercy, so punishment that operates through external possessions and the body establishes no smarting contact and does not fasten upon the viciousness itself, but is for the most part addressed to opinion and the senses. But whoever comes here from the world below unpunished and unpurged, is fastened upon by Dikê, exposed to view and naked in his soul, having nothing in which to sink out of sight and hide himself and cloak his baseness, but on all sides plainly visible to all in all his shame. In this state she first shows him to his good parents and ancestors—if such they are—as one execrable and unworthy of them, while if they are wicked, he sees them punished and is seen by them; he then undergoes prolonged chastisement, each of his passions being removed with pains and torments that in magnitude and intensity as far transcend those that pass through the flesh as the reality would be more vivid than a dream.

"The scars and welts left by the different passions are more persistent in some, less so in others. Observe," he said, "in the souls that mixture and variety of colours: one is drab brown, the stain that comes of meanness and greed; another a fiery blood-red, which comes of cruelty and savagery; where you see the blue-grey, some form of incontinence in pleasure has barely been rubbed out; while if spite and envy are present they give out this livid green, as ink is ejected by the squid. For in the world below viciousness puts forth the colours, as the soul is altered by the passions and alters the body in turn, while here the end of purgation and punishment is reached when the passions are quite smoothed away and the soul becomes luminous in consequence and uniform in colour; but so long as the passions remain within there are relapses, attended by throbbings and a convulsive motion which in some souls is faint and soon subsides, but in others produces a vehement tension. Some of these, after repeated punishment, recover their proper state and disposition, while others are once more carried off into the bodies of living things by the violence of ignorance and the 'image' of the love of pleasure. For one soul, from weakness of reason and neglect of contemplation, is borne down by its practical proclivity to birth, while another, needing an instrument for its licentiousness, yearns to knit its appetites to their fruition and gratify them through the body, for here there is nothing but an imperfect shadow and dream of never consummated pleasure."

After this explanation Thespesius was swiftly taken by the guide over what appeared an immense distance, traversing it easily and unerringly, buoyed up by the beams of the light as by wings, until he came to a great chasm extending all the way down and was deserted by the power that sustained him. The other souls too, he observed, were thus affected there, for they drew themselves in like birds and alighted and walked around the circuit of the chasm, not venturing to pass directly across. Within, it had the appearance of a Bacchic grotto: it was gaily diversified with tender leafage and all the hues of flowers. From it was wafted a soft and gentle breeze that carried up fragrant scents, arousing wondrous pleasures and such a mood as wine induces in those who are becoming tipsy; for as the souls regaled themselves on the sweet odours they grew expansive and friendly with one another; and the place all about was full of bacchic revelry and laughter and the various strains of festivity and merry-making. This was the route, the guide said, that Dionysus had taken in his ascent and later when he brought up Semelê; and the region was called the place of Lethe. On this account, although Thespesius wished to linger, the guide would not allow it, but pulled him away by main force, informing him as he did so that the intelligent part of the soul is dissolved away and liquefied by pleasure, while the irrational and carnal part is fed by its flow and puts on flesh and thus induces memory of the body; and that from such memory arises a yearning and desire that draws the soul toward birth (*genesis*), so named as being an earthward (*epi gēn*) inclination (*neusis*) of the soul grown heavy with liquefaction.

Proceeding as far again, he saw in the distance what he took to be a large crater with streams pouring into it, one whiter than seafoam or snow, another like the violet of the rainbow, and others of different tints, each having from afar a lustre of its own. On their approach the crater turned out to be a deep chasm in the ambient, and as the colours faded, the brightness, except for the white, disappeared. He beheld three daemons seated together in the form of a triangle, combining the streams in certain proportions. The guide of Thespesius' soul said that Orpheus had advanced thus far in his quest for the soul of his wife,[4] and from faulty memory had published among men a false report that at Delphi there was an oracle held in common by Apollo and Night—false, as Night has partnership in nothing with Apollo. "This is instead," he pursued, "an oracle shared by Night and the Moon; it has no outlet anywhere on earth nor any single seat, but roves everywhere throughout mankind in dreams and visions; for this is the source from which dreams derive and disseminate the unadorned and true, commingled, as you see, with the colourful and deceptive.

"As for Apollo's oracle," he said, "I hardly know whether you will be able to catch sight of it; for the cable of your soul gives no further upward play and does not grow slack, but holds taut, being made fast to the body." At the same time he endeavoured to draw Thespesius near and show him the light that came (he said) from the tripod, and passing through the bosom of Themis, rested on Parnassus, but it was so bright that Thespesius, for all his eagerness, did not see it. But he did hear, as he passed by, a woman's high voice foretelling in verse among other things the time (it appears) of his own death. The voice was the Sibyl's, the daemon said, who sang of the future as she was carried about on the face of the moon. He accordingly desired to hear more, but was thrust back, as in an eddy, by the onrush of the moon, and caught but little. . . .

They now turned to view those who were suffering punishment. At first these presented only a disagreeable and piteous spectacle; but as Thespesius kept meeting friends, kinsmen, and comrades who were being punished, a thing he never would have looked for, and these lamented to him and raised a cry of wailing as they underwent fearful torments and ignominious and excruciating chastisements, and when he at last caught sight of his own father emerging from a pit, covered with brands and scars, stretching out his arms to him, and not allowed by those in charge of the punishments to keep silent, but compelled to confess his foul wickedness to certain guests he had poisoned for their gold, a crime detected by no one in the lower world, but here brought to light, for which he had suffered in part and was now being taken away to suffer more, Thespesius in his consternation and terror did not dare to resort to supplication or intercede for his father, but wishing to turn back and escape, saw no longer that kindly kinsman who had been his guide, but certain others of frightful aspect, who thrust him forward, giving him to understand that he was under compulsion to pass that way. He observed that while the torment of those who had been recognized in their wickedness and punished on the spot was not so harsh or so prolonged in the other world, as it now dealt only with the irrational and passionate part of the soul, those who on the contrary had cloaked themselves in the pretence and repute of virtue and passed their lives in undetected vice were surrounded by a different set of officers who compelled them laboriously and painfully to turn the inward parts of their souls outward, writhing unnaturally and curving back upon themselves, as the sea-scolopendras turn themselves inside out when they have swallowed the hook; and some of them were skinned and laid open and shown to be ulcered and blotched, their wickedness being in their rational and sovereign part. He told of seeing other souls coiled like vipers around each other in twos and threes and yet greater number, devouring one another in rancour and bitterness for what they had endured or done in life; moreover (he said) there were lakes lying side by side, one a seething lake of gold, a second, piercing cold, of lead, and a third of rugged iron, with certain daemons in charge, who, like smiths, were using tongs to raise and lower alternately the souls of those whose wickedness was due to insatiable and overreaching avarice. Thus, when the souls had grown red hot in the gold from the blazing heat, the daemons plunged them into the lake of lead; when they had there been chilled and hardened, like hailstones, they were removed to the lake of iron. Here they turned an intense black and were altered in appearance, as their hardness caused them to become chipped and crushed; and after this they were once more taken to the gold, enduring, as he said, the most fearful agonies in the course of each change.

Most piteous of all, he said, was the suffering of the souls who thought that they were already released from their sentence, and then were apprehended again; these were the souls whose punishment had passed over to descendants or children. For whenever the soul of such a child or descendant arrived and found them, it flew at them in fury and raised a clamour against them and showed the marks of its sufferings, berating and pursuing the soul of the other, which desired to escape and hide, but could not. For they were swiftly overtaken by the tormentors and hastened back once more to serve their sentence, lamenting from foreknowledge of the penalty that awaited them. To some, he said, great clusters of the souls of descendants were attached, clinging to them like veritable swarms of bees or bats, and gibbering shrilly in angry memory of what they had suffered through their fault.

He was viewing the final spectacle of his vision, the souls returning to a second birth, as they were forcibly bent to fit all manner of living things and altered in shape by the framers of these, who with blows from certain tools were welding and hammering together one set of members, wrenching another apart, and polishing away and quite obliterating a third, to adapt them to new characters and lives, when among them appeared the soul of Nero, already in a sorry plight and pierced with incandescent rivets. For his soul too the framers had made ready a form, that of Nicander's viper, in which it was to live on eating its way out of its pregnant mother, when suddenly (he said) a great light shot through and a voice came out of the light commanding them to transfer it to a milder kind of brute and frame instead a vocal creature, frequenter of marshes and lakes, as he had paid the penalty for his crimes, and a piece of kindness too was owing him from the gods, since to the nation which among his subjects was noblest and most beloved of Heaven he had granted freedom.

Thus much he beheld. He was about to turn back, when he was driven frantic with terror, for a woman marvellously beautiful and tall took hold of him and said: "Come hither, sirrah, the better to remember everything," and was about to apply to him a red hot rod, such as painters use; but another woman interposed, and he was suddenly pulled away as by a cord and cast in a strong and violent gust of wind upon his body, opening his eyes again almost from his very grave.[5]

Here we find the majority of the descriptive elements that are defining characteristics of the medieval visions, and which also nurtured those that appear in the work of Virgil and Ovid.

Proclus, a Greek philosopher of the fifth century, recorded the vision of Cleonymus, who told how his soul "disengaged" from his body and rose to a height that allowed him a vision of the world below:

> Cleonymus, the Athenian, . . . becoming very sorrowful on the death of one of his associates, and giving himself up to despair, apparently died, and was laid out according to custom; but his mother, as she was folding him in her embraces, taking off his garment, and kissing him, perceived in him a gentle breathing, and, being extremely joyful on the occasion, delayed his burial. Cleonymus in a short time afterwards was restored to life, and narrated all that he saw and heard when he was in a separate state. He said, that his soul appeared, as if liberated from certain bonds, to soar from its body, and that having ascended above the earth, he saw in it places all-various both for their figure and colour, and streams of rivers unknown to men; and that at last he came to a certain region sacred to Vesta, which was under the direction of dæmoniacal powers in indescribable female forms.[6]

In book six of the *Aeneid* (ll. 233ff), Virgil tells the story of Aeneas's visit to the underworld under the guidance of the Sibyl of Cumae. He also has to cross a river, the Acheron, but he must take the boat of Charon and not a bridge. He then sees the Fields of Mourning and comes to a crossroads. The road on the right is the way to Elysium and that on the left looks over the "theater of torture reserved for the wicked and leads to unholy Tartarus." He sees a river of fire, the Phlegethon, and an iron tower from which comes the sounds of moans, metallic noises, and the clanking of chains.

This story enjoyed great popularity and was translated into French around 1160 and into Middle High German by Heinrich von Veldeke around 1170; these two works contributed to spreading the image of Hell as it was seen in antiquity. This type of description of the beyond

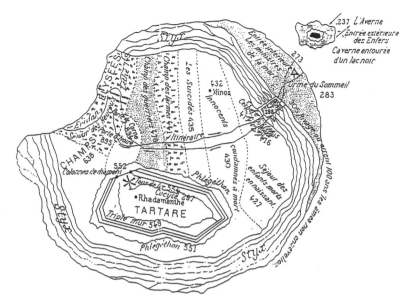

Map of Hell from Virgil's *Aeneid*, book VI.

faithfully reflects many of the fundamental elements of the literature of revelations. Virgil's text also influenced Dante Alighieri's (1265–1321) *Inferno*, which was the inspiration for this image of hell by Botticelli.

Chart of Hell by Sandro Botticelli, circa 1480–1490, from Dante's *Inferno*, Vatican Library.

And everyone is most likely familiar with the illustrations made by Gustave Doré of the Virgilian hell and its gate.

Gates of the Infernal City by Gustave Doré, circa 1861, from Dante's *Inferno,* canto VIII.

The River Styx by Gustave Doré, circa 1861, from Dante's *Inferno,* canto VIII.

In Flaming Spirit of the Evil Counsellors by Gustave Doré,
circa 1861, from Dante's *Inferno*, canto XXVI.

The Latin poem *Architrenius* ("The Arch-Weeper"),[7] which Johannes de Hauvilla dedicated to Walter de Coutances in 1184, was composed in imitation of the writers of classical antiquity. It tells the story of a young man's journey into hell where he meets figures who were well known to authors in the ancient world: Megaera and Tisiphone of the Furies, and for Tisiphone's name he follows Fulgentius's etymology: "Avenger of Murder." According to Johannes de Hauvilla, Lucifer's fall had divided the world, but Tartarus overflows onto the earth. Hell had "become the hyperbole for the moral suffering present there and a sign of the world's disorder," Catherine Klaus rightly notes.[8] But the hero also visits Tylo, an island paradise—which should not be confused with Thule—that resembles the Garden of Eden.[9]

TWO

THE BEYOND AS SEEN IN MYTHOLOGIES AND RELIGIONS

The Greeks believed that Hades "the invisible" and Persephone ruled over the dead in the underworld, assisted by demons and spirits. This underground realm includes Tartarus, the deepest region, which is located beneath the underworld and is the place where the greatest

Hades and Persephone. Bibliothèque nationale de France, ms français 143, fol. 136v (fifteenth century).

criminals are tormented. According to Hesiod's *Theogony* (ll. 775ff), it is surrounded by a bronze river. There are several rivers: the Styx; the Acheron, an almost stagnant river that souls are ferried across by Charon; the Cocytus, "River of Lamentation"; the Pyriphlegethon, "River of Flames"; and the Lethe, "Oblivion," from which the dead must drink to forget their lives on earth. The early Christian writers retained these descriptions in their memory, and Prudentius (d. ca. 405) spoke of Tartarus, Avernus, and Phlegethon in his *Psychomachia* (Battle of Souls).

Fortunately, however, hell is not the only thing that awaits human beings! In *Works and Days,* Hesiod speaks of the reward for the heroes who make their way to the Isles of the Blessed, the paradisiacal home of the just:

> *But on others Zeus . . .*
> *settled a living and a country*
> *of their own, apart from human kind,*
> *at the end of the world.*
> *And there they have their dwelling place,*
> *and hearts free of sorrow*
> *in the islands of the blessed*
> *by the deep-swirling stream of the ocean*[1]

They would later be given the name of the Fortunate Isles (μακάρων νῆσοι). The geographer Ptolemy (ca. 90–ca. 168) describes them as "inaccessible" and Diodorus Siculus (writing in the first century BCE) says they are "impossible to find."

In 380 BCE, Plato noted in the dialogue *Phaedrus*:

> But the others receive judgment when they have completed their first life, and after the judgment they go, some of them to the houses of correction which are under the earth, and are punished; others to some place in heaven whither they are lightly borne by justice, and there they live in a manner worthy of the life which they led here when in the form of men.[2]

A depiction of the Fortunate Isles. Bibliothèque nationale de France, ms français 1378 fol. 2 (fifteenth century).

We can see that the notion of judgment has already been established. In his refutation of the works of Celsus (*Contra Celsum,* bk. XXV), Origen writes:

> It is in the precincts of Jerusalem, then, that punishments will be inflicted upon those who undergo the process of purification, who have received into the substance of their soul the elements of wickedness, which in a certain place is figuratively termed "lead," and on that account iniquity is represented in Zechariah as sitting upon a "talent of lead."[3] (cf. Zechariah 5:7–8)

This idea of judgment and punishments corresponding to sins can be seen repeatedly throughout the centuries, especially in those mythologies in which hell appears in a variety of guises. For the Babylonians, it is the Aralu, the "land where people cannot see anything" (*mat la namari*), which coincides semantically with the Greek term Ἅιδης (Hades). It was also called the "land of no return," or the land from which no one ever returns (*mat la tayarti*). It was governed by Nergal and his wife Allat. One of the oldest examples of a descent into hell is that of the goddess Ishtar, whose journey was impeded by seven different doors that she could only cross through by gradually stripping off her garments.[4] This is a lightless place where the inhabitants sit in darkness with dust and mud as their only sustenance.

For the Jews, the name Sheol designates an underground region where the dead exist in a lethargic state, where there is no distinction made between the good and the wicked, and where there is no reward or punishment. Sheol is akin to the Hades of the Greeks and the Aralu of the Babylonians. In this kingdom the dead cannot even praise God, who is only God for the living (cf. Psalm 6; Psalm 30:10; Psalm 88:6 [Vulgate]). The Hebrew scholar Moses Gaster translated the *Gedulath Mosheh* (Revelation of Moses), a text that relates how the biblical figure of Moses left his body, which was changed into fire and traveled through the seven heavens.[5]* He saw hell and the men there "tortured by the angels of destruction." Some were hung up by their eyelids, others by their ears, hands, tongue, sexual organs, or feet, and covered in black worms.

Another Jewish revelation informs us that hell has three gates. The first opens onto the sea, the second onto a savage land, and the third onto the inhabited part of the world. According to the Vision of Ezekiel (I, 10), this place of damnation has seven names: Adamah, "the Bottom"; Erez, "Earth"; Nehsiyyah, "Forgetfulness"; Dumah, "Silence"; Sheol; and Tit ha-Yaven, "Miry Clay." these names correspond to their seven compartments in the Babylonian Talmud: Sheol; Abaddon, "Destruction," "Abyss"; Beer Shahat; Tit ha-Yaven; Sha'are; Mawet, "Shadow of Death"; and Gehinom, "Gehenna." In the visions cited by Gaster, the names are different so we get Hatzar Maveth, which in Hebrew means "the dwelling place of death," Beer Tahtiyah, and Beer Shaon. They have nine different kinds of fire, and rivers of pitch and fuming and seething sulfur.[6]

In the Muslim religion, the beyond (الآخِرة) has an abode of the

---

*Each heaven corresponds to a day of the week.

damned that has several names, contains several levels,* and is supervised by nineteen archangels. Its names include Furnace (Jahīm), Inferno (Sa'īr), and Gehenna (Jahannam). Other names refer to its depth (Hutama, Hāwiya). The principal characteristic of this Hell is that it is Fire (Nār), a fire that is seventy times hotter than earthly fire. Hell has seven gates guarded by angels; the souls that are damned there suffer from fire and thirst. The elect enter paradise after the Last Judgment; some people say there are four heavens and others eight. Called the Garden of Retirement, the Garden of Eternity, Eden, the Dwelling of Salvation, and the True Life, and so forth, this dwelling place of the blessed is a veritable palace in which the elect are clad in silk, wear gold and silver bracelets, and sleep in golden beds encrusted with precious stones.[7]

In the Persian Zoroastrian religion, during a seven-day ecstatic trance caused by a potion and under the guidance of Srosh the Pious and the angel Adar, the soul of Arda-Viraf crossed the Chinvat Bridge to reach the otherworld. There he saw heaven, purgatory (Hamistagan) and the places of damnation.[8] In other accounts, he is led by the Yazatas to Garōdemāna (the House of Song) reserved for the just.

The Mandaean religion of Mesopotamia, which is characterized by a gnostic dualism, opposes the world of Light (nhura) to that of Darkness (hshuka). The first is presided over by a kind of unknown god, who is given various names: "Life" (hiia, or "Great Living One," Hiiyē rbē), Lord of Greatness (mare rbuta), and "Powerful Mana" (mana = receptacle, spirit). He is surrounded by a vast number of beings of Light called the Uthra (wealth), who remain in the many worlds of light (almē).[9] The principal Mandaean work, the Ginzā (Treasury),[10] a compilation devoted to the teaching of the mythology and cosmology, describes the ascension of the soul toward the domain of light and hymns. Guided by two Uthra, the soul rises past the guards of the sun, moon, fire, the seven planets, the Ruhā (Wind),[11] and some rivers. The place of punishment is called "Burning Fire," "Darkness," and "Sea of the End," and the sinner falls into it.[12]

---

*These are: Jahannam, Saqar, Ladha, Al Hutamah, Jaheem, Sa'eer, and Al Haawiyah; the latter is endless and has no ground.

For the ancient North Germanic peoples, the world is tripartite and consists of the "Middle Enclosure" (Miðgarðr), the world of the gods (Ásgarðr), and that of the giants, (Jötunheimr or Risaland), a mythical place without a precise location or definition. The latter realm is another world that is sometimes located in the east or to the northeast, beyond the ocean. Hel is the realm of the goddess Hel, "the Concealed One," and it has the name of Niflhel, "Dark Hel," and Niflheimr, "Dark World." To get there, a person had to cross over a bridge and get through a wrought iron gate. It was reserved for people who had not died on the field of battle. Odin gave the goddess Hel authority over nine worlds, such that she has to administer the lodging for those who are sent to her: the ones who died from sickness and old age.

Curiously, after the apocalypse of Ragnarökr (later popularized by Richard Wagner as the "Twilight of the Gods" [*Götterdämmerung*]) there will exist "the Obscure Plain, the Dark Fields, and the Shore of Corpses." This hell contains several halls, two of which, opening to the north, are particularly terrible. In one, woven from the backs of serpents and reserved for oath-breakers and murderers, venom flowed down through the smoke hole. In the other hall, the serpent Nidhöggr devours the corpses of the dead. There is also another empire of the dead, that of the goddess Ran, which is reserved for the drowned.

In Finnish mythology Kalma is the goddess of death and decomposition, and Kipu-Tyttö the goddess of death and illness. The land of the dead was called Tuonela,* kingdom of Tuoni and Tuonetar, king and queen of the dead, or named Manala and governed by a queen answering to the name of Manalatar. In most traditions, Tuonela is an underground kingdom, or it is located beneath a lake,[13] or on the other side of a black river that the boat of Tuonen tytti or Tuonen piika makes it possible to cross. Tuonela is a dark and lifeless place, where the dead rest in eternal slumber. It is located somewhere in the north and is sometimes confused with Pohjala, which takes its name from *pohja,* "the north." I will have more to say about this when I discuss the journey of Väinämöinen in these regions.

---

*Tuonela is the customary translation of the Hades (Ἅιδης) of the Bible.

One mythology that has generally received little attention is that of the Lapps, which, however, sheds a very interesting light upon the beyond because of its shamanic substratum. It is called Jábmiidaibmu, a word coined from otherworld (*áibmu*) and death (*jábmi*). During the Middle Ages, under the influence of Catholic missionaries, the otherworld consisted of a hell, the Rotaimo; a purgatory, the Jábmiidaibmu; and a celestial beyond, the Radienaimo. The master of Hell is Rota; he welcomes all those who have not obeyed the local gods. The righteous are given a new body and enter the Radien, where they live for a time. But a soul may also end up in the kingdom of the dead before the human dies. Then the shaman "has to hunt for his soul and return it to the sick person so that the latter can regain health and life."[14]

For the ancient Celts, the beyond was a pleasant land that bore a variety of names: Tír na n-Óg (Land of the Young), Tír na mBéo (Land of the Living), and Tír Sorcha (The Shining Land), among others. This is not a kingdom of the dead, as these names clearly indicate. Yet the historian Procopius of Caesarea (ca. 500–565 CE) informs us that the souls of the dead were transported to Brittia. In Ireland, they were led to the small island of Tech Duinn, off the coast of the Isle of Dursey. The most famous of these isles is that of Avalon (the Apple Orchard) where King Arthur was taken. And when a mysterious woman invited Bran mac Febail to join her in another paradisiacal island, it was located "in the ocean, to the west of us" (*isind oceon frinn aníar*).

The otherworld is to be found beneath the mound and it is written in the *Book of Taliesin*: "Annwfn is below the world" (*Annwfyn is eluyd*), under a lake (the Loch na nÉn, for example), in the sea, on an island in the middle of a lake, or off the seacoast.

The isolation of the otherworld is already present in the legends concerning Alexander the Great that feature the Islands of the Blessed.[15] We should again note that the ancients located it beyond the Land of Darkness, in the north of the earth. Furthermore, this placement in the north is a recurring phenomenon, both in the mythologies and in the visions, and sometimes the east and northeast are added. The orientation of pagan burial sites provides a confirmation

Arnold Böcklin, *The Isle of the Dead* (1886).

for the belief that the beyond was located in these regions. This situation is sometimes alluded to indirectly, as in the story of the revenant Garnier, who says: "Alas for me, since, coming from remote countries through many dangers, I have suffered from storms, snow, and the cold. How many fires have I burned and how much bad weather have I put up with in coming here."[16]

THREE

From the Christian Beyond to the Literature of Revelations

Christians' knowledge of the beyond essentially rested on the Bible and the apocryphal texts. The foundational texts of the literature of revelations are the descent of Jesus into Hell (*Descensus ad inferos*); the *Vision of Ezra,* which has been dated to the second century; the *Apocalypse of Paul,* most likely written in the third century; and the *Gospel of Nicodemus,* written in Greek around 361. The latter text had a considerable impact and was used in preaching as well as in the exempla and *The Golden Legend* of Jacobus de Voragine.

According to the Gospel of Matthew (12:40), "the Son of Man shall be three days and three nights in the heart of the earth." The apocryphal texts interpreted this as a katabasis between death and the Resurrection. In the second-century text the *Questions of Bartholomew,* Christ states: "For when I vanished away from the cross, then went I down into Hades that I might bring up Adam and all them that were with him."[1] In the fourth to fifth century, the *Acts of Philip* clearly announce what shape the literature of revelations will take: a young man tells the story of his descent into hell, during which he witnessed the punishments inflicted on sinners.[2]

The *Vision of Ezra* shows the hero visiting hell, to which he descends by six thousand and seven hundred stairs under the guidance of seven angels who were responsible for him. There he see the punishment of adulterers, the incestuous, and the greedy, and so forth. He crosses a bridge spanning a river of fire that is swarming with serpents and scorpions, and then he climbs to the heavens and argues with God.[3]

The *Apocalypse of Paul* enjoyed considerable success and was translated into eight languages. It was the primary inspiration for the vision literature of the eighth to thirteenth centuries, notably the visions of Fursey, Tnugdalus, and Alberic. It tells of the apostle's raptures in the third heaven where he sees paradise, the city of Christ, and a river in which a multitude of men and women are bathing, some immersed up to their knees, and others to their navels, lips, and scalp. He then catches sight of another river of fire, pits that are three hundred cubits deep, and humans standing on top of an obelisk of fire and being torn to pieces by beasts. The pits of the abyss give off a terrible stench. In the north he sees men and women immersed in the cold. At the end, Paul enters paradise.[4] Traces of the influence of this text can be found in Aldhelm in 709 and, five centuries later, in a German poem with the title *Sanctus Paulus*.[5]

Christ in Hell, after Michael Burghers (d. 1727).

The *Gospel of Nicodemus* tells the story of Jesus's descent into hell, how he brought it under his dominion, and his meetings with Adam, Elijah, and Enoch. André de Coutances translated this text into French in the twelfth century.[6]

The apologist and moralist Tertullian (ca. 197–222) regarded hell as a jail, which corresponds to the Platonic image of the prison and the bonds of the body: "it is an immensity located within a deep trough of the earth and hidden within its very depths" (*in fossa terrae et in alto vastitas et in ipsis visceribus eius abstrusa profunditas* [*Ad nationes* 7, 4]). Here the soul will await judgment and the gates of this prison will only open at the time of Christ's second coming. For Tertullian, the Gehenna, a "treasury of a subterranean and mysterious fire intended as punishment" (*ignis arcani subterraneus ad poenam thesaurus* [*Apologeticum* 47, 12]), replaces the Phlegethon. The infernal fire is divine in essence, thus incorruptible, and it is the vomiting of volcanoes (*Apologeticum* 48, 14).

The *Life of Anthony* (Βίος καὶ πολιτέια τοῦ ὁσίου πατρὸς ἡμῶν Ἀντονίου),[7] a hagiographic legend written around 360 by Athanasius, the bishop of Alexandria, and translated into Latin in 373 by Evagrius of Antioch, supplied an image of the devil that inspired quite a few subsequent authors. Flaming torches came out of his mouth and his hair was on fire; smoke poured out of his mouth. He disguised himself as an old man or even as Christ.

Aurelius Prudentius Clemens (348–405/410), better known as Prudentius, concentrated on the fate of sinners after death and in his *Hamartigenia* (The Origin of Sin), he writes:

> The Father, in His foreknowledge, set alight the fires of pallid Tartarus (*liventia Tartara*) blackened with molten lead, and at the bottom of dark Avernus He dug out the pitch-filled pits in the bitumen of the infernal waters, and in the gulf of Phlegethon He prescribed that swarms of gnawing worms (*inolescere vermes*) provide an eternal punishment for crimes. (Ἁμαρτιγένεια, ll. 824–30)

A little further on, Prudentius gives a sketch of what is awaiting the righteous in paradise (ll. 856–59). For him, hell is an abyss with a landscape of lakes and caverns that resembles a volcanic region. The souls there are plunged into pits,[8] and on the night that is the anniversary of Christ's descent, the raging flames subside for a time.[9] We should note that the works of Prudentius were much studied and commented upon during the Middle Ages. His influence can still be felt in *The Adventures of Telemachus* and *The Dialogues of the Dead* by François Fénelon (1651–1715).

PHYSICAL RAPTURE

A distinction must be established between the accounts of the witnesses that speak of coma or catalepsy, as opposed to the stories of those persons who are believed to be dead because their spirit or soul had left their body, which we may refer to as "discorporation."[10]

In the first case, the people present undertake an examination of the body with two different results: there are either a few signs that make it possible to show that death has not occurred and what is happening is a trance, or all the clinical signs present speak in favor of death.

The second case gives rise to a great number of accounts. Gregory of Tours, a Frankish historian of the sixth century, recorded the testimony of Salvi, who, after being thought dead, came back to life, crying:

"Merciful Lord, why have You done this to me? Why have you decreed that I should return to this dark place where we dwell on earth? I should have been so much happier in Your compassion on high, instead of having to begin once again my useless life here below. . . . When my cell shook four days ago," he went on, "and you saw me lying dead, I was raised up by two angels and carried to the highest pinnacle of heaven, until I seemed to have beneath my feet not only this squalid earth of ours, but the sun and the moon, the clouds and the stars. Then I was led through a gate which shone more brightly than our sunshine and so entered a building where the floor gleamed with gold and silver. The light was such as I cannot describe to you, and the sense of space was quite beyond our experience. The place was filled with a throng of people who were neither men nor women, a multitude stretching so far, this way and that, so it was not possible to see where it ended. The angels pushed a way for me through the crowd of people which stood in front of me, and so we came to a spot to which our gaze had been directed even while we were still a long way off. Over it hung a cloud more luminous than any light, and yet no sun was visible, no moon and no star: indeed, the cloud shone more brightly than any of these and had a natural brilliance of its own. A Voice came out of the cloud, as the voice of many waters. Sinner that I am, I was greeted with great deference by a number of beings, some dressed in priestly vestments and others in everyday dress: my guides told me that these were martyrs and other holy men whom we honour here on earth and to whom we pray with great devotion. As I stood in the spot where I was ordered to stand there was wafted over me a perfume of such sweetness that, nourished by its delectable essence, I have felt the need of no food or drink until this very moment. Then I heard a Voice which said: 'Let this man go back into the world, for our churches have need of him.' I heard the Voice, but I could not see who was speaking.". . .

As he said this, all those who were with him were amazed. The holy man of God wept. Then he said: "Woe is me that I have dared to reveal such a mystery!"[11]

The Venerable Bede (673–735), the Anglo-Saxon historian, recorded the vision of Dryhthelm[12] in his *Historia ecclesiastica gentis Anglorum* (History of the English Church and People; bk. V, chap. 12).[13] Stricken one day by a quickly worsening illness, Dryhthelm died in the early hours of the night, but returned to life at the break of day. He sat up and all the weeping people gathered around him fled except for his wife. He entered the monastery of Melrose, received the tonsure, and lived out his days in penance. There he recounted his vision: a guide clad in a garment of light had taken him on a visit of the beyond.

This text enjoyed enormous distribution. Otloh of Sankt Emmeram (d. ca. 1067) included it in his *Liber visionum* (Book of Vision).[14] We find it recounted again in the homilies of Ælfric (ca. 950–1010), the abbot of Eynsham; in the work of the Cistercian monk Hélinand of Froimont (ca. 1160–1230), author of *Les Vers de la Mort* (Verses of Death); in the work of Stephen of Bourbon (ca. 1180–1261); and in *The Golden Legend*. Bede also reported two other visions, which, like the one experienced by Dryhthelm, found a place in the works of Otloh of Sankt Emmeram.[15]

In 678 or 679, Barontus, a monk of the monastery of Saint Peter in Langoretus (Lonrey, later known as Saint-Cyran, located in the *département* of Indre, France), fell ill after singing matins and found himself "taken to the brink of death" (*ad extremum funere ductus*).[16] He had the deacon Eodan summoned, who found him unable to speak, and then he ceased to move all together. The community went into mourning and recited the psalms until vespers. At daybreak Barontus woke up, yawned, opened his eyes, and told of where he had been and all that he saw there.

In a letter addressed to Eadburga, abbess of Thanet in Kent, Saint Boniface (died 754) recounted the vision of a monk of Wenlock who went into an ecstatic trance although he was gravely ill. The account opens with a description of "evil spirits" who fought over the soul with angels, each devil embodying a sin. Then the monk saw hell with its pits of fire and the miserable souls in the form of wailing and shrieking black birds, crossed over a wooden bridge spanning a river of fire and reached the heavenly Jerusalem.[17] Otloh of Sankt Emmeran repeated this vision almost word for word.[18]

In the seventh century, the Galician hermit Valerio of Bierzo (ca. 630–695) told of what had befallen Bonellus, who died "as the result of a serious illness, struck with a physical deficiency, and then, several hours later, returned to his body, which had recovered all his lost health" and recounted the story of his vision.[19] An angel of light had shown him heaven and then hell, from which emanated all horrible howls and moans. Bonellus went on to live for some time before giving up his soul. Valerio tells of another experience, undergone by the Visigoth Maximus, who, ill, was carried off by an angel of light and saw the heavenly paradise and the abyss of hell before reentering his body on the command of his guide.[20]

In the eleventh century, Hincmar (806–882), archbishop of Reims and counselor to Charles the Bald, recounted the story of Bernold, whose precarious health had left him at death's door. For four days he was unable to drink, eat, or speak, and then he asked for a priest to be summoned and shared with him his vision during which, conducted by a guide, he had seen the tortures inflicted on prelates and noblemen. One of them said to him: "You will leave this world to return to your body," and he also informed him that after fourteen years spent in his body, he would return here.[21]

Around the year 900, the *Vision of Emperor Charles III* (*Visio Karoli Tertii Imperatoris*), who was also known as Charles the Fat, made use of a motif that shows up in folklore: a ball of thread. Essentially, the anonymous author tells us:

A glorious being appeared to Charles holding a ball of thread that emitted a beam of light.[22] He unwound it and ordered Charles to wind one end around his thumb because he was going to take him into the labyrinth of hell. They descended into fiery valleys where demons attempted to snatch away the thread; when these attempts failed, the demons attacked Charles in order to throw him into a flaming pit, but the angel cast the thread around the emperor's shoulders and drew Charles toward him. They ascended fiery mountains, from which flowed down burning rivers. On their banks were furnaces filled with serpents. They then entered a valley that was dark on one side and luminous on the other, and Charles saw two casks, one filled with lukewarm water and the other with boiling water. In the boiling cask he found his father, Louis II the German. Thanks to the intercession of Saint Remigius, Louis could find relief by moving into the lukewarm cask every other day. After hearing his uncle Lothaire's predictions for his future, he undid the thread from his thumb and his spirit returned to his body.

Peter Damian (ca. 1007–1072), bishop of Ostia, recounts the story of an ailing young man who soon found himself on his deathbed (*ad extremum pervenit*). He looked like a corpse (*quasi defunctus*), but nevertheless, life could still be felt in his cadaver (*cadaver exanime*) and a palpitation in his chest (*motus in ejus pectore palpitaret*); this is when the vision took place, at the end of which Saint Peter led his spirit back into his body (*reddensque spiritum corpori*).[23]

On September 29, 1125, Orm, a thirteen-year-old lay brother, fell ill and remained so for eight weeks, during which time he was unable to eat or drink. His body was lifeless (*exanime*), cold and stiff (*corpus frigidum et inflexibile*), as if he were dead (*simillimum mortuo*). Everyone thought that his vital spirit (*vitalis spiritus*) had left. He remained inert for thirteen days and thirteen nights, then stirred and sat up as if he was coming out of slumber, and he related what had happened to him: the archangel Michael had dragged him to the gates of heaven, then toward hell, and had showed him paradise, sealed off by a wall.[24] Orm remained alive from December 16 to June 1 in great suffering, and then he died after thirty-six days without speaking or eating.

In 1148, the knight Tundale (Tnugdalus)[25] "fell to the ground, stiff as death as if he had never lived, and he showed all the signs of having died because his soul had been carried away from him. . . . There he was, lying prone as if dead on the tenth hour of Wednesday until the same time on Saturday. There was no thought given to burying him because there was a bit of warmth on the left side of his chest. At the aforementioned hour, the body recovered its soul and remained in the same condition save for a very faint breathing. After an hour had passed, Tundale began breathing normally again.[26] He felt himself coming back into his body" (*se sensit induere corpus suum*).

Alberic of Settefrati (1101–1146) fell gravely ill at the age of nine years and remained immobile and completely senseless for nine days and nine nights as if dead. He sees a dove stick its beak into his mouth and pull something out, and then the bird carries him away. In his journey under the guidance of two angels, he discovers purgatory, hell, and paradise. Like the aforementioned Barontus, he was stricken by fever and "led to the brink of death" (*ad extremum funere ductus*).[27]

In 1190, Godescalc, an inhabitant of the village of Horchen near Neumünster (Schleswig-Holstein), "fell ill for a full seven days. On the eighth day he was taken from the light of this world and regained his body some five days later. Having noticed that his lips were moving slightly although he was lying rigid and cold as if dead, those present did not dare to bury him, deeming that his soul was still within him and only made numb by the heavy burden of the illness." Godescalc then recounted the story of his journey in the beyond. The cleric who wrote down his story after hearing it from Godescalc added the following remarks of his own:

When the soul of this man rejoined his body, he remained for five weeks so languid that he had neither sense nor reason, and he no longer took any food or drink. Having tasted the delights of the higher world and feeling as if he was drowning in the bliss of what he had seen, he greatly cursed being imprisoned in his shell of perishable flesh. He continued to aspire to rid himself of the bonds of his body and desired with all his might to enjoy the splendor of the freedom such as he had seen.

But he had been poisoned by having

breathed in the vapors rising from the road that led to hell. This was why pus oozed from his nose and ears, and he had to long suffer such oozings caused by the infernal pestilence. He was also afflicted by a sharp pain on his side, which he explained this way: when he drew close to the furnace, its flames had burned his flank. On this point, as on the others, the reason remained hidden why he could feel on his body what he had suffered in his soul.[28]

This last remark expresses all of the cleric's uncertainty as to whether Godescalc had journeyed *in corpore* or *in spiritu*. Instead of a discorporation, we should view this as some sort of disassociative state (*dédoublement*), which is the only way to explain the presence of these stigmata on Godescalc. We should note that, from the perspective of psychoanalysis, the visions engendered in a state of diminished health are a projection of mental content, and the fact that Godescalc was ill would fit in with such an interpretation. It is still necessary to explain the stigmata that he bore upon awakening, which is a point we will return to later.

The *Vision of Fulbert* (*Visio Philiberti*), attested to in a Latin poem dating from the eleventh or twelfth century and translated into Middle High German by Heinrich von Neustadt,[29] brought a major novelty into this genre by including a debate between the soul and the body in the narrative.[30] The basic outline is simple: While dreaming, a hermit sees a corpse; the soul that has parted from it is cursing it and accusing it of being the cause of its damnation. The debate ends when the devils arrive and drag the soul off to hell. This debate had a major resonance and both Hildebert of Lavardin (1056–1133), archbishop of Tours, and the philosopher and theologian Peter Abelard (d. 1142) mentioned it in their works.

Ansellus Scholasticus offers us this story from the twelfth century:

On the day of Easter, a monk of Reims saw Jesus come down off the cross, who invited the monk to follow him if he believed in the Resurrection. The monk obeyed and plunged into the depths of hell. The fright of the devils on seeing the arrival of Jesus is described in vivid fashion: they fled in every direction, roaring like lions whose cubs have been taken away. On the other hand, the angels exulted and welcomed the souls freed from hell. The Christ commanded the monk to return to his cloister and gave him a black demon to be his guide, which is quite an unusual detail. On the return path, devils surrounded the monk, gnashing their teeth and trying to grab him with their red-hot pincers in revenge for the liberation of the souls. Once they were back at the monastery, the demon asked him why Jesus had come down to hell to take away guilty souls. "It was at the request of the bishops, abbots, monks, and nuns, who, throughout the year, say masses for the deceased and give alms," the monk replied. "The only ones left are the thieves, adulterers, parricides, oath-breakers, and impenitent sinners. Isn't it possible to be freed from infernal punishment by repenting?" "That's impossible," responded the demon, who then gave him some pernicious advice: "Don't get up too early when the bell sounds matins; rest a bit longer, you will get there in time for Mass." But the monk rejected this counsel in horror and the demon vanished.[31]

We may mention a final example. In 1467, in Perugia, Isabetta di Luigi fell ill and "died." She lay at rest with her eyes weeping (*gli occhi inbambolati*), feeling nothing, and making no movement (*sença senso et sença movimiento*).[32]

In all the cases I've mentioned, the texts say the soul or spirit leaves the body following an illness—this occurs in twenty-five out of thirty cases—and sets off on a journey into the beyond that reveals hell and purgatory to the visionary, and then lets him catch a glimpse of heaven from afar. When Tnugdalus told of his experience, he began by saying, "When my soul left my body and it was dead" (*cum anima mea corpus exueret et illud mortuum esse cognoscere*), and it was similar when Niccolò de Guidoni "suddenly fell down dead" (*cadde in terra de morte subitana*) and experienced a vision in 1300.[33] What we have here is the medieval form of the near-death experience (NDE) and out-of-body experience (OBE). We will revisit this topic.

Common to all these visions is the Christian background that leaves a deep imprint on the narratives in which the visionary meets demons and saints, as well as angels or the Virgin. It is useful to note that the visionaries of the twelfth and thirteenth centuries are clergymen, and that from the seventh to eleventh centuries only three laypeople are cited as having such visions. In total, fifteen lay people (eight peasants and seven nobles) and nineteen monks are visionaries. It is as if the Church realized the potential of such tales and made use of them while accentuating their pedagogy of fear. In his *History of the English Church and People,* Bede wrote the following about Dryhthelm's vision: "For, in order to arouse the living from spiritual death (*ad excitationem viventium de morte animae*), a man already dead returned to bodily life and related many notable things that he had seen."[34] In the thirteenth century, an anonymous author dedicated a *Vision of Saint Paul's Descent into Hell* to the English Templar Henry d'Arci. It is based on older texts, and says in the prologue [answering the question of who caused the souls in hell to have respite on Sundays]:

It was Paul the apostle, and the archangel Michael, for God wanted Saint Paul to see the punishments borne by those who suffer [there], so he showed him all the punishments of hell.[35]

In *The Golden Legend* by Jacobus de Voragine, an angel urges Saint Fursey to look at the world, and the latter sees "a valley filled with shadows, and in the air four fires some distance apart from each other," and the angel explains to him that the fires are those of mendaciousness, cupidity, discord, and impiety.[36] The pedagogical message is clear because these fires examine each person in accordance with the merit of their works.

The texts dwell at length upon the tortures that await sinners after their death. Additionally, these stories were illustrated in church frescoes, similarly to depictions of the Last Judgment, such as in the Cathedral of Albi. It is not difficult, then, to comprehend the influence they had, as the images would be used to instruct the illiterate peasants.

JOURNEYS IN DREAM

For two are the gates of shadowy dreams, and one is fashioned of horn and one of ivory. Those dreams that pass through the gate of sawn ivory deceive men, bringing words that find no fulfillment. But those that come forth through the gate of polished horn bring true issues to pass, when any mortal sees them.

HOMER, *THE ODYSSEY*, XIX, LL. 562–67
(TRANS. MURRAY)

Although much rarer than the visions that arise during an illness, those that come in dreams deserve our attention. In order to get a better grasp of them, it would be a good idea to recall a few basic concepts.[37]

For the Greeks, Hypnos (Sleep) and Thanatos (Death) are two twin brothers, in other words, the transitional state is closely connected to actual death, and even precedes it. More than one ancient author noted that dying in one's sleep was the most desirable way to end one's life, and there are even prayers that call for this.[38] For example, one of them says: "Remember that sleep is the portrait of death."[39] Tales and legends are not remiss in this matter, such as those that depict Brynhild put into a deep sleep by Odin on Hindarfjall (Hind Mountain),[40] and Sleeping Beauty.

The lexicon has preserved this kinship between sleep and death since the word *cemetery* derives from *koimētērion* (κοιμητήριον),[41] "dormitory," which has its basis in the Greek verb κεῖμαι, "to lie asleep." The Germans regarded sleep as a visitor, which is expressed by their word *Sandmann*, "the emissary," which inspired the French term *marchand de sable* (sand-merchant), and the English *sandman*. These latter terms resulted from a mistaken identification of the German word *sand-* (which derives from the verb *senden*, "to emit," "to send") with the French word *sable* (sand) and the English *sand*.

There are several classical words for designating what takes possession of you when you sleep: Greek *enupnion* (ἐνύπνιον), the dream, which corresponds with the Latin *visio*, and lastly Greek *oneiros* (ὄνειρος). Since the time of Saint Augustine (354–430),[42] the Church has made a distinction between three kinds of visions: the intellectual vision that is a communication with no tangible image; the imaginative vision, a representation produced by God that does not go through the eyes; and physical vision, which does appear through the sense of seeing. Later on, the beatific vision, and lastly the mystical vision, which only addresses the spirit, were added to this list. In the cases we are concerned with, the vision is no longer a tangible understanding but a supernatural knowing, which some regard as an illusion or hallucination: it implies an act of faith.

According to the Christian interpretation, dreams are dangerous. The soul does not leave the body but receives images by way of what was then called *visio spiritualis* (when applied to concrete things) or *visio intellectualis* (when remaining in the domain of abstraction). The dream is suspect, in conformance to Ecclesiastes (5:6),* because it "short-circuits the ecclesiastical intermediary role," to borrow the words of Jacques Le Goff.[43]

---

*["Where there are many dreams there are many vanities and words without number: but do thou fear God" (Douay-Rheims trans.). In modern numbering this corresponds to Ecclesiastes 5:7. —*Ed.*]

The narratives set the scene of the dream visions basing them on a thought that Lactantius illustrated perfectly when he said: "[God] left to Himself the power of teaching man future events by means of the dream."[44] Dream visions are therefore pedagogical, and the future of which he speaks is, in fact, that of the dead.

Saint Augustine made a thorough examination of the question of visons and took the following position:

> Like dreams, moreover, are also some visions of persons awake, who have had their senses troubled, such as phrenetic persons, or those who are mad in any way: for they too talk to themselves just as though they were speaking to people verily present, and as well with absent as with present, whose images they perceive, whether persons living or dead. But just as they which live, are unconscious that they are seen of them and talk with them; for indeed they are not really themselves present, or themselves make speeches, but through troubled senses, these persons are wrought upon by suchlike imaginary visions; just so they also who have departed this life, to persons thus affected appear as present, while they be absent, and whether any man sees them in regard of their image, are themselves utterly unconscious.
>
> Similar to this is also that condition when persons, with their senses more profoundly in abeyance than is the case in sleep, are occupied with the like visions. For to them also appear images of [the] quick and [the] dead; but then, when they return to their senses, whatever dead they say they have seen are thought to have been verily with them: and they who hear these things pay no heed to the circumstance that there were seen in like manner the images of certain living persons, absent and unconscious.

At this point he describes in detail what happened to a certain Curma:

> A certain man by name Curma, of the municipal town of Tullium, which is hard by Hippo, a poor member of the Curia, scarcely

competent to serve the office of a duumvir of that place, and a mere rustic, being ill, and all his senses entranced, lay all but dead for several days: a very slight breathing in his nostrils, which on applying the hand was just felt, and barely betokened that he lived, was all that kept him from being buried for dead. Not a limb did he stir, nothing did he take in the way of sustenance, neither in the eyes nor in any other bodily sense was he sensible of any annoyance that impinged upon them. Yet he was seeing many things like as in a dream, which, when at last after a great many days he woke up, he told that he had seen. And first, presently after he opened his eyes, "Let some one go," said he, "to the house of Curma the smith, and see what is doing there." And when some one had gone thither, the smith was found to have died in that moment that the other had come back to his senses, and, it might almost be said, revived from death. Then, as those who stood by eagerly listened, he told them how the other had been ordered to be had up [i.e., appear], when he himself was dismissed; and that he had heard it said in that place from which he had returned, that it was not Curma of the Curia, but Curma the smith who had been ordered to be fetched to that place of the dead. Well, in these dream-like visions of his, among those deceased persons whom he saw handled according to the diversity of their merits, he recognized also some whom he had known when alive. That they were the very persons themselves I might perchance have believed, had he not in the course of this seeming dream of his seen also some who are alive even to this present time, namely, some clerks of his district, by whose presbyter there he was told to be baptized at Hippo by me, which thing he said had also taken place. So then he had seen a presbyter, clerks, [and] myself, persons, to wit, not yet dead, in this vision in which he afterwards also saw dead persons. Why may he not be thought to have seen these last in the same way as he saw us? that is, both the one sort, and the other, absent and unconscious, and consequently not the persons themselves, but similitudes of them just as of the places? He saw, namely, both a plot of ground where was that presbyter with the clerks, and Hippo where he was by me seemingly baptized: in which spots assuredly he was not, when he seemed to himself to be there. For what was at that time going on there, he knew not, which, without doubt, he would have known if he had verily been there. The sights beheld, therefore, were those which are not presented in the things themselves as they are, but shadowed forth in a sort of images of the things. In fine, after much that he saw, he narrated how he had, moreover, been led into Paradise, and how it was there said to him, when he was thence dismissed to return to his own family, "Go, be baptized, if thou wilt be in this place of the blessed."[45]

This text is noteworthy because it presents a disassociative state, a bilocation, while at the same time it attempts to conceal any troubling elements that the phenomenon might have. In deciphering the facts, we find that there is only one Curma. Pope Gregory the Great (ca. 540–604) would later borrow the story of Curma, whose name he changed to Stephen. This man was led down to hell where he was turned back by the judge because he was not the right Stephen. Gregory left out the passage that mentioned a second Curma (*Dialogi,* bk. IV, chap. 37, 5–6).

This theme of the resuscitated dead man, which is reminiscent of shamanic journeying, resurfaces in the fifth century in the *Miracles of the Protomartyr Stephen,* which speaks of a man named Dativus:

Half crushed by the collapse of his house, he was left for dead, but his wife begged Stephen, who resuscitated Dativus. Once he was retored to consciousness, he told of what he had seen in the beyond: He had been surrounded by a multitude of dead people, some of whom he knew and others he did not, and then a young man clad in white approached and ordered them to retreat, and they immediately vanished (*statim illas mortuorum turbas non comparuisse*). Finally, the youth resuscitated him.[46]

The difference between sleep and death is scarcely apparent in the *Vision of Salvius* (Saint Salvi of Albi, d. 584), which Gregory of Tours recounted in the sixth century. One day, in the grip of a high fever, he lay in his bed gasping for breath, when all at once his cell began to shake and became filled with a great light. With his hands lifted to heaven, he gave thanks and breathed forth his spirit. Plans for his burial were underway when "he stirred himself as if awakened from a deep sleep, opened his eyes, raised his hands and spoke," regretting that he had been obliged to return to the world, and he recounted his vision to all who were present.[47]

Around the year 656, an anonymous author wrote the *Vita Sancti Fursei* (Life of Saint Fursey),[48] the Irish founder of the Cnobheresburg monastery in East Anglia, and later the founder of the monastery at Lagny near Paris, where he received a vision. Falling ill and enveloped in darkness, he gave his last sigh and saw himself picked up by two angels with a third preceding them, armed with a shield and a sword to protect the visionary from attacks by demons. His spirit then rejoined his body because they could not take him with them until he had completed an action. Fursey took communion, and the next day his feet grew cold again, and he fell into a deep sleep on his bed (*in lectum quasi somno gravatus obdormivit*). It is understood that the angels expected him to receive communion. In the course of his journey through the beyond, he met two bishops who gave him instructions and advice. During his return trip to earth, Fursey was burned on the jaw and shoulder by demons. When his soul rejoined his body, he saw his chest open (*vidit pectore illius corpus aperiri*). This detail is absent in the account of Fursey that appears in *The Golden Legend* (chap. 140). On the other hand, it said that "the devil struck Fursey so hard that after he returned to life, the marks from those blows remained forever" (*tunc dyabolus tam graviter eum percussit, ut postmodum vitae restitutus semper percussionis vestigium retineret*). And the writer noted: "In a surprising manner, what the soul had suffered had manifested in the flesh."

Heito (d. 836), the bishop of Basel and later the abbot of Reichenau, recounted the vision the monk Wettin experienced during an illness. He slept "as much from fatigue of the soul as from that of the body" (*post tantam lassitudinem tam animae quam corporis in somno resoluto*) and saw evil spirits carrying instruments of torture, and then an angel. He awoke then, told of what he had seen, and then died shortly after.[49]

In 824, the Carolingian poet Walahfrid Strabon (808/809–849) put the vision into verse form. Folcuin of Lobbes (d. 990),[50] superior of Lobbes Abbey in the Hainaut (Wallonia), followed by the Benedictine monk Arnold of Sankt Emmeram,[51] spread the text of the vision yet further.

In a manuscript dating from the eleventh century in the National Library of Rome[52] there is a story that has been given the name *Vision of a Monk Who Went into a Trance and Witnessed the Death of a Sinner and That of a Righteous Person*. This is the story of his two visions:

When he was close to death, his soul hesitated to leave the body because of its fear. It could see the demons that were offering it a globe and threatening it by saying: "Why are we delaying to take this soul? Perhaps the archangel Michael will come with his angels to carry it off while we have it shackled." "Have no fear that he will intervene," replied one of the demons, sure of the fate of the soul, whose presence he had never left. The soul lamented: "Alas, poor me, what did I do to deserve being put into such a dark and evil body?" and hurled abuse at the body. The soul concluded its speech by saying that the body would be food for the worms and that it was going to be carried off to hell. The demons at the headboard of the dead man's bed ordered: "Stab his eyes that coveted all that they saw; cut off his ears; pierce his heart that never knew mercy, charity, or piety! Tear off his feet and hands that were so quick to do evil!" And gradually the body changed its appearance. They then pulled out the soul and carried it off. On the way, the soul caught sight of a great brightness and learned from its abductors that it was paradise. The soul was finally led into hell, where a demon in the form of a dragon swallowed it then spat it into the flames.

After this first vision, the monk went back to sleep and saw in a dream that he had been transported to a monastery where a poor monk was dying alone on a straw mattress. The visionary heard the song of the angels that had come to collect the monk's soul, which came out of his mouth, and then turned toward the body and told him it was time to part. The soul thanked him for having suffered hunger, thirst, and all sorts of deprivations. Saint Michael then carried the soul away on his gleaming wings.[53]

One day in 1196, Thurkill, a peasant of Stisted in the diocese of London, sank into a deep slumber. Saint Julian woke him up (*a sompno excitavit*) and invited him to follow him. Thurkill wanted to get dressed, but his visitor told him there was no need because his body would remain in bed and only his soul would accompany him (*sola enim anima tua mecum abibit*). Julian went on to say: "So that no one thinks you are dead, I will leave your vital breath" (*vitalem in te flatum dimittam*). Surprised by her husband sleeping much longer than usual, Thurkill's wife shook his head, his arms, and his legs, all in vain. The local inhabitants and the parish priest were alerted, and the latter ordered that Thurkill's mouth be forced open so that some holy water could be poured into it. Thurkill's jaws were spread apart with a wedge and the holy water was administered to him. Thurkill rose up and leapt naked from the bed, and went to open the window. Then, seeing the people gathered in his bedroom, he got back into bed, covered his nakedness, and complained that he had been woken up, for he would have received the testimony of his vision (*testimonium visionis sue*). He finally told of what he had seen, concluding that he "had been guided back into his body without knowing how" (*ad corpus proprium nesciens quo ordinis reductus*).[54]

Even though the *Vision of Thurkill* follows the canons of the genre, it clearly distinguishes itself from other vision accounts by its circumstances; the deep sleep is suggestive of catalepsy. It should be noted that these phenomena occur when the subject is in a state of reduced awareness or has been overwhelmed by a fainting spell, a coma, or sleep. Lethargy is the *sine qua non* for the experience of a vision.

An Icelandic poem written around 1200, the *Sólarljóð* (Song of the Sun) features a father who, after his death, returns to visit his son and give him advice. He describes hell to him, as well as the punishments inflicted on thieves, murderers, and so forth, and the welcome into paradise for men who have led good lives.

39

The Sun I saw,	*Sól ek sá*
True star of day,	*sanna dagstjörnu*
Droop in worlds of din;	*drúpa dynheimum í;*
But hell's gate	*en Heljar grind*
I heard on another path	*heyrða ek á annan veg*
Creaking heavily.	*þjóta þungliga.*

40

The Sun I saw,	*Sól ek sá*
Set with bloody staves,	*setta dreyrstöfum,*
Much was I then leaning out of	*mjök var ek þá ór heimi hallr;*
the world;	
Mighty it looked to me	*máttug hon leizk*
In many ways	*á marga vegu*
from how it was before.	*frá því er fyrri var.*

41

The Sun I saw,	*Sól ek sá,*
It seemed to me,	*svá þótti mér,*
As if I were seeing worshipful God;	*sem ek sæja göfgan guð;*
I bowed to it	*henni ek laut*
For the last time	*hinzta sinni*
In the world of men.	*aldaheimi í.*

42

The Sun I saw,	*Sól ek sá,*
It shone so brightly,	*svá hon geislaði,*
That I seemed to lose my senses;	*at ek þóttumk vætki vita;*
But the streams of Gjölf	*en Gylfar straumar*
Roared in the other way,	*grenjuðu á annan veg,*
Greatly blended with blood.	*blandnir mjök við blóð.*

43

The Sun I saw	*Sól ek sá*
Trembling in my sight,	*á sjónum skjálfandi,*
Dread-filled and downcast;	*hræzlufullr ok hnipinn;*
for my heart	*þvíat hjarta mitt*
was so greatly	*var heldr mjök*
torn asunder in shreds.	*runnit sundr í sega.*

44

I saw the Sun	*Sól ek sá*
Seldom more sorrowful,	*sjaldan hryggvari,*
I was then greatly leaning from	*mjök var ek þá ór heimi hallr;*
this world;	
My tongue	*tunga mín*
Was like wood,	*var til trés metin,*
And all chilled on the outside.	*ok kólnat alt fyr utan.*

45

I saw the Sun	*Sól ek sá*
Never again	*síðan aldregi*
After that dreary day,	*eptir þann dapra dag,*
For the waters of the mountains	*þvíat fjallavötn luktusk*
Closed up before me,	*fyr mér saman,*
And I turned away, called from	*en ek hvarf kallaðr frá kvölum.*
torments.	

46

A star of hope flew	*Vánarstjarna flaug,*
—Then I was born—	*—þá var ek fæddr,—*
Far from my breast;	*brot frá brjósti mér;*
High it flew,	*hátt at hon fló,*
Nowhere did she set down,	*hvergi settisk,*
So that she might have rest.	*svá at hon mætti hvíld hafa.*
. . .	*. . .*

51

On the Norns' seat	*Á norna stóli*
I sat for nine days,	*sat ek niu dagu,*
From there onto a horse I was heaved;	*þaðan var ek á hest hafinn;*
. . .	. . .

52

From without and within	*Utan ok innan*
It seemed to me that I fared all	*þóttumk ek alla fara*
Seven victory-worlds;	*sigrheima sjau;*
Above and below	*uppi ok niðri*
I sought better ways,	*leitaða ek œðra vegar,*
Where the roads would be clearest for me.	*hvar mér væri greiðastar götur.*

53

It must be told,	*Frá því er at segja,*
What too I first saw,	*hvat ek fyrst of sá,*
When I came into the worlds of torment:	*þá er ek var í kvölheima kominn:*
Singed birds,	*sviðnir fuglar,*
Which were souls,	*er sálir váru,*
Flew as many as midges.[55]	*flugu svá margir sem mý.*

As is typical of the Icelandic literature of the period, this text offers a mixture of pagan and Christian elements. The metal gates of the death are those of the beyond, which were called Helgrind in the mythology. Gjölf refers to the river of hell, perhaps Gjöll (Tumult), the river that in Norse cosmology was closest to the underworld.[56] The Norns are the goddesses of fate; the dead man apparently makes his way to the beyond on horseback and his journey there takes nine days. As for the souls in the form of birds, this motif was borrowed from the Latin literature of revelations.

Around 1450, an eleven-year-old boy named Blasius remained

lifeless for five days and then came back to himself "as if someone had pulled him from a sound sleep" (*tamquam a somno excitatus*).[57]

In Norway, the *Draumkvæde* (Dream Song), whose date of composition is unclear, tells the story of the dream journey of Olav Åsteson* in the beyond. The poem has fifty-two verses and was reconstructed by Moltke Moe in 1890 from ancient versions.

On Christmas night Olav Åsteson is carried off into the clouds and then at the bottom of the sea he can see hell and catch a glimpse of heaven. He has to travel through a land of thorns and cross a bridge over the Gjöll (Gjallarbrú); he wades through a marsh, comes to a crossroads, and he turns to the right and sees paradise. He makes his way to Brokksvalin, where the judgment of souls is taking place with Saint Michael weighing the souls. Olav then sees the various tortures of the damned:

> 40. *I came to several men*
> *They walked upon the burning ground:*
> *God have mercy on these poor souls*
> *Who have moved the boundary markers*
> *in the woods! . . .*

> 41. *I came to several children*
> *Who stood upon a blazing fire*
> *God have pity on these sinful souls*
> *Who cursed their father and mother . . .*

> 42. *I came to a toad and a serpent*
> *Who bit each other with their teeth:*
> *They were a sinful brother and sister*
> *Who had cursed each other . . .*

> 45. *It is hot in hell,*
> *Hotter than anyone can imagine . . .*[58]

---

*Depending on the region, his name may also appear as Olaf Åknesonen, Olaf Håkinson, or Olav Åknesi.

The *Dream Song* ends with a description of the rewards of the righteous (ll. 46–51).[59] Researchers have determined that the author of this ballad must have been familiar with the *Dialogues* of Gregory the Great, the visions from Bede's *History of the English Church and People,* and the vision of Tundale, which was translated into Icelandic (*Duggals leizla*).[60]

THE TESTIMONY OF A DISASSOCIATIVE OR "DOUBLED" STATE (*DÉDOUBLEMENT*)

If the case of Godescalc remained unparalleled, there could be good reason to doubt the account. But his vision was collected by two different clerics and the A version describes at length his aching feet and back (chap. 58 and 60), his headaches (chap. 59), his weakness, and his loss of appetite (chap. 61). One interesting detail is the fact that the cleric noted the similarities between the experience of Godescalc and those of Er of Pamphylia.[61]

The Venerable Bede tells of the vision received by Laurentius while he slept. Saint Peter appeared and scourged him for a long time for his plan to leave the flock that had been entrusted to him. On the next day, Laurentius showed the lacerations on his skin.[62]

In *The Golden Legend* (chap. 142), "the encyclopedia of the Christian religion" (André Boureau) compiled between 1261 and 1267, Jacobus de Voragine recounts the vision of Saint Jerome[63] who "about mid-Lent was taken with a sudden and burning fever, that all his body was cold, in such wise that there was no vital heat save a little which he felt in his breast."[64] During the time when preparations were being made for his funeral services, Jerome was hauled before the "tribunal of the Judge" (God) who accused him of being a Ciceronian and struck him quite hard. When he came back to life, his shoulders were all black and blue from the blows he had received in front of the tribunal.[65]

In this same collection, Jacobus de Voragine wrote the following about Fursey (chap. 140): "Then the devil smote him so grievously that, after, when he was re-established to life, the token and trace of the stroke abode ever after" (*tunc dyabolus tam graviter eum percussit, ut postmodum vitae restitutus semper percussionis vestigium retineret*).[66]

But in the *Visio Fursii*, he returned with a burn on his shoulder and on his jaw because a devil had grabbed him and held him over the flames. It is also interesting that the compiler of the vision also brought up the problem of the soul's "corporeal nature" (*Mirumque in modum quod anima sola sustinuit in carne demonstrabatur*). Yet when Barontus left his body, he was given another one made of air.

If Godescalc, Fursey, and Jerome were only carried away in spirit, then their bodies should not have shown any trace of it: we have to understand that it was their double that had been spirited away into the beyond. "In this way, the double can move and take action in a universe that can be described as a mental virtual reality," as Michel Nachez has rightly perceived.[67] This belief is not the prerogative of Christian literature, and numerous traces of it can be found in the literature of entertainment.[68] But the clerics rarely made note of the injuries brought back from an ecastatic journey, and this is for a good reason: For Christians, the soul is incorporeal and cannot be marked in any way. Ecstatic trance is a spiritual phenomenon, and one that is solely spiritual; this is what they would have us believe, since the witnesses have a body before them that is in a lethargic state.

In fact, there is not much difference between the journeys of visionaries and those of shamans who have gone into the otherworld in search of a patient's soul. We may note that the former, the visionaries, have no need to use the method of going into a trance (as can done via psychotropic drugs, dance, or using a drum) for entering the otherworld, and they are not "trance professionals" like shamans. But there is this detail which they share: both bear traces of the ordeals they went through while in the otherworld.[69]

FOUR

HELL, PURGATORY, AND PARADISE

Little by little, hell became more and more terrifying to Christians. In Ireland, the *Vision of Adamnán,* abbot of Iona from 679 to 704, paints a horrifying picture of the torments awaiting the sinner in hell. The Dominican preacher and inquisitor Stephen of Bourbon (1180–1261) gives an equally dreadful description. It is a dark place (*tenebrosus*), blazing with fire, without any springtime (*intemperatus, unde dicitur Avernus, quasi sine vernantia temperamentis*), frightful (*horridus*), parched (*aridus*), foul (*fetidus*), unclean (*immundus*), hidden (*occultus*), smoke-filled (*fumosus*), poisoned (*veneficus*), noisy (*tumultuosus*), a furnace (*caminus*), dangerous (*periculosus*), an abyss (*baratrum*), and a land of oblivion (*terra oblivionis*) named Lethe.[1] It was inspired by the stories of Dryhthelm, Fursey, Saint Jerome, the *Purgatory of Saint Patrick,* and the *Vision of Paul* as well as that of Ezra.[2]

Hell is a place that fully justifies the inscription Dante placed at its entrance: "Abandon hope all ye who enter here" (*Lasciate ogni speranza, voi ch' entrate*). In the *Vision of Saint Paul,* an apocryphal text from the end of the second century, the angel declares: "There is naught here but cold and snow."[3] Vincent of Beauvais (d. 1264) reduced the horror that this place inspired down to one gripping phrase: "Snow, night, voices, tears, brimstone, thirst, heat; hammering and harsh sounds, lost hope, shackles, serpents" (*Nix, nox, vox, lachrymae, sulphur, sitis, aestus; malleus et stridor, spes perdita, vincula, vermes*).[4]

Purgatory, from the *Très Riches Heures du Duc de Berry* (circa 1440).

Common to all of the accounts, from antiquity to the Middle Ages, is the presence of a guide accompanying the traveler who has made his way into the beyond: the Yazatas for the Persians, the Uthras for the Mandaeans, Virgil for Dante, and a saint or an angel in the visions. Every time, the guide protects the soul from attacks by demons who want to carry it off.

THE LOCATION OF HELL

The visionaries remain vague about the location of hell. For example, Orm and Laisren believe it is in the north, while Dryhthelm maintains it is in the northeast and Godescalc claims it is in the west. Some people believe it is in the middle of the earth, full of brimstone and fire, which is why it is often described as a "lake of fire and brimstone." It bears a variety of names: the Lake or Land of the Dead, the Night Lands, the Land of Oblivion, Tartarus, Gehenna, Erebus. It is filled with dragons and reptiles. Its mouth is a volcano—and, speaking of volcanoes, Isidore of Seville claimed that Mount Etna was Gehenna.[5]

Gottfried of Viterbo (died 1191) noted: "It is where the head of the Tartarus is found."[6] Concerning the Sicilian Aeolian Islands, Gregory the Great claimed that they "spit up the fire of torment" (*Dialogi*, IV, 36, 12). He noted that: "King Theodoric had died. . . . 'Yesterday, at three o'clock, Pope John and the patrician Symmachus led him, disrobed and barefoot, with his hands in chains, up to the brink of a neighboring volcano and cast him into its flaming abyss'"

The Mouth of Hell. Fresco in the Church of Saint-Méard-de-Dronne (Dordogne, France, twelfth century).

(*Dialogi*, IV, 31, 3).[7] This tradition is also cited in the *Kaiserchronik* (Emperors' Chronicle; ca. 1150), which retraces the life of Theodoric (ll. 13825–14193), but it never became well established outside of the Germanic-speaking areas. In a sermon, Julien de Vézelay observed that those who burned in Gehenna were called "Etniques," a word coined from the name Etna.[8] Caesarius of Heisterbach was speaking of a Mount Gyber [= Etna] when he was asked by a novice: "Isn't that purgatory or hell?"[9] In *The Voyage of Saint Brendan*, hell was located on a mountainous island whose inhabitants were black and hideous, and Brendan told his shipmates: "We are in the neighborhood of hell (*sumus in confinibus infernorum*)."[10] When the saint's boat passed close to the island, the devils threw huge heaps of burning slag at it:

> While sailing toward a mountain, the monks caught sight of a being that filled them with terror, a gigantic devil who emerged covered with flames from Hell. He was holding an iron hammer in his hand that was so large it could have been used as a pillar. When his intense, sparkling eyes caught sight of the monks he hastily went off to prepare the torture he intended to give them. Spitting fire from his mouth, he made his way back to his forge in a few giant steps. He came back out almost immediately with a red-hot blade that he held in his tongs, the weight of which would have caused ten oxen to fold. He lifted it up in the air and then violently cast it straight at the monks.[11]

Today we know that what Brendan witnessed was a volcanic eruption. Thus, we remain in the same category of phenomena. The Hekla volcano in Iceland was regarded as a gateway to hell during the Middle Ages.

Reference should be made here to the *Lucidarius*, which Honorius of Autun wrote around 1100. When a student asks, "Where is hell?" a schoolmaster replies:

> "There are two hells, a higher one and a lower; the first is that land full of torments. . . . The inner hell is at the end of the world, there where no man can live because of the clouds and darkness."

"Does hell have a bottom?"

"Hell is narrow at the top and wide at the bottom, so much so that no one but God alone knows how wide. No one has ever reached the bottom. The books say that a good many souls have been falling there for eternity, but that they have never seen the bottom."

"How many names does hell have?"

"[The first is] Gehenna."

"You have to tell me what they mean."

"Hell is called *lacus mortis,* which is to say, fatal lake. When souls come there, they will never leave again. It is also called *stagnum ignis,* which means lake of fire, because in the same way that the bottom of the sea will never dry up, the souls that enter it will never find refreshment. It is also called *terra tenebrosa,* which is to say the dark land, because the path that leads there is always filled with smoke, stench, and vapors. It is also called Tartarus, which means martyr, because the smoke causes the eyes to weep endlessly and the cold causes the gnashing of teeth. It is also named Gehenna, which means fire of the earth, because the fire of hell is so strong that our fire is but a pale shadow of it. It is called Erebus, meaning dragon, because the access to hell and its depths are filled with fiery serpents that never die. Another name is Baratrum, to wit, gaping darkness, because it will yawn until the Last Judgment so it can swallow more souls. It is also called Styx, meaning sorrow, because sorrow reigns there eternally. It is named Acheronta, which means groan, because the devils there are as busy as the sparks from furnaces. It is also named Flegeton because of a river that crosses through it. From it rises a stench of pitch and brimstone and it is also so cold that it exceeds all the other torments of hell."

"Where is the upper hell located?"

"It can be found at many places in this world, on high mountains and islands in the sea. Pitch and brimstone burn there and the souls that need salvation are tortured there."[12]

Honorius of Autun here recycles Gregory the Great's idea that the dead can atone for their sins on earth, hence the notion of two hells.

Albertus Magnus made a distinction between the lower hell, the Gehenna reserved for the damned, and the higher hell, the limbo for children.[13] For Mechthild of Magdeburg (d. 1238), who was a great mystic, hell was divided into three parts: one part was reserved for Christians, one for Jews, and one for pagans.[14]

In his *Image du Monde* (Mirror of the World), Gossouin de Metz (thirteenth century) poses the questions "Where does hell lie and what is it?" and answers that it is enclosed inside the earth, and is ugly, dark, hideous, full of stench, full of fire and brimstone, full of filth and "every evil venture," fear, pain, anguish, sorrow, hunger and thirst. Its names are abyss, land of perdition, land of oblivion, and land of death, because the souls that are cast there remain there eternally: "all die there while still living and still live while dying." Perilous rivers of fire and ice are found there, filled with venom and beasts that make a great racket while they molest souls.[15]

It would not be until around 1304, with the appearance of *Placides et Timeo ou Li secrés as philosophes* (Placidus and Timeus, or the Secrets of the Philosophers), a small encyclopedia, that we discover anything new about hell: "The ancients say that the gulf of Satrenie goes down there,"[16] a gulf that the text calls "the navel of the sea," which freezes and flows by the Lake of Hell. The author is using here a transformed version of the myth of Medusa that had enjoyed considerable popularity since it was first disseminated in 1181; the gulf, whose name was distorted into Satalie, Satilie, Sathame, and so forth, came into being when the head of a monster, born of the intercourse between a dead and a living person, was tossed into the sea.[17]

THE TOPOGRAPHY OF HELL

In the French version of the *Vision of Saint Paul* by Henry d'Arci, a thirteenth-century Templar of Lincolnshire, Paul comes to a furnace:

All about were seven cruel tortures, and the devils were casting the souls in [the oven]. The first is snow, the second is fire, the third is snakes, the fourth is blood, the fifth is ice, the sixth is lightning, and the seventh is pestilence.

In medieval times the Jaws of Hell were often envisioned as the gaping mouth of a monster.

The Gateway to Hell in the *Visio Tnugdali*.

It is easy to see that a veritable impressionistic tradition was formed over the centuries, which determined the essential elements of the descriptions of hell. In the fifteenth century, the *Visio Lazari*, written in Middle High German, describes hell as five cells corresponding to five torments deserved by sinners; the characteristics of this hell are fire, ice, total darkness, stench, smoke, brimstone, and pitch. The damned are attached to pillars with chains of fire, and the devils tear off bits of their flesh with flaming tongs.[18] In this vision there is no purgatory because the time of the narrative is before the death of Christ. An original detail is that even the devils suffer from the fires they are fanning. We may note, incidentally, the use of the acronym SALIGIA, which is a mnemonic device for remembering the sins that lead to hell: *superbia, avaritia, luxuria, invidia, gula, ira, acedia* (pride, avarice, jealousy, envy, gluttony, wrath, sloth*).

The *Vision of Alberic*,[19] which I mentioned earlier, has the merit of offering us a precise topography of the beyond that contains an entire series of places, not to mention the punishments attached to each of them. Here they are, in the order in which we cross through them with Alberic:

✻ The purgatory of the souls of one-year-old children; they remain there for seven days, those who are two years old remain for fourteen days, and so on (*Purgantur ergo in hoc igne pueri unius anni septem diebus, duorum quatuordecim, ita deinceps*).

✻ A terrible, glacial valley (*vallem terribilem, in qua innumeros quasi congelate glaciei*).

✻ A valley with trees that are pointed like spears; they are one hundred fathoms high, with sharp tops and covered with thorns (*capita acsi sudes acutissima erant et spinosa*).

✻ An iron ladder that is 365 cubits long and aflame; at its base is a pool full of oil, pitch, and resin (*vidi scalam ferream trecentorum sexaginta quinque cubitorum longitudinis, ita ardentem et scintillas emittentem acsi ferrum, cum de fornace trahitur. Ad cuius pedes vas quoddam magnum oleo, pice ac resina refertum pernimium bulliens fervebat*).

✻ Some globes of fire and sulfurous flames (*ignium globos sulphureasque flammas*).

✻ A lake of fire.

---

*Sloth is an evil of the soul that is expressed by ennui, as well as disdain for prayer, penitence, and spiritual reading.

✳ A pool full of bronze, tin, and lead fused together (*plenum quoque erat ere, stagno, plumbo, sulphure et resina, ita omnibus liquescentibus et ferventibus*); at one end there is an iron horse, at the other is a door where the souls enter who are destined to be tortured here.

✳ The mouth of hell that looks like a dark and stinking pit (*os infernalis baratri deductus sum, qui similis videbatur puteo*), from which emerge groans and moans.

✳ A valley with a circular lake spitting flames (*flammas emittentem*).

✳ A great pit that is casting out flames (*os putei magnum, flammas emittentem*).

✳ A horrible dark place that is on fire and reeking; it is full of serpents and dragons, wailing and groaning (*vidi locum horridum et tenebrosum, fetoribus exhalantibus, flammis crepitantibus, serpentibus, draconibus, stridoribus quoque et terribilibus repletum eiulatibus*).

✳ A lake of sulfurous water (*aqua sulphurea plenum*).

✳ Two evil spirits in the form of a dog and a lion, vomiting sulfurous flames (*vidi duos malignos spiritus in figura canis et leonis. De quorum ore flammeus ac sulphureus exibat flatus*).

✳ A river of burning pitch that has an iron bridge[20] crossing over it (*vidi flumen magnum de inferno procedere, ardens atque piceum. In cuius medio pons erat ferreus multam habens latitudinem*), which is wide for the righteous but narrows for the sinners, who fall into the river and are tortured there until, purified of their sins, they are able to cross the river.

✳ An immense field that takes three days and three nights to cross on a pass covered with thorns and thistles (*tantaque spinarum ac tribulorum densitate coopertum, ut ne vestigium quidem pedis nisi in illis punctionibus poni potuisse*); an enormous dragon serves as a mount for the devil, who is holding a snake that he uses to flog the soul that is fleeing down the thorny path until the time when, purged of its sins, it can escape him.

✳ The soul finally makes its way to a pleasant, flower-filled field where joy reigns (*Plenus est enim omni iocunditate et gaudio et letitia*); its wounds are healed and its clothes are repaired; in the middle of this countryside is paradise.

The *Vision of Alberic* by Settefrati gives us a good glimpse of the beyond and offers a foretaste of what purgatory will be a little later. In fact, there are three purgatories: the one for children (chap. 2), the one represented by the river and the bridge (chap. 17), and the field of thorns and thistles* (chap. 19), but the word "purgatory" is never used. It only involves the purgation of sins; the verb used is *purgare* ["to cleanse, purify"] (chaps. 2 and 17), and we find the expression *a peccata emundare* ["purifying sins"] (chap. 19).

For his part, Dante, who was familiar with the *Vision of Alberic*,[21] made a distinction between nine circles in hell, each of which was guarded by a mythological monster: Charon, Pluto, Minos, Cerberus, and so on. These circles form an inverted funnel; the deeper one goes, the greater the punishments.

Except for the descriptions of heaven, the countryside of the beyond is inhospitable and marked by the omnipresence of fire. The principal characteristics of this countryside are icy valleys, flaming mountains from which flow rivers of fire (Charles the Fat), a valley of fire spanned by a bridge (Laisrén), a valley that is surrounded by flames on the left and by hail and snow on the right (Dryhthelm), a glacial valley and another full of spiky plants (Alberic), a land of thorns (Adamnán), and a pestilence rules over these places. Tnugdalus and Fursey see frozen mountains on one side and burning ones on the other.

Hell is an abyss, and, in 1480, in *Le Baratre infernal*, Regnaud le Queux (circa 1440–1500)[22] compiled pagan and Christian stories about hell based on the *Vision of Tundale* and Boccacio's *On the Genealogy of the Gods*. All of the elements combine to inspire terror, to force the

---

*An Austrian legend describes a dead person who, to keep a promise, comes back to see his friend and says: "Do not remind anyone of eternity, the path is long and leads through thorns and thistles. Look at my injured feet, where the thorns are still stuck" (Depiny, *Oberösterreichisches Sagenbuch*, 84).

most obdurate souls to repent. Who would want to face these conditions of the afterlife? And we are not even mentioning the torments of the damned that are described so minutely by the trance journeyers and which horrified and terrified them so. You must choose to behave on earth as a good Christian or else risk damnation with its frightful torments. The Benedictine Nicholas of Clairvaux (d. 1176 or 1178) noted in one of his sermons: "Going from heaven to hell, from angel to beast, from God to the devil! What an abominable conversion: changing glory into destitution, life into death, peace into combat, and this through a captivity that is final" (Sermon 42, 2). The exempla contain quite a few stories in which, for example, a dead man tells of his fate in the beyond and asks that a wrong he has done be righted so as to mitigate his punishment. The great popularizers of visions were Jacques de Vitry (d. 1240)[23] and the Cistercian Caesarius of Heisterbach, whose *Dialogus miraculorum* (Dialogue of Miracles), written between 1219 and 1223, includes fifty-five exempla: twenty-five concern hell, sixteen purgatory, and fourteen paradise. The didactic intent is clear. In Bede's *History of the English Church and People,* an angel tells Dryhthelm: "You must now return to your body and live among men once more; but, if you will weigh your actions with greater care and study to keep your words and ways virtuous and simple (*in rectitudine ac simplicitate*), then when you die you too will win a home among these happy spirits that you see." Of another monk's vision, Bede writes: "through his own perdition he might bequeath a means of salvation to the living who learned of his fate."[24] One could not state it any more clearly!

PURGATORY

In general, purgatory is located next to hell; it is a receptacle of souls (*receptaculum animarum*). It is underground but, as believed by Gregory the Great, Saint Bonaventure, and Saint Thomas, it can be found anywhere on earth.[25] I have no desire to recreate the fine analysis that Jacques Le Goff has made of the birth of purgatory,[26] but I can bring in a few elements that complement his investigation.

In the vision dedicated to him that I have already mentioned,

Charles the Fat crosses through vast empty, dark spaces, and then together with his guide comes to an immense valley that *d'uny costé estoit doulce et resplendissant et d'autre part toute ardant et bouillant. Et lors se tira devers le Costé bouillant* (on the one side was sweet and gleaming, and on the other was bubbling and burning hot. And then he was guided to the bubbling side). Charles realizes that this is purgatory:

> Nothing on earth can give an idea of just how desolate this region is, except perhaps some of these beaches of the African desert covered with a yellow, burning sand, where nothing breaks the view, where nothing green is growing, where sprout only a few pale plants with sparse foliage. Furthermore, in this place there were blackish hills here and there formed like the dross of iron and cooled lava. Charles saw two fountains there whose water first filled the lakes appearing in the mouths of dead volcanoes, and then spread into the distance, forming two streams. *"L'une estoit trop chaulde, l'autre estoit clere, mais fort impétueuse"* (the one was too hot, the other was clear but raging). The latter stream rolled large glowing stones in its waters and covered its banks with an abundance of foam; the first one had the color of boiling oil and a dense vapor snaked over the entire course of the stream.[27]

Then he saw two vats; in one he found his father, Louis the German, who informed him that they were in purgatory.

In the twelfth century, the Cistercian monk Henry of Saltrey (Bedfordshire) wrote the *Tractatus de Purgatorio Sancti Patricii* (Treatise on the Purgatory of Saint Patrick), which records the visit of the knight Owen to the beyond.[28] It enjoyed considerable popularity, and the book has been translated into numerous languages since the Middle Ages. There are several French prose versions and seven in verse, including one by Marie de France, *L'Espurgatoire seinz Patriz,* which we will examine.

Here, the knight Owen first sees fire, then a valley from which plaintive moans were rising, four fields in which sinners were tortured, a smoking house that had pits filled with molten metal in which souls were being bathed, and a mountain at the foot of which were individuals *si cume une genz mort attendanz* (like a folk awaiting death; l. 1233); a gust of wind carries them off and casts them into a stinking and glacial river. Next, Owain catches sight of a *flame oscure, sulphrine e puant outre mesure* (dark flame, sulfurous and reeking beyond measure; ll. 1265–66), the entrance to hell. He crosses over a bridge that spans this infernal river where devils lie in wait for passersby, and he comes to a very high wall made from rare gems, with a gate of precious metal. The gate opens and gives him access to an earthly paradise. A bishop tells him:

> *Icist païs e icist estres,*
> *Sachiez c'est Parïs Terrestres.* (ll. 1689–90)

> [Here is peace and here is life
> Know it is the earthly paradise.]

L'Espurgatoire seinz Patriz incorporates all the elements we have already had an opportunity to discover in the literature of revelations. Marie de France added some exempla at the end of the text, such as the one by a monk whom devils abducted and held captive for three days and three nights. They whipped him and nearly beat him to death (*Tut flaëlé e debattu / Des qu'a la mort e navrez fu*; ll. 2035–36). When he returned to the dormitory at the monastery, he was covered with wounds that could never be cured (ll. 2019–56): proof that he had been carried off to the beyond. The opinions of authors and theologians tell us that purgatory is in the air or below ground, and the sinner remains in the common purgatory during the day then returns to the places where he sinned at night.

Analyzing the *Pèlerinage de l'Âme* (Pilgrimage of the Soul), which Guillaume de Digulleville, the prior of Chaalis Abbey (Senlis Diocese), wrote in 1355–1358, Fabienne Pomel has retraced the soul's journey through the beyond as follows:

The between-world of the souls in purgation therefore fits into a vertical structure, which, going successively from top to bottom, starts with heaven, then the bosom of Abraham, purgatory, the earth, the limbos, and then the hell of the damned. The pilgrim's movements along this ladder are sometimes up and sometimes down; if we accept the validity of the spatial placement that I have suggested, after having climbed to the entry of the curtain wall, behind which the tribunal sits, the soul descends back down by stages: implicitly traveling through the bosom of Abraham, it makes its way to purgatory where it meets its body that is going through its own purgatory there. Next, it launches off on a subterranean descent: after crossing through the limbos, it makes its way to the hell of the damned. From there, it climbs back up by stages.[29]

Around 1321–1327, The Dominican Fillipo of Ferrara wrote his *Liber de introductione loquendi*, the fifth book of which is devoted to death. Here we find the purgatory of the sailors: those who pursued this profession while they were alive will perform their purgatory while sailing on the sea.[30]

Fillipo of Ferrara introduces us to another, quite original, purgatory. A Dominican prayed continuously for a dead colleague. One day, his former brother appeared and told him that his prayers had saved him from the torment of purgatory, which consisted of being trapped on the moon with a fear of falling.[31]

Another Dominican, Jean Gobi, tells the story of a revenant that a prior interrogated about his fate. At the twenty-second question, the dead man spoke of purgatory and answered by using as an example a brother who had just died in Bologna:

> After his angel told the soul of this brother that he would have to stay in the common purgatory for three months, the Virgin Mary interceded with her Son on behalf of this brother. She was so successful that his soul remains today in the darkened air for two hours.[32]

Last, the clerics sometimes situated purgatory on earth, sometimes under the earth, sometimes on the sea, and sometimes in the sky. This latter spot brings to mind the troops of the dead that travel the earth on certain dates, the most famous of which is the Mesnie Hellequin.* These hosts represent a wandering purgatory, as the figures that appear in them, and the words which the latter exchange with witnesses, show beyond any doubt.[33]

PARADISE

In general, a glimpse of heaven, characterized by light, harmonious singing and sweet fragrances, brings the journey of the entranced visionary to a close.

Light is the predominant feature in the beyond, as we read in the *Life of Saint Ansgar* (801–865): "It was a miraculous radiance, an

The Entrance to Paradise. Fresco in the Church of Saint-Méard-de-Dronne (Dordogne, France, twelfth century).

---

*[The Mesnie Hellequin is the French name for the folklore phenomenon of the Wild Hunt. For more on this, see Lecouteux's study *Phantom Armies of the Night* (2011). —*Ed.*]

inaccessible light of intense clarity and made of the rarest of colors, from which happiness radiated. . . . They were so bright that it dazzled the eyes while filling them with pleasure" (*in ipso vero orientis loco erat splendor mirabilis, lux inaccessibilis, nimiae atque immense claritatis*).[34] In the book by Otloh of Sankt Emmeram, the visionary sees "walls of a blinding brightness, immensely long and high,"[35] and the angels tell him: "This is the holy and renowned Heavenly Jerusalem."[36] Retelling the vision of a monk of Cîteaux, Peter the Venerable (d. 1156) describes paradise as an edifice constructed of precious stones, flanked by towers topped by pinnacles, with two doors in the wall, one in ruins and the other decorated with precious stones and pleasantly lit.[37] The vision of Gunthelm[38] depicts heaven as a golden city whose entrance is a gate also decorated with precious stones. This opens onto a delightful place (*locus amoenus*) with plants, trees, birds, flowers, fruits, and running waters. This is where the four rivers that water the four parts of paradise have their source.

The story of Tundale recapitulates to some extent the descriptive elements we have seen earlier. The knight comes to a door, which opens of its own accord onto a magnificent world that is spilling over with flowers and delectable smells. There are so many souls in bliss to be seen there that they cannot be counted. Here it is never night and the sun never sets, and there is a well of living water. "I forgot all my suffering because bliss and happiness reigned supreme here," Tundale reported. Without knowing how he did it, he scaled a silver wall and saw "the choir of saints and angels, men and women dressed in white, singing praises to God. . . . Their voices were wonderfully sweet, echoing like the melodies of stringed instruments, and they gave off an aroma of holiness more delectable than that of the most exquisite herbs." A little farther away, another wall that was just as high, but made of gold this time, then a castle, and tents from which escaped the sound of organs, harps, and many stringed isntruments. And then yet another wall, higher and more beautiful than any of those before it, made of gems of all colors—the model followed is that of the heavenly Jerusalem. Tundale climbs over the wall and hears the choirs of angels and ineffable words.

We see that paradise contains several spaces, which mirrors the words of Jesus: "In my father's house are many mansions" (John 14:2). In the majority of the visions, we find a city and garden comparable to that of Eden. Jacqueline Amat realized that its model is the Eastern *viridarium* (park, garden), and she notes that the fruits most mentioned are apples, grapes, and figs.[39] The visions I have cited add songs and music to the heavenly ambiance.

According to medieval cosmographical conceptions, the earthly paradise was located in various places, either on a mountain in the East or on an island in the Atlantic Ocean. In the *Alexandri Magni iter ad paradisum* (Journey to Paradise of Alexander the Great),[40] the anonymous author borrows the geographical fable about the four rivers that originate in paradise—the Gihon, the Pishon, the Tigris, and the Euphrates—and the idea that said paradise can be reached by following the course of the rivers back to their source. According to legend, Alexander the Great followed the Pishon:

> Then at length, on the thirty-fourth day, they [Alexander and his companions] saw in the distance what appeared to be a walled city of remarkable height and extent. They approached it with great difficulty. Near the shore, the river ran somewhat less fiercely and the noise of the waves was a little less; but the narrowness of the shore and the muddy ground prevented them from advancing on foot to the wall. They therefore continued to sail for almost three days, with great difficulty, along the side of the city where it stretched from its northern extremity towards the south, looking for a way in.
>
> The wall was very smooth, with no towers or ramparts in its circuit. The entire surface was covered with ancient moss, so that the stones and their joins were completely invisible. On the third day they caught sight of a tiny window shuttered on the inside, a sight which instantly relieved the spirits and strength of the tired travellers with hope.
>
> Alexander immediately had some of his men embark in a boat to see if anyone might answer when they knocked, and gave them a message for the inhabitants. As soon as they reached the wall they knocked loudly and shouted to those inside to open up. After a time

they heard someone slide the bolt, and a gentle voice inquired of them who they were and where they had come from, and asked them to explain their unusual and unheard-of demand.[41]

Once they gave their answer, the voice told them to wait and, two hours later, they were given a gemstone for Alexander and an order to leave. The next part of the story tells of the return of the Greeks to Susa and how the Macedonian learned the secret of the gemstone.

A fourteenth-century Portuguese text relates the legend of Saint Amaro (*Conto de Amaro*),[42] which is a curious mixture of Celtic, Portuguese, and Spanish elements. It is very similar to *The Voyage of Saint Brendan*. The story is presented as Amaro's journey when he set off to find heaven on earth and traveled through different worlds before achieving his goal.

Amaro set sail and reached an island eleven weeks later, where he met a hermit that led him to a monastery in front of which were lying many dead lions and other beasts. They had been there for eight days, and had gathered together as they did every year for their tournament. After giving him some bread and water, the hermit sent Amaro, who was not allowed to remain long, away. At midnight the hero weighed anchor.

He came to a second island with five castles on it. The men there were large and handsome, and the traveler stayed there for seven weeks until he heard a voice one night ordering him to continue his voyage. Amaro then crossed the Red Sea and came to a large island called Clear Fountain (Fonte Clara), which was filled with all that anyone could desire, and he disembarked there. The inhabitants were very beautiful and courteous, and the country was so healthy that no one was ever sick. People only died of old age after living an average of three hundred years. Amaro stayed there for seven weeks and then an old woman advised him to be on his way; else his companions would never again wish to leave.

Amaro and his crew left at night, heading into the sea not knowing where they were until one morning they spotted seven large ships without sails that had approached and then been trapped by the congealed sea (*mar quoalhado*). Sea monsters pulled the bodies of sailors who had died of starvation from the boats and devoured them. Amaro and his companions pleaded, and the old woman showed the hero in a dream the way to hitch his boat to the monsters and escape the congealed sea.

Three days later, another island came into view, full of ferocious beasts that had depopulated it. It was called the Desert Island (Insso deserta). Amaro alit on the ground to procure food and water. He met another hermit there who supplied him with provisions and pointed out the route to follow, to the east, where a beautiful country was located. Amaro made his way there and found large rivers, numerous springs, a cloister, and a monk named Leomites "because the lions and the other animals came to ask him for his blessing" (*E o frade avya nome Leomites porque os leõões e as outras alimaryas vinhã demãdar que os benzese*). A dream had forewarned him of the arrival of Amaro, who stays for forty days in the Vale das Flores monastery before leaving. After having traveled along the coast, Amaro reaches a valley, where he finds two hermits whom he asks where the earthly paradise is (*vos rrogo senhores que me digades se sabedes hu he aquel parayso terreal*), and they tell him: "The paradise you speak of is truly on earth, but no one knows where, except for Bralydes, and he will only reveal it to the holiest of men." Amaro continues his journey, and he comes to a monastery of women named Flor das Donas (Flower of the Ladies). There, after a long period of penitence, he receives a visit from Lady Valides and puts back on the monastic habit of the hermit's niece. Then Valides (variant: Bralydes) leads him to the foot of the mountain of the earthly paradise, from which a river flows, carrying fruits and flowers.

In the high mountains, Amaro comes to a marble castle; rivers flow out of its five towers. The door-warden refuses to let him in, but opens the door so he can see its wonders. Amaro contemplates them for a moment that in fact lasts for two hundred and sixty-seven years, and he then returns to our world with a bit of soil, retires to a monastery, and dies.

The story is meant to be an allegory of human life, and the story-teller gives it the shape of a journey that conforms to medieval representations of life, which the miniatures of the manuscript often depict in the form of a sea voyage: the sea represents the world, and its temptations or dangers are evoked by various monsters, such as sirens, for example. The hermits are ferrymen who relaunch Amaro's quest by urging him not to tarry anywhere.

The voyage to paradise was known in Japan. The inhabitants believe that heaven was located beyond the sea. Monks embarked at Kumano to go there in coffin boats that were nailed from the outside.

The religious elements should not mask the mythical basis of this kind of story, however, and for the sake of comparison I want to mention a little-known text, *Herzog Ernst* (Duke Ernst),[43] a romance of adventure—and education!—written in Germany around 1190. Banished by Kaiser Otto, Ernst sets sail for the Holy Land, but a storm pushes him off course and from that point on he is embroiled in one adventure after another, each marking a stage of the evolution of his character, which grows from egoism to altruism, from ardor to reason. Ernst travels through other worlds, such as the one of the crane-men, the one of the Arimaspes (Cyclops), and the one of pygmies and giants. As with the tale of Amaro, his ship is blocked by the congealed sea (a mythical vision of the ice field!), but here this is located at the base of the Magnetic Mountain. The transitions from one site or world to another are remarkable. There is the great classic tale of the tempest and then the transport by griffins once the hero and his faithful vassal Wetzel are sewn into hides, and the crossing of a mountain by means of an underground river.

FIVE

BETWEEN VISIONS, TALES, AND LEGENDS
The Chivalric Romances

For a long time now, the chivalric romances have been recognized as the resurgence, in the midst of the medieval world, of mythological themes and structures, and more precisely, those of the Celtic universe. It is by reading them in relation to the beyond and to other worlds that we shall confirm this.[1]

THE DIABOLICAL SPACES

In the romances of the Middle Ages, hell is not evoked directly but is most often suggested, albeit in a fairly transparent way, and we have to get past the marvelous or fantastical nature of the narrative sequences to discover the author's source of inspiration. Cemeteries and graves are a border zone where strange manifestations occur. In the *Prose Lancelot*, burning graves are indications of the punishment of the damned (XXXVII, 34–35); LXV, 24–26), smoke pours out of them (XXXVII, 34) and tombstones rise up—in other words, cemeteries are veritable antechambers of hell or purgatory. Traditions have a tenacious existence, and, in Corsica, for example, there was a distinction made between three frontiers separating the world of the living from that of the dead: the entrance of the church, the river, and the threshold of the cemetery.[2]

In the thirteenth-century romance *L'Âtre perillous* (The Perilous Cemetery), it is a demon that rules over the cemetery's premises. Anyone who spends the night there is found dead in the morning. Gawain is sitting on a gravestone when the slab rises up. He moves several steps away and sees a maiden in the open grave, who gives him the following explanation: because she was sick, she allowed the devil to heal her, and he made her his mistress and comes to visit her every night. Gawain confronts this demon, over whom he triumphs thanks to his faith. The cemetery, therefore, is in communication with hell. One passage from the *Prose Lancelot* confirms this point: the hero is invited to lift up a tombstone. He does so and sees a hideous, winged serpent. The reptile hurls fire at him, which burns up his chain mail and weapons, and then it leaps into the cemetery, setting aflame the bushes of the enclosure. The presence of the reptile and the fire suggest images of hell to the reader. Farther on, Lancelot comes to a bleeding tomb; next to the grave the head of white, hoary man is floating in a spring: "The water was boiling as if all the fires of hell were gathered there." It is a kind of purgatory, as is the case in another passage of the romance: when Lancelot succeeds in reaching Corbenic, the Grail castle, he hears the cries of a woman and finds her immersed in a marble vat in which the water alternates between boiling and icy cold—the punishment that God has inflicted on this sinner.[3]

With *Amadas et Ydoine,* written between 1190 and 1220, we enter into a realm where deviltry has become entwined with faery. Ydoine is abducted in the middle of the day by a *faés* (fay or magical) knight, who then drops her and vanishes. She falls ill a short while later and dies (*morte est Ydoine a grant dolar*). After her burial, her lover Amadas comes one night to collect his thoughts by her grave in a cemetery that is enclosed within a wall. He then hears the sound of a troop approaching, and he grows scared: he thinks that the devil has come to carry off Ydoine's body (ll. 5604–5). Two troops arrive, one carrying a casket. A "large and handsome" knight mounted on a steed leaps over the wall of the cemetery—a Christian would have entered by the gate— and approaches Amadas, whose love he tests by claiming to be Ydoine's lover. He wishes to carry away her body. Amadas fights him and wins, and learns that his beloved is not dead and that her catalepsy is due to an *anel faé* (fay or magic ring; l. 6444). He takes the magical ring off of Ydoine's finger and she comes back to life. A careful examination of the text allows us to see that what we are reading is a variant of the myth of Orpheus. The cemetery has replaced the underworld; the unknown knight, Hades; the battle, the song of the lyric poet; and, as in *Sir Orfeo*, Amadas brings Ydoine back to this world: "Now, it is because of you that he escaped from the hands of the devil, whom— thanks to his friend—he discomfited and vanquished."

> *et or est por vor escapée*
> *Des mains de maufé par son dru,*
> *Qu'il l'a desconfit et vaincu* (ll. 6885–87).

Maufé, as it happens, is another name for the devil. The ring that caused the apparent death of Ydoine allows the author to introduce the world of faery. We should also note that the anonymous author was familiar with the *Aeneid* and the *Odyssey* (ll. 5836–48) in which, as we have seen, there are two descents into hell.

Chrétien de Troyes recounts the abduction of Queen Guinevere by Meleagant in *The Knight of the Cart*. Three clues reveal that he carried his prey off to the otherworld.

1. Many researchers are certain that the name of his country, Gorre, is identical to the Ile of Voirre (*verre*, "glass"), which is another Avalon; but Philippe Walter points out that the word *gorre* belongs to the same Indo-European family as Latin *gurges*, "abyss, gulf," and concludes: "It is a kind of mouth of hell . . . that swallows the souls of the dead."[4]

2. The reactions of the spectators to the abduction: "At their departure, all the men and women present assumed she would never return alive, and they grieved as deeply as though she lay dead on her bier."[5]

> *Au departir si grant duel firent*
> *Tuit cil et celes qui l'oïrent,*
> *Con s'ele geüst morte en bier:*
> *Ne cuident qu'el reveigne arriere*
> *Ja mes an trestot son aage.* (ll. 215–19)

She will return, and Lancelot will kill Meleagant in single combat.

3. The kingdom of Bademagu, Meleagant's father, is called the "land from which no one returns."

One final point, in the *Life of Gildas* by Caradoc of Llancarfan, the name of Guinevere's abductor is King Melvas. "Etymologically, Mael-was would be a king of the land of the dead,"[6] Philippe Walter reminds us.

In the Vulgate *Queste del saint Graal* (Quest of the Holy Grail), Galahad (Galaad) makes his way to an abbey and learns that a voice speaks from one of the tombs of the cemetery. "Its power is such that those who hear it lie shorn of strength and wits for a long season." The knight approaches the tomb that is beneath a great tree: "as he drew near he heard a rending shriek as of a being in torment, and a voice which cried: 'Stand back, Galahad, thou servant of Jesus Christ, and come not nigh me, for thou wouldst yet oust me from that place where I have lodged so long.'" Galahad went to lift the headstone away from the tomb, but he then saw "smoke and flame belch out, followed at once by a thing most foul and hideous, shaped like a man." The knight made the sign of the cross, for he knew this was the Evil One (*l'anemis*), and, thus protected, removed the tombstone and saw a body in the hole. An old man that was there said: "[The body] must be taken from this graveyard and cast out, for since this ground has been blessed and hallowed, no body belonging to a wicked and recreant Christian ought to lie here."[7] This was done. Here again, the grave is a passageway to hell.

The *Prose Lancelot* confirms this.[8] The knight enters a cemetery sealed off by a rampart whose crenellations are adorned with the heads of the gallant knights interred there. He enters a chapel and then goes down into a crypt (*une cave desos terre*), hears a loud noise and sees a door guarded by two knights of copper, each holding a sword. He manages to pass by them and arrives at another door and a well *moult puans, noir et hideus* (very foul, black and hideous), from which the noise he heard is coming. He runs into a man with a black head that is spitting flames, has eyes like embers, and red teeth, who is carrying an axe. Lancelot manages to toss him down the well and then he sees before him a copper maiden holding the key to the enchantments. He grabs it, goes toward the copper pillar standing in the center of the room, opens it, and makes his way close to the *coffre perilleus* (perilous coffer) and listens: howls are coming out, and he sees two copper pipes that are communicating the sounds of these horrible voices. He opens the perilous coffer and from it comes *un grans estorbellons et une si grant noise* (a big whirlwind and a great noise) that makes him think that all the devils in hell must be making it. He loses consciousness and when he comes back to his senses, he takes the key to the pillar and the one to the coffer. He goes toward the well, which has sealed itself back up. The copper pillar, the maiden, and the guardians have all sunk into the ground. When he emerges into the cemetery, all the graves and heads have vanished.

This fantastical adventure leisurely demonstrates that points of communication exist between this world and the infernal beyond. The cemetery is both hell and purgatory; here, its very unique fence tells us that this *dormitorium* is not a sanctified space that has been consecrated as Christian ground.

In the adventure* of the Sains Cimentiere (Holy Cemetery), Lancelot goes down into a crypt, at the back of which he sees a flaming tomb. He is preparing to lift up the slab when a voice stops him and reveals that the sepulcher is that of Simeon, Joseph of Arimathea's nephew, and that his son Moses lies in a perilous place. But thanks to the prayers of Joseph, this is what happened to Simeon and Moses: "God has granted us salvation of our souls in exchange for the damnation of our bodies, so each of us was placed in a grave where we would have to endure this torment until someone came to deliver us." Lancelot attempted to free him but failed.[9] The grave clearly seems to be an intermediary space between heaven and hell, a purgatory from which the dead can be freed by the prowess of a knight who is free of any sin.

Li Hauz Livres du Graal (The High Book of the Graal) mentions the Cemetery Perilous, in which knights who die without repenting and whose bodies do not rest in hallowed ground, appear every night:

---

*This Old French term *aventure,* derived from the Latin verb *advenire* ("to arrive"), possesses a wide semantic field and, depending on the context, can mean "event, destiny, inevitability." In the courtly romances, it is regularly associated with *querrir, acomplir mener a chief* ("seeking, accomplishing an end"). In Middle High German, *âventiure* has the meaning of "unheard-of event, wonder, enchantment."

These evil spirits continued to make their racket all around the cemetery, and they dealt themselves such violent blows it made the entire forest echo, and it seemed to catch fire from the flames that sprung out of these creatures (branch XV, title xix).

As the cemetery was protected by Saint Andrew, the damned held their sabbat on the outside. In the adventure of Lancelot at the Chapel Perilous, which was located in a deep valley in the center of a forest, an old and entirely enclosed cemetery surrounded the monastery. On the other hand, when Perlesvaus conquers a certain castle, we learn that it bore three names: Eden, Castle of Joy, and Castle of Souls. It was given the latter name "because no one ever died there whose soul did not go to heaven" (branch X).

Perceforest, a prose romance that was rewritten in the fifteenth century,[10] tells how a spirit brought Passelion to the gates of hell on the orders of Zephir the *luiton* (sprite), a fallen angel sent to earth to tease and test human beings.[11] The entrance to hell was in a mountainous area cut off from the valleys. When he drew near to it, the knight heard a loud noise and he questioned the spirit:

The spirit replied: "That is because when a soul leaves its mortal body, it is brought here and cast into that hole from which you can see the smoke pouring. The soul then sinks into the hole based on the weight of its sins, and the heavier its misdeeds, the deeper it sinks and the greater its torments."[12]

The spirit soared into the air with Passelion and stopped at a spot where the smoke was intolerable because of the new souls that the demons had just brought there. The smoke dissipated and Passelion saw *une abysme tres espoantable* (a very horrendous abyss) and Lucifer. The influence of the medieval Christian visions on this scene is undeniable, but *Perceforest* shows its originality by introducing us to the Isle of Evil Spirits, which is mountainous and dark, and the Isle of Life, both of which are found in an Irish lake. Saint Patrick made the first island the site for his purgatory and the second belongs to the Fairy Queen

Saint Patrick venturing into purgatory.
Bibliothèque nationale de France, ms français 1544, fol. 105r
(fourteenth century).

and possesses the elements of a pagan Celtic paradise: the four elements have been brought into accord so they do not fight with one another (XLVIII, 816–18), death has no access to this isle, nothing decays, and water and fruits have a regenerative power.

INFERNAL KNIGHTS

The devil sometimes appears as a knight who has signed a contract with the devil. Gerbert de Montreuil introduces us to the Dragon Knight, so named because his coat of arms bears a dragon's head spitting fire, which is one of the many forms taken by the devil. In the adventure of Pui de Montesclaire, Perceval sets off to defeat him and is confronted with thunder, lightning, and rain—signs that herald a diabolical encounter. He covers himself with his shield, which bears a cross, and frightens the devil, who *brait et crie comme un tors* (brays and cries like a bull; l. 9564). Fire consumes the knight's lance, but he strikes the devil with his heraldic shield and the demon flees *en guise d'un corbel tout noir* (in the guise of an all-black raven).[13]

In *Wigalois,* which Wirnt von Grafenberg wrote in the middle of the thirteenth century,[14] the hero of the story learns there is a flaming castle nearby where a crowned animal makes a regular appearance. As he does not want to later regret missing this opportunity, he follows the animal. While on his way, he watches a tournament:

> As all they allowed to be heard were cries of distress, Wigalois assumed that they were not true knights, and once he had seen their coats of arms, their feats seemed fictitious to him, for they were all of the same color, all as black as coal and their tinctures depicted glowing flames the color of vermilion.

He throws himself into the joust, but his spear burns up on contact with the knights. He departs then and catches up with the animal he had been pursuing. Once they reach the depths of the woods, this animal transforms into a man. He reveals that he was King Lar, the former sovereign of Korntin, and explains what he has seen:

> I still want to tell you something about the assembly of knights you saw a little while ago on the road: their penitence is infinitely heavy and so painful that their distress is without equal. Whatever joy they may exhibit while riding, the truth is that they are always in the flames of hell without respite.

These knights are therefore the damned from hell who have spilled out into this world, something which occurs quite frequently in the romances of the Middle Ages. In Renaut de Beaujeu's *Le Bel Inconnu* (The Fair Unknown), the hero confronts a *grans et corsus* (big and stout) knight mounted on a charger *si oil luissoient cum cristals* (whose eyes blaze like crystals), with a horn in the middle of its forehead and flames shooting out of its nostrils. When Guinglain cuts him down, "a hideous and repulsive smoke pours from his mouth." Then, to learn if he was still alive, [the knight] placed his hand on his chest; everything changed into hideous, rotting flesh.

Por savoir s'il ert encore vis,
Sa main il met deseur ke pis;
Tos fu devanus Claire pure,
Qui molt estoit et laide et sure (ll. 3065–68)

All of these encounters with devils and diabolical knights did not represent an innovation. As the Arthurian cycle attests, the authors were certainly inspired by exempla, which they knew quite well from the religious literature. Now, the exempla employed notions that avoided the strict framework of Christian cosmology, allowing elements to surface "from between two worlds," which in turn find reflection in the romances.

Otloh of Sankt Emmeram (ca. 1010–1067) relates the adventure of a minstrel named Vollarc. While he is traveling with some companions, they encounter a good fellow named Nithard, who offers to give them lodging. They cross through a valley, then a dark forest, and arrive at a dwelling where they are forbidden to speak to anyone. Little by little, Vollard realizes that he is in the house of the devil and asks to leave. Their host lavishes his guests with gifts and provides them with guides who lead them back to the place in the forest where they had met Nithard and then suddenly vanish. Vollarc and his companions find themselves all alone, dying of hunger, and the gifts they had been given are nothing but spider webs.[15]

The plot of this story can be found in the work of Jacques de Vitry (1160/70–1240), an Augustinian canon:

An abbot and some Cistercian monks become lost one night, and some demons that have the appearance of monks offer them the hospitality of their abbey in the middle of the forest. The Cistercians accept, but once they are there, alerted by the behavior of their horses, they eat only the food they have brought with them. The next day they say Mass and see the chapel gradually empty. When they question the abbot there, he tells them: "We are the angels that fell with Lucifer." The monastery and monks vanish, and the Cistercians find themselves in the middle of a swamp[16] (*et statim tota illa abbacia evanuit. Et illi invenerunt se devia et paludes*).

A close variant of this story can be found in the work of the Dominican inquisitor, Stephen of Bourbon (1180–1261),[17] indexed by F. C. Tubach under Exemplum nr. 1655: "The Monastery of the Demons: A defrocked monk gets lost in the forest and comes to a strange monastery in which only a single monk is living. The fugitive sees devils torturing the dead monks, and, when they sink into the ground in terror, he seeks refuge in his own monastery." We also find this story in the *Scala coeli* by Jean Gobi.[18]

Thanks to a legend collected around 1830–1840 by Johann Jacob Musäus[19] and retold by Ludwig Bechstein,[20] we can see that Otloh, Jacques de Vitry, and others were inspired by the same oral tradition. A young knight and his squire are traveling though a forest haunted by a ghost with the evocative name of Count Schwarzenberg (of the Black Mountain). Suddenly, the squire cries out:

"Milord, someone is riding behind us. The shoes of the horse sound hollow, and look—there is a fiery froth dripping from its bit!"

The count invited them to follow him to his castle. They went inside.

The knight courageously followed his guide into a spiral staircase. From time to time a griffin's claw holding a lit candle came out of the wall. The candles were black and white. The walls were black as coal, as was the count's armor, which was also made in the style of the past. He was entirely covered in a hauberk and wore a strangely shaped helmet on his head. The crest was neither cast nor forged. It was alive and in the shape of a small dragon, similar to a little salamander, whose claws were solidly embedded in the helmet. At times he turned his head, and his sparkling black eyes flashed like the points of diamonds. The dragon's long tail fell from the helmet on to the nape of the count's neck and twitched from side to side. At the bottom of the staircase the count stopped and turned toward his guest. His face was wan, pale, and emaciated, and his eyes, which were sunk deep into their sockets, spoke of murder. They had no lashes, and no eyebrows shaded them. He panted loudly and his breath was as hot as the wind of the scorching African desert.

He was atoning for a terrible sin, as we shall see:

"Follow me now and see what I have done and how much I suffer!" he said to the knight. "I am bound to show all those I meet at midnight my infamous crime. It is useless to pray for me! I cannot atone, neither by repentance, nor suffrages,[21] nor by prayers."

He showed him a coffin, inside of which lay a little old woman, a dagger stuck in her chest.

"Here is my mother!" cried out the count, "and here stands before you her murderer."

During a fantastic scene in which the cadaver rose up and assumed gigantic size, the knight invoked the name of Jesus: a terrifying cry echoed through the building causing its frame to crack, the castle shook, and coffin and wall and count and countess sunk out of sight. And the knight sunk deeper into the impenetrable night.

The Black Count is therefore a damned soul who pays the price for his sin on earth, and his castle is a form of hell. The details of the text leave no doubt about this: everything is black, and the presence of the dragon on the helmet represents the devil. The count's breath is hot, a sign that he is burning on the inside. The damned man explicitly states that he is beyond redemption and, finally, from the room in which the corpse of his mother is lying, there emerges "a breath so cold it could have come from a glacier."

THE OTHERWORLD OF FAERY

It is in the lays of the twelfth and thirteenth century that we most frequently encounter the otherworld inhabited by faeries or *faés* (fay) men. Among the works of the great Marie de France (circa 1160–1210), the first French woman of letters, there are two lays that deal with this subject. The lay of *Guigemar* relates the following:

One day while hunting, Guigemar looses an arrow at a white hind, but the shot ricochets and wounds him. The hind then sorrowfully tells him that none can cure his wound but the lady who would suffer for his sake. The knight resumes his journey, crossing through a forest, a moor, and a plain, and passes a mountain from which a river flowed, and he then reaches a harbor where he finds a splendid ship that is totally deserted (*ni aveit nul, ne nul, ne nul ne vit*; l. 46). He falls asleep and is transported up to the palace of a lady who was sequestered there by her jealous husband. She takes in Guigemar and cares for him. They fall in love and are discovered, and the knight is forced to leave. Before leaving him, the lady makes a knot in his shirt: no one but herself can untie it. Guigemar climbs back into the boat and returns to his own country. The lady eventually escapes, sets sail, still in the same boat, and makes it to Guigemar's home, and unties the knot. . . .

This lady is never called a "fairy." However, certain clues indicate her supernatural character, such as her ability to read the future or her connections with the magic boat. Furthermore, the details of the hero's itinerary could not fail to grab the attention of the hearers of this lay and let them know that he had experienced a singular encounter. The lay contains the majority of the motifs that relate to a journey to the otherworld, from the description of the hero's path and his encounter with the hind, to his journey on a wondrous ship without a pilot. Philippe Walter is not misled and notes that the lady's country "corresponds completely to a place in the otherworld that is beyond the sea and inaccessible to humans."[22]

Muldumarec, the hero of *Yonec*,[23] another lay of Marie de France, is obviously a king of the otherworld. In the form of a bird,[24] he rejoins the woman that he has chosen—who has been imprisoned in a tower by her husband and watched over by an old woman—and changes before her into a handsome and noble knight. He tells her that he has loved her for a long time and goes on to say: "But I could not have come to you or left my country if you had not invited me" (ll. 131–33). As it happens, the lady had simply been lamenting the fact that it was no longer the age when women could find gallant and courteous lovers (ll. 95–98). Is this to say that he was able to read her mind? They were loving each other when they were surprised and the lover, wounded, was forced to flee. The woman miraculously escapes from her prison, follows the trail of blood left by Muldumarec, enters a mound, advances through the darkness, and finds herself in a beautiful meadow, crosses through a town devoid of any inhabitants, comes to a palace, and finds her beloved. He gives her a sword for her son and a magic ring to slip on to her husband's finger so he will forget everything that happened. The path followed by the lady clearly shows how a person travels from one world to the other, and it is no coincidence that the entrance is located in a mound: this is a well-known motif in Celtic literatures, which abound with fairy (*sidh*) mounds.

Folk traditions always have surprises in store for us. A folktale collected by Alexander Afanasyev, "The Feather of Finist, the Fair Falcon," is practically the Russian version of the Breton lay. But judge for yourself:

> The heroine begs her father for the feather of Finist; he agrees to buy it for her. When she opens the case, the feather soars out, hits the ground, and changes into a handsome prince. Her sisters, hearing them talking, cause the prince, who turns into a falcon, to flee. The scene happens again, and to put an end to it they take sharp knives and needles and stick them to the edge of the window. Finist wounds himself and goes back to the otherworld "beyond the three-times-ninth country in the thirtieth kingdom. Before finding me, you must wear out three pairs of iron shoes, you will break three cast-iron canes, and you will eat three loaves of bread made of stone." At the end of a very long journey, the young girl finds her prince again.[25]

Philippe Walter has demonstrated the Celtic origin of the lay of *Yonec*, whose parallel can be found in the story of Conaire, the legendary king of Tara. But he cites another story taken from the collection of Somadeva, written between 1063 and 1081, in which the supernatural being corresponding to Muldumarec is a *rakshasa*, an ogre of Indian mythology. The similarities between this story and *Yonec* are too numerous for them not to represent a shared fragment of our Indo-European heritage.

One of Marie de France's best-known lays is *Lanval*. This text was even translated into Old Norse during the reign of King Hakon Hakonarson (1217–1263),[26] and several times into early English. The story relates the following:

Unhappy and forgotten in the gifts distributed by King Arthur, Lanval wanders in the forest. When he reaches the banks of stream and lies down in a meadow there, two maidens come up to him and invite him to follow them because their mistresses wish to see him. He follows them to a beautiful tent where he meets a young woman who tells him: "I have left my own land because of you; and have come in search of you from afar . . . because I love you above all else" (ll. 110ff). She gives him a gift and forbids him from ever revealing her existence:[27] "You would lose me forever if our love were to become known" (ll. 147–48). Lanval becomes a rich man and attracts the attention of the queen who, like the wife of Putiphar, offers him her love. He rejects her advances and she tells her husband how Lanval has offended her. Summoned to prove his innocence, the knight confesses that he already has a girlfriend superior to the queen. The sovereign demands proof of his statement on pain of death. The fairy arrives, accuses the queen of lying, and turns around. Lanval leaps on the back of the fairy's horse and she carries him off to Avalon. *Nul hom n'en oï plus parler* (No man has heard any more of them again; l. 646).

It is not hunting here but disappointment that compels the knight to seek solitude in the wild. There is no journey to the otherworld; the meeting takes place on the frontier (the river) of this world. The lady is never called a "fairy," but she makes her love rich and imposes a prohibition on him, much like what we find in the legend of Melusine. All he needs to do is think about her and she will come to him. All of these elements are evidence of her being a supernatural being. And the Norse text indicates that she rode off with him to the island named Ualun (Avalon).

An Italian *cantare*,[28] *La Ponzella Gaia* (The Joyful Maiden)— folktale type 400 and 401—features an opening that is close to that of Lanval, before it diverges onto another path:

Galvano and Troiano go hunting. While Troiano is capturing a white hind (III, 3–4), Galvano confronts a serpent that asks him his name and, on hearing it, transforms into a beautiful maiden: a daughter of the fairy Morgana who has been in love with him for as long as she could remember. She offers him her love and wealth. He becomes her lover and she gives him a magical ring that will bring him anything he desires, but he should never reveal the existence of his lover to anyone. They are living happily together, but the queen Ginevra (Guinevere) offers her love to Galvano. He rejects her and she reacts like the queen of Lanval, and organizes a contest during which Galvano reveals his lover's existence. He is on the verge of being hung when the fairy appears. However, because she has disobeyed her mother, she is condemned to be locked away in a tower so dark that she will never see any light—whether of the sun, moon, or stars—and to be immersed in water up to her breasts.

Galvano sets off in search of her and performs miracles in order to reach the mysterious city of Pela-horsso, which seems to be the point of entry for Morgana's kingdom. He slays the defenders, breaks down the gate, imprisons Morgana in her daughter's stead, and returns with the Ponzela Gaia to Arthur's court.[29]

We may note the reversal of the motif here: the fairy does not carry her lover into the otherworld, but follows him to the court. Furthermore, there are a number of folktale motifs detectable in this story that are characteristic of tales in which a fairy falls in love with a mortal: the animal guide (B563), the one who shows the way (B151) and leads the hero to adventure (N774), the imprisonment in a tower (R41.2), and, of course, the taboo (C423.3).

In *The Crown* by Heinrich von dem Türlin, Gawain meets Enfeydas, the queen of Avalon, in the month of May, inside a tent that has been erected in the middle of a meadow:

This lady was a fairy	*Dje frawe ein götinne was*
And King Arthur's aunt	*Vnd was künig Artus base*
She wore a splendid crown	*Vnd truog die riche krone*
In Avalon	*Da zü Aualone*
She was called Enfeydas	*Enfeydas was sie genannt.*

But let us return to France. Chrétien de Troyes, the author from Champagne who was born around 1130 and died between 1180 and 1190, left us two romances that should hold our attention in this regard. Although he strives to provide rational explanations for the wondrous aspects in his work, what he allows to remain, which was imposed by his sources, gives us a good view of the forms taken by the otherworld. Let us look at *Yvain, or The Knight with the Lion*[30] and its Welsh counterpart *Owain, or The Lady of the Fountain*.[31] One fine evening, the knight Calogrenant—who is named Kynon in *Owain*—tells of the misfortunes he suffered in the forest of Broceliande, where he encountered a wild man.

Yvain	Owain
A peasant that looked like a Moor, disproportionately ugly and hideous . . . was sitting on a stump and holding a large club in his hand. I approached the churl and saw that his head was bigger than that of a packhorse or any other animal, his hair grew in tufts and his bare forehead was nearly two spans wide. His ears were hairy and as large as those of an elephant; he had enormous eyebrows and a flat face, the eyes of an owl, a cat's nose, a mouth as wide as that of a wolf, sharp and yellow teeth like a boar, a red beard and twisted whiskers, and a chin that looked like it merged with his chest. His large backbone was arched and humped. Leaning upon his club, he was wearing very strange garb made not of linen or wool but from two freshly flayed bull or ox hides hanging down from his neck.	You will follow the road until a large clearing occupied by a field in the middle of which is a mound. On the top of the mound you will see a large black man, twice as big as two men of this world. He has only one foot and only one eye in the center of his forehead. He has an iron club, and you can be sure it weighs as much as would take two men of this world to carry, whoever they might be. He is the guardian of this forest. You will see a thousand wild beasts grazing around him. Ask him the way out of the clearing. He will treat you curtly, but he will show the path to find what you seek.

In the conversation that ensues, the ugly character gives a demonstration of his power over animals. Both texts offer a well-known folktale motif here, that of a supernatural figure haunting the forests with wild beasts as his flock.[32] Calogrenant/Kynon has reached the border of the otherworld, and this rustic figure is its doorkeeper. He indicates the path for the knight to follow that will let him pursue his adventure:

Near here you will soon find a path that will take you there. Go straight if you wish not to walk overmuch, for there is a great risk of getting lost; there are many other paths! You will see the bubbling spring whose waters are colder than marble. It is shaded by the most beautiful tree Nature ever created. It keeps its foliage through all seasons and even winter cannot strip away its leaves. An iron basin hangs there on a chain that is so long it reaches down to the spring. Next to the fountain, you will find a stone slab. . . . On the other side you will see a small but very beautiful chapel. If you draw some water from the spring and spill it over the stone, you will see a storm come up that will cause all the beasts of the forest to flee . . . [33] and you will see the unleashing of such lightning bolts and wind, and crashing trees, rain, and thunder, and flashes of light that if you are able to escape without great harm and hardship, you will be the luckiest of any knight to have ever gone to this spot.

Take the path at the top of the clearing and climb the hill there until the top. There you will see a very large valley and in the center of this valley, you will see a huge tree, whose branches are greener than the greenest fir tree. And beneath this tree is a fountain, and at the edge of this fountain is a large stone slab. On this slap sits a silver bowl so securely attached to a gold chain that it cannot be taken away. Pick up the bowl and spill its contents on the stone. You will then hear a loud clap of thunder, so strong that it will seem to shake heaven and earth. A very cold rain shower will follow after this clap of thunder. You will have a good deal of trouble of escaping it alive because of the hail. After the rain, the sky will brighten. Not a single leaf will be left in the tree that has not been carried off by the storm. Next, a flight of birds will come and land in the tree; never in your land have you heard music as beautiful as their song. When you are feeling the greatest pleasure from listening to it, you will hear great sobbing and groaning coming toward you from the valley. Next, you will see a horseman riding on a completely black horse, and completely dressed in black silk, with an entirely black pennon made of linen on his lance. He will attack you . . . .

Calogrenant/Kynon spills the water on the stone—Chrétien de Troyes explicitly states that the stone is an emerald resting on four rubies—and a knight appears, who unseats him and steals his horse. Once he has heard this tale, Yvain decides to pursue this adventure personally. He follows the same path, has the same encounters, mortally wounds the black knight, and follows him back to his castle, where he is caught in a trap. A young woman rescues him and brings him to safety. On the day of the knight's funeral, Yvain/Owain sees the chatelaine and falls in love with her. He marries her and becomes the guardian of the spring.

But Gawain urges him to ask his wife for some time away. She reluctantly agrees to allow him to leave, but makes him promise to return in one year and eight days at the very latest. He forgets to return at the appointed time and, once he has lost his wife, he goes mad and leads the life of a wild man:

He goes mad. He tears and rends his garments. . . . He lies in wait for the animals of the forest and kills them. He eats raw venison. . . .	Owain left for the ends of the earth and the mountainous wasteland. And he wandered for so long that his clothing wore out as did his body, so to speak. Long hair grew all over his body. He traveled with the wild animals, and ate in their company. . . .

Yvain remains in this state until the day he is cured by the fairies, who, obviously in service to his wife, gave him an ointment that brought the madman back to his senses. After numerous adventures, he finds his wife again.

All the decorative elements of the adventure of the fountain point in the direction of the otherworld, even though Chrétien was reluctant to use the word "fairy" for the lady of the fountain and her maid, Lunette.[34]

In one of his romances, *Erec and Enide,* Chrétien de Troyes draws the picture of another fairy world that has a close parallel in the Welsh story *Geraint and Enid.* The environment of the adventure of the Joy of the Court is a marvelous orchard that a knight has promised to defend and the approach to which is quite alarming: Geraint sees a hedge, "on each stake of the hedge there was a man's head except for two stakes." In Chrétien's story, the stakes stand inside the orchard, and one of them holds a horn.

Erec	Geraint
No wall or palisade surrounded the orchard except for a layer of air. In fact, by the art of magic this garden was entirely enclosed by a wall of air with but one sole opening. It was such that no person could enter, save through the door, as if the wall had been made of iron. Inside there were flowers and ripe fruits all summer, which had the virtue of only being possible to eat inside the garden.	"Farther down, there was the Enclosure of the cloud, where enchanted games took place. Of all the men that have gone there, not one has ever returned," Gwiffret told Gereint. Geraint entered the cloud. When he emerged from it, he found himself in a large orchard, in the middle of which stool a silk pavilion with a red top. He saw that its door was open. Facing the pavilion's door was an apple tree. Hanging from one of the apple tree's branches was a large horn. He got down from his horse and entered the pavilion.

Seeing a wondrously beautiful maiden, Erec starts to approach her, but a knight of extraordinary size and clad in red armor, Mabonagrain, threatens him, and combat ensues. Erec is the victor, as it should be. It is at this point that the text allows us to grasp what this adventure is concealing. Mabonagrain has been imprisoned in this orchard by his girlfriend, and he has sworn to her that he will not leave so long as he remains undefeated by a knight. In the Welsh story, the adversary's gigantic nature is not evident, and he remains anonymous. The succession of motifs—a magic enclosure, heads on stakes, a wondrous orchard—nevertheless signal that this place is clearly another world, and researchers have long recognized that this adventure overlays one in which a giant is the prisoner of a fairy. In the Middle High German adaptation that Hartmann von Aue (d. ca. 1110–1120) made of Chrétien de Troyes's romance, the orchard is fenced off within a cloud (*ein Wolken*, l. 8751), it is a paradise (*daz ander Paradise*, l. 9542) and Mabonagrain's horse is red, which underscores the supernatural nature of its rider. His gigantic nature is expressed by a cliché that is constantly seen in the descriptions that the German romances give of giants:

"Now Erec heard a voice, strong and grim, that echoed like a horn" (ll. 8992–94).

> *Nû gehôrte er eine stimme*
> *Starc unde grimme,*
> *Diu lûte same in horn dôz.*[35]

Written in the thirteenth century, the verse romance *Floriant et Florete* follows a plot that is well known in the lays, but brings with it one great novelty:

Floriant is abducted by *III. fees de la mer salee* (three fairies of the salty sea; l. 549), one of whom is Morgana, the sister of King Arthur. Like Lancelot, he is raised and educated by the fairy transformed into his adoptive mother. One day he leaves to go hunting at the foot of a mountain and flushes out a large stag that is as white as quicksilver. He pursues it for ten leagues or more, and then spies a magnificent castle that the stag enters. He dismounts, enters, and looks everywhere, but there is not a trace of the beast. In the castle he finds Morgana, who tells him: "I cannot leave this place without losing my life." She then explains to him that she lured him to the castle because "he has to die and leave the world. No one can help you, and medicine is powerless. Truthfully, you should know that this castle is enchanted . . . the person who stays within it cannot die."

(ll. 8177ff)

In other words, she has rescued him and given him a kind of eternal life on condition that he never leaves the castle. Essentially, what is being suggested is that time is suspended here but will reclaim its rights if Floriant sets foot outside.

In *Gauriel von Muntabel, The Knight with the Goat*, an Arthurian romance by Konrad von Stoffeln (thirteenth century)[36]—which, alas, is missing its opening lines—we have a new otherworld. The eponymous hero of the work transgresses the taboo imposed by the queen of Fluratrone, which literally means "Throne of Flowers," and is punished by the fairy (ll. 258–62).

Your beauty will be taken from you	*diu schœne wirt iu gar benomen*
And you will have such an appearance	*und ir werdet ein sölich bilde,*
all misshapen and savage,	*gar ungetân und wilde,*
That men and women shall fear you.	*daz iuch vürhtent wîp und man.*
This I impose on you as penance.	*Daz wil ich iu ze booze lân.*

Gauriel remains ill for six months. A letter from his lover tells him of the conditions he must fulfill to win her back: defeat King Arthur's three best knights. After he has accomplished this feat, he sets off with Walwan, Gawan, Iwein, and Erec to Fluratrone, a land whose gate is defended by two dragons. Once they have slain these two monsters, they enter a very beautiful forest and come to a raging river spanned by a bridge guarded by two giants, whom they kill. These details indicate that the knights have made their way to the frontier of the otherworld. They next ride toward the fairy's castle, Frîapolatûse, a name that merits a closer look: it is composed from *frîâ*, "freedom, privilege, courting," and *palast*, "palace." One of the fairy's followers comes to meet them, and she gives Gauriel a balm that restores his beauty: "She spread the balm all over him. The hideousness of his face vanished in front of everyone. He transformed and became the most beautiful man ever seen."

> *Mit der salben si zehant*
> *Allenthalben (in) bestreich.*
> *Zuo ir aller angesihte im entweich*
> *Sîn antlütze griulich*
> *Und wart der schœnste man*
> *Den man kunde ie gewan.* (ll. 3046ff)

The fairy comes to meet him, accompanied by a troop of monsters,* a detail that further supports her supernatural nature. The romance comes to a close with the happy ending of a fairy tale.

THE DEMONIZATION OF THE FAIRY KINGDOM

Sometimes the world of fairies is demonized, and any stay there will bring about eternal damnation. This can be seen as the reaction of the Church when faced with something it perceived as a remnant of paganism. Thomas the Rhymer, a Scottish poet and soothsayer of the thirteenth century, tells how a knight followed the queen of fairies into her kingdom.

> She led him to the foot of the Eildon Tree and into the secret place within the hill, where it was dark as any midnight. They waded through water up to their knees, crossing through blood red waves because all the blood that flows on earth shall blend into the streams of this land. For three days, Thomas heard naught but the murmur of the river.

They came to a beautiful orchard. Thomas went to eat a fruit, but the fairy shouted: "Stop, for these fruits contain all the wounds of hell! I tell you, in all truthfulness, if you pick them your soul will be cast into the infernal flames." She made him lay his head in her lap so that he could have a vision, which gave him a view of the beyond:

> Do you see that fair path that crosses through the high mountain? It is the road taken by the souls of the sinners once they have found redemption. Now, do you see that other path below it that crosses through the greenery? That is the one that leads to the joys of paradise. And do you see the third path that crosses over the green plain?

---

*It consists of four giants; hybrids that are half man, half animal, or even half snake; *amanes,* creatures without heads; and horned beings with multiples eyes and hairs that sting like awls.

That is the one where the souls of sinners suffer. And do you see the fourth path at the bottom of this deep valley? It is the one on which the howls from the infernal furnace emerge. And finally, do you see that splendid castle on the high hill? There is none other like it on earth. It belongs to me as well as to the lord of this land.

When Thomas left his beloved, she promised to come see him if she could.[37] The theme of this story is akin to that of the thirteenth-century German troubadour Tannhäuser, who was transformed into a figure of legend around 1440, and it can also be seen in the story *Le Paradis de la reine Sibylle* (The Paradise of Queen Sibyl) by Antoine de la Sale (d. 1460/61).

Located at the end of a perilous road through mountains, caves, and narrow passes is a paradise of love and delight ruled by a queen. It is reached by crossing through a cavern full of wind, and a bridge thrown across a *tresgrant et tres hydeux abisme deparfondeur, et au fons oyt une tresgrosse riviere* (most wide and hideous deep abyss, at the bottom of which flowed a very great river). At the end of this cave there are two dragons whose shining eyes illuminate the area. A knight and his squire find their way into this otherworld and are hosted by beautiful women who transform into vipers every night. They remain there for three hundred days before going to Rome to ask the pope forgiveness of their sins, but he refuses to absolve them, and the knight returns to Queen Sibyl's paradise.[38]

Andrea de Barberino wrote the romance *Guerino detto il Meschino* (Wretched Guerrin) around 1410. It enjoyed great popularity and was even turned into a chapbook in 1638.

Having set off in search of his parents, Guerrin decided to question the fairy Alcina and made his way into the mountain where she lived. The entrance was a labyrinthine cavern. The path there was "rocky, with ravines, surrounded by deep vales and terrible precipices. Its peaks were lost in the clouds. Light barely penetrated the deep ravines, and not a tree or even a tuft of grass was growing there. This area could only be entered during three months of the year. . . ."

Guerrin arrived at the gate to the fairy's kingdom, above which was written: "He who enters here will remain one full year without leaving. He will remain alive until the Day of the Last Judgment, then lose both his soul and his body, and be damned for eternity." The land of the fairy is therefore an antechamber of hell.

Guerrin would be subjected to temptation but victoriously resists the voluptuous charm of Alcina. He learns that the inhabitants of the city he is in suffer a weekly transformation: "Know that when the pope speaks the Mass," he is told by a person he meets, "everything found in the fairy's house changes appearance—everyone including men and women, the young and the old, all will become beast, dragon, serpent, basilisk, scorpion, toad, or worm. But you have nothing to fear for they are not able to harm or wound you. Once we have all been transformed, if you are hungry, take pains not to eat in our presence! Find a place where you will be alone until tomorrow. We shall remain transformed until the Mass has been said on Monday morning, then we shall regain our human forms. The same thing occurs on every Saturday of the year."

A little later, Alcina let him know that the form of the transformation depends upon the sin of the individuals. Guerrin manages to leave the place and resumes his quest.[39]

In this romance we have a singular blend of two worlds: the world of the fairies, which barely conceals the world of hell. A space like this, in which people are suffering from a punishment, is suggestive of purgatory as the text does not speak of damnation.

SIX

THE OTHERWORLD IN MEDIEVAL SCANDINAVIAN LITERATURE

Norse literature has a wealth of accounts about journeys to the otherworld. I will provide an overview starting with the oldest texts that have a mythological resonance. Snorri Sturluson's (1179–1241) *The Beguiling of Gylfi* (chap. 49), tells how Odin sent his son Hermod to the realm of the goddess Hel to bring back his dead brother, Baldr:

> Hermod rode nine days on Sleipnir, Odin's eight-legged steed, through dark and deep valleys until he came to Gjöll, a river that flowed beneath a golden bridge, reached the gates of Hel, jumped over them, and entered a building in which he found his dead brother. The next day he begged Hel to let Baldr return home. She accepted, on the condition that all things in the world would weep for him. Hermod returned to the gods, but one giantess refused to weep and Baldr did not return.[1]

The *Gesta Danorum,* written by the Danish historian Saxo Grammaticus between 1212 and 1216,[2] and in which the mythology of the ancient Scandinavians is transposed into history and into a novelized form, tells of Thorkil's two journeys in the otherworld. This is presented as a country located somewhere to the northeast of the known world, but a number of details allow us to discern the underlying patterns with even greater facility, since we possess the "mythological redaction" of the same journey, passed down by the *Prose Edda* of the great Icelandic poet, Snorri Sturluson:

> Having heard of the riches of Geruth [a giant], King Gorm decides to send Thorkil to find these, but "the entire road thither was said to be fraught with peril for mortals almost impassible. Those who were knowledgeable claimed that you had to sail across the ocean which girds the earth, putting the sun and stars behind your back, journey beneath the realm of night and pass finally into the regions which suffer perennial darkness without a glimmer of daylight."
>
> Thorkil and his men eventually reach a shore, and Guthmund, "a man of extraordinary stature" (*inusitatae magnitudinis vir*), gives them a place to stay. The travelers see a gold bridge spanning a river, and when they want to cross it it, Guthmund calls them back, saying that: "the bed of this stream formed a natural boundary between the human and the supernatural worlds. No mortal was permitted to step beyond it" (*naturam nec mortalibus ultra fas esse vestigiis*). The land of the dead thus lies on the other side of the bridge.
>
> Thorkil escapes Guthmund's snares of hospitality when he offers them his daughters; four of the men sleep with them and go mad. Then Guthmund offers them fruit from his garden, but the ingestion of food would cause the visitors to lose all recollection of their earlier life. After his attempts fail, Guthmund conveys the travelers to the other side of the river, thus performing the duties of Charon.
>
> On their route they see a sinister decayed town not far in the near distance. It has all the appearance of a misty cloud. Severed heads are planted on stakes set up between the ramparts. In front of the gates, they see extremely savage dogs keeping vigilant guard over the entrance.[3]

All of these details are motifs indicating that we are at the entrance to hell. The dog Garm keeps watch here in Scandinavian mythology, just like the Greek Cerberus. After visiting the foul and putrid premises, teeming with snakes, and being stripped of their wealth, twenty men manage to escape.

The second voyage—heavily Christianized—starts with an entirely different intent (*Gesta,* VIII, 15):

> "After he [the king] had spent his days with the utmost regard for his own safety and almost reached the end of his existence, because certain individuals had persuaded him with convincing proofs that souls were immortal, he kept turning over in his mind what sort of dwelling he would repair to when the breath had left his body, or what reward was earned by a ready devotion to the gods."

As he meditated on these problems, some who were ill-intentioned toward Thorkil informed the king that it would suffice to ask the gods, namely Uthgartha-Loki. Thorkil sets off with the ill-intentioned men, and they reach a land "that knew neither stars nor the light of day but was shrouded in everlasting night" [this could be a description of the Far North]. They disembark on a shore, discover a cave and stumble upon two black, beak-nosed giants, who inform them that their voyage will be long and dangerous. Thorkil and his companions reach their goal four days later. They enter a cavern where they find Uthgartha-Loki fettered. "His rank-smelling hairs were as long and tough as spears of cornel-wood. Thorkil kept one of these as a more visible proof of his labours by heaving at it with his friends till it was plucked from the chin of the unresisting figure." They then all leave. They are attacked by spirits, but thanks to the prayers that Thurkill addresses to the "god of the universe"—the Christian God, of course—they are eventually able to get back home.[4]

Here the otherworld takes the form of a cave, but the most interesting thing is the way in which Saxo Grammaticus differentiates and transforms the myth of the journey of the god Thor to the home of Útgarðaloki, "Loki of the Outer Enclosure" (in other words, Loki of the otherworld), a giant that is a master of tricks and illusions.

The *Gesta Danorum* (I, 8) presents another subterranean world:

Then while he was dining, Hadingus saw a woman emerge beside a brazier bearing stalks of fresh hemlock. He asked her where it was able to grow in the middle of winter. She then took him underground (*sub terras abduxit*), and Saxo notes: "It was, I believe, by the design of the underworld gods that she took a living man to those parts which he must visit when he died." They first went through a smoky veil and came to a sunny region, and then a bridge over a swirling river with weapons spinning about in its blackish waters. On crossing it, they saw two armies of the dead confronting each other. Next they were halted by an unsurmountable wall; the woman tried to leap over it and, when that failed, she tore off the head of a rooster she had been carrying with her and tossed the fowl over the wall. The bird came back to life immediately (*statimque redevivus*) and crowed.[5]

What is described here is clearly a journey into the beyond, as is proven by all its descriptive elements. Furthermore, the wall is reminiscent of what we have seen earlier in the medieval visions, especially that of Tundale, and the resuscitated rooster suggests that on the other side of the wall is the world of eternal life.

One final passage (*Gesta*, III, 4) is very reminiscent of what we have seen earlier in the Breton lays of Marie de France:

Hotherus lost his way in the forest while hunting and came upon the home of the forest maidens (*silvestrium virginum*); they saluted him, calling him by name, and revealed that they were the ones who decided the outcome of wars. Then their dwelling vanished and he found himself alone in the middle of a plain.

Icelandic saga literature offers a variety of forms of travel in the otherworld; we will take two as examples. In the *Þorsteins þáttr bæjarmagns* (Tale of Thorstein House-Power),[6] Thorstein makes his way to the otherworld twice. One day he comes to a mound and hears a boy asking his mother for a staff because he wants to take a ride. The term that is used, *gandreið*, has the literal meaning of "staff-ride." It involves a magical form of transportation that is reminiscent of that used by witches. Thorstein finds himself a staff and follows the boy. They dive into a large river. Thorstein has the impression of crossing through a cloud of smoke (*líkast sem þeir væði reyk*), then he catches sight of a town, enters a palace, takes a gold ring, and then flees with the boy. This latter casts his staff into the mound and enters it, while Thorstein finds himself back in the world of men.

On another occasion he is crossing through a forest and arrives at the home of Goðmundr, a man of enormous size who rules over Glæsisvellir,[7] the "Shining Plains," a name that reflects another paradisiacal world and is reminiscent of Irish traditions. It can be compared to Glasislundr, the "Gleaming Grove," mentioned in the *Poetic Edda*, and of Glasir, which, according to the *Prose Edda* of Snorri Sturluson, is located by the gates to Valhalla. The same conception of a shining land appears in the Anglo-Saxon poem *Beowulf*,[8] where we find the name of the "Splendid Meadow" (l. 93: *wlitebeorhtne wang*), and the context shows that the author is here following the story of creation (Genesis 1–2:25). This otherworld consists of three realms: a country named Risaland, "Land of Giants," a second named Jötunheimar, "Land of Ogres," and a third, Grundir,* located between the other two and governed by the jarl (earl) Agdi, who is well versed in sorcery, and where the men look more like giants than they do men (*menn hans váru tröllum likari en mönnum*).

The fourteenth-century *Egils saga einhenda ok Ásmundar berserkjabana* (Saga of Egil One-Hand and Asmund Slayer-of-Berserkers)[9] provides us with a curious story in which Arinnefja, a female troll capable of changing into a fly, goes down into an underground world (*undirheimr*). This saga is one of those that are called either *fornaldarsögur* ("legendary sagas") or *lygisögur* ("lying sagas"), and in which a number of motifs from folktales come into play:

Arinnefja uses all means to prevent Hringr's marriage with Ingibjörg. Captured, she must buy back her life by going into the

---

*Plural of *grund,* "field, grassy plain."

underworld and bringing back three valuable objects: "a cloak that fire couldn't burn, a drinking horn that could never be emptied, and a chess set that would play by itself whenever someone challenged it."[10] Arinnefja makes her way into the underworld, buys the drinking horn, and kills two of the three giants guarding the chess set. She spares the third giant, who gives her the chess set and a glass that Arinnefja describes as having the following virtues: "If a man looks into it, I can give him the shape of anyone I chose. If I want I can blind whoever looks into it."[11] She goes down even deeper in search of the cloak and encounters the "Prince of Darkness" (*Fann ek pá höfðingja myrkanna*), apparently Odin, who wants to sleep with her and tells her the test she must pass in order to win the cloak: jump across a huge fire. Arinnefja takes possession of the garment, returns home, and gives the objects to Hringr and Ingibjörg.

The *Samsons saga fagra* (Saga of Samson the Fair) offers a new otherworld, access to which is gained by going to the bottom of a body of water.

At the request of Jarl Finnlaugr, Samson sets off in search of Princess Valentina, who has disappeared. He comes to the place of a miller, whose mill stands close to a waterfall, under which is a deep hole with a great whirlpool. Suddenly, a troll-woman (*tröllkona*) drags him into the water. He slays her, dives beneath the whirlpool, discovers a cave, and enters it. Upon inspection he finds much wealth, and the clothing and adornments of Princess Valentina, who had been abducted by the troll-woman. He opens a stone door that was "shut, but not locked," and leaves. At the end of four days, he makes his way back to the main roads and returns to Jarl Finnlaugr.

When he shows the jarl what he has brought back with him, the story states that: "It seemed most likely to them that she was dead" (*þótti þeim líkast, að hún mundi dauð vera*).[12] The text therefore suggests that Valentina has gone on into the otherworld and that the cave of the troll-woman is its entrance.

The otherworld can also be found in a mountain. The Icelandic *Landnámabók* (Book of Settlements) recounts how Thorolf Mostrarskegg chose to settle near Mount Helgafell ("Holy Mountain") because he and his family believed that they would go there after their death.[13] Other settlers like Sel-Thorir and Kraku-Hreidar held similar beliefs.[14]

In the *Saga of Snorri Goði* (as recounted in the *Eyrbyggja saga*),[15] a shepherd bringing his flock back from the Helgafell saw the northern slope of the mountain open up, saw large fires inside, and heard a joyful noise. Making out some words, he realized a warm welcome was being given to some men who had just drowned and that someone was inviting Thorstein to sit on the seat of honor facing his father.[16] The *Brennu Njáls saga* (Saga of Burnt Njall) reports how Svan died at sea, and some fishermen believed they saw him go into the mountain of Kaldbakshorn and receive a warm welcome there.[17]

Henrik Ibsen wrote his famous play *Peer Gynt* (1876), basing it on a Norwegian folktale:

> In quest of love and adventure, the ne'er-do-well Peer Gynt leaves the village of his birth and meets the lady in green, one of the daughters of the king of Dovrefjell, a mountain range in central Norway. Seduced by Peer, she leads him him into the world of the trolls. They pay a visit to the king of the Dovre Mountains, whose other daughters are gnomes. But in order to wed the princess, and gain goods and honor, he must let the king mutilate his eyes so he can have the same visual perception as trolls. Peer refuses and flees.

The otherworld here is that of the trolls,[18] who are no longer the giants of ancient Scandinavian mythology (the *bergrisar*), but dwarfs. Ibsen also does not mention the propensity of trolls to have several heads (they can have anywhere from three to nine), or their stupidity, which allows the heroes of the folktales to deceive or kill them, but he does keep their habitat, the inside of a mountain. In the Norwegian folktale "About the Giant Troll Who Never Carried His Heart with Him" (*Om risen, som ikke havde noget Hjerte pass sig*) collected by Peter Christen Asbjørnsen (1812–1885), the narrator speaks of a steep mountain.

Hvorledes Jomfruland af Havet overskygges,
Ved Underjordens Folk es første Dag bebygget
Og siden ligget skjult i mange gode Aar,
Die en in namned Saoe i Børnelavets eaax.

Det af Søfarend Mand es kaldet godt
Men som i fordüm Tid hes Jomfruer des boed
Som deres Jomfrüdom behærede ingen Mand,
Da deh vq eftir dem blev kaldet Jomfrüland.

The *Three Virgins of Huldreland*.
Engraving by Theodor Kittelsen (1857–1914).

In more recent legends, the otherworld is a ghostly island, Utrøst,* which sometimes emerges into the open and whose existence was first mentioned in 1676 by Dieterico Brinckio. He locates it near to Lofoten and adds that the Norwegians call this Huldreland (*Talem terram Nordlandi Huldreland vocant*), the "Land of Huldra/Hulder," a female forest nymph. According to the great folklorist Asbjørnsen, this land is where the subterranean folk who also called the "people of Hulder" (Huldrefolk) live.[19] This same scholar notes that three young women live on Utrøst, and that their land is called "Virgin Land" (Jomfruland), which the sailors have named the "Promised Land" (Landet gode).[20]

It is difficult not to see the similarity of Utrøst with the Isle of Avalon in Celtic literature. According to another account, a voice sometimes commands: "No one should come ashore" (*ingen skal gå i land no heller*), and a final text makes it clear that spirits and/or subterranean dwellers (*tuftefolk*), another name for dwarfs, that inhabit this spot, are the dead.[21]

---

*A name that can be analyzed as consisting of *ut* ("outside") + *røst* ("voice").

A word needs to be said about Huldra/Hulder, whose name is derived from the Indo-European root *kel-, "to conceal." She is a beautiful and dangerous forest nymph who is endowed with extraordinary strength and has a horse or cow tail. This attribute vanishes if she weds a man in a church. She rules over the animals, over the fish in ponds and lakes, and has her own sheep, goats, and cows.[22]

There are other phantom islands: Brasil to the west of Ireland, which was depicted on Italian maps since 1325; Zemlya Sannikova (Земля Са́нникова), in the Arctic Ocean; and, of course, Utopia, the ideal state on the island of the same name invented by Thomas More (1478–1535).

Utopia, de optimo rei publicae statu deque nova insula Utopia,
Thomas More, 1516.

We see that various concepts of the otherworld have existed simultaneously: from islands and paradisiacal meadows to dark caves and sometimes splendid, sometimes horrible castles. Water is omnipresent, and is certainly no coincidence that drowned fishermen enter a mountain after their death, as the beyond is often reached at the end of a journey by sea.

SEVEN

THE PATHS TO THE OTHERWORLD

People do not make their way into the land of the fairies by accident, but most often by following an animal that serves as a guide (a white hind, a pig, a wild boar, etc.), without the hero's knowledge.[1] In general, it is as a result of getting lost while hunting a cervine creature[2] that a person arrives in the otherworld, after having crossed a river.

THE ANIMAL GUIDE

In the lays of the twelfth and thirteenth centuries, which were deeply imprinted by Celtic culture, this unfolding of the adventure is perfectly illustrated by the story of *Graelent* and that of *Guingamor*.

Graelent was pursuing a white hind that led him onto a moor, toward a spring in which a maiden was bathing. She informed him: "It is for you that I came to this spring" (*por vous ving jou a la fontaine*; l. 315). He breaks the prohibition not to speak of her, but when he is threatened by death, she rescues him and then leaves. He follows her and comes to a river that she has crossed. Despite her warnings he throws himself into the water. Just when he is on the verge of drowning, the fairy takes pity on him and brings him back to the land. "Some people of this land still say that Graelant is living there" (ll. 709–10). It is easy to presume that the white hind is the animal form that the fairy in love with the knight has used to attract him to her. It is not uncommon for the beings of faery to also have the shape or attributes of a deer. The *Dindshenchas* of Rennes, etymological tales based on toponomastic legends, describes the battle between two groups of supernatural beings that had assumed the shapes of stags; their combat was so violent that two mountains were formed from the hooves and antlers of these creatures.[3]

Guingamor, meanwhile, had set off to hunt a white boar, a dangerous undertaking from which no one had ever returned. He catches sight of the beast and follows it through the risk-filled moor and the perilous river (ll. 357–58), and eventually comes to a castle. He sets off again and makes his way to a spring in which a maiden was bathing, who invites him to her home, which is to say, the castle he had seen earlier. He intends to stay no more than two days, but things do not go at all as planned (l. 540). When he returns to our world he does not recognize a thing.[4] Starving, he eats an apple and starts to age rapidly because time had reclaimed its rights.[5] Two servants of the fairy then come and take him back to the otherworld.

This difference between the time he exists in this world and that of the otherworld is attested by Walter Map, who was born between 1135 and 1140 in Wales and died in 1209 or 1210. In his *De nugis curialium* (Courtiers' Trifles), written between 1180 and 1186, we find the following story:

Invited by a dwarf to his wedding, Herla entered a hollow mountain. Before he left, the dwarf gave Herla a bloodhound to carry in his arms and then forbid him and his comrades to set foot on the ground, under any pretext, before the dog had jumped down first. When Herla returned to his kingdom, he was astounded to learn that two hundred years had gone by since he left to visit the dwarf. "The King, who had thought he had made a stay of but three days, could scarce sit on his horse for amazement. Some of his company, forgetting the pygmy's orders, dismounted before the dog had alighted, and in a moment fell into dust" (*Quidam autem ex sociis suis ante canis descensum immemores mandatorum pygmæi descenderunt, et in pulverem statim resoluti sunt*).[6]

The hollow mountain is not only another world, but it is also a kingdom of the dead, as the last sentence shows. We should note that the different passage of time in the otherworld was a very well-known motif in the Middle Ages and was spread via exempla, such as those by Jacques de Vitry (*De quodam valde religioso abbate*) or by Maurice de Sully (*Il fu un bons hom de religion*).[7] It can be seen in the folktale type "the land where no one dies" (AT 470B) and in the tale of "The Man Who Did Not Want to Die":

> Peter did not wish to die and set off in search of the land of immortality. He came to a country where no one had died since the Creation, but a bird was devouring the land and this world was doomed to disappear. He set off again and came to an island that possessed the same virtue, but a fish was drinking the sea, and when it was gone it would be the end of the world. Peter met a fairy who transported him onto the star where she lived and where no one ever died. He remained there for centuries, but he grew bored and wanted to see his village again. Unable to dissuade him, the fairy gave him a horse to carry him there and ordered him not to dismount. He came to the village that had replaced his and whose inhabitants could barely understand his language. He pushed on farther and saw a cart stuck in the mud whose driver asked him for help. He set foot on the ground, but the carter was Death. The cart transformed into a pile of shoes: all the ones that Death had worn out looking for Peter.[8]

There are two points here to emphasize: the world of the fairy, which is that of immortality (like Avalon), and the psychopomp horse.

In 1888, François-Marie Luzel collected a travel tale—in this case concerning a journey to the earthly paradise—which blended clearly pagan elements together with Breton beliefs:

> The young Goazic set off in search "of the unknown beauties whose home is paradise on earth." An old woman told him what she knew and gave him a wand that led him to the woman's two sisters in succession. The third one told him what he needed to do: go to a grove

where there is a pond in which four princesses come to bathe; at these times they deposit their clothes and wings near the pond. Goazic had to steal the garments and wings of the youngest princess. "You will then mount upon her back and she will carry you to the earthly paradise." Goazic followed her instructions and attained his goal, and liked it so much "that at the end of five hundred years he thought he had only been there for five." Because he wanted to see his father again, the princesses brought him back to earth, where he no longer recognized anything, so he decided to return to the pond. As he approached the grove, he saw a cart mired in a rut; it was loaded with the old rags of people of all ages and social status. The carter, an old man white with age and armed with a scythe, asked him his name. Goazic gave him his name and the other replied: "Here it has been a good five hundred years, or thereabouts, that I have been looking for you." This old man was Death (the Ankou) and he cut off Goazic's head with his scythe and threw his corpse into his cart.[9]

Compared to the previous tale, this story is presented, as it were, either as the "original" version that has been Christianized, or as a secular (lay) version of the Christianized one. It is difficult to choose between the two hypotheses. Certainly, we are dealing with heaven on earth here, but it is the dwelling place of the bird-women, who represent a type of swan-maiden (*femme-cygne*).

THE TRAIL TO FOLLOW AND THE ABDUCTION

When a fairy, or a "*faé*" (fay), falls in love with a mortal, he or she can also draw the object of their affection toward them, either by abduction, or by sending him or her a wondrous boat—as subject we will revisit later—or with a kind of scavenger hunt.

1. By means of abduction: *The Wooing of Étaín* (*Tochmarc Étaín*, ninth century),[10] tells how Midir of the *síd* of Brí Léith, a king of the otherworld, abducted Étaín, the wife of Eochaid Airem, the king of Ireland. He grabbed her by her right arm and carried her through the smoke hole in the roof, from which two swans were then seen flying

away.[11] This text is interesting because it implies that swan-maidens could be mortal women who have entered the otherworld by one means or another, which would explain their dual nature as both swan and woman. It certainly suggests that a reconsideration and more extensive examination be made of tales and legends in which the husband or wife takes the shape of an animal by starting from this hypothesis.

In the Germanic regions, *Frederick of Swabia* recounts the quest of a knight who, having violated a taboo, lost his lover who had flown away after being transformed into a dove. Thanks to a young woman changed into a hind, he managed to find his wife whose kingdom bore the evocative name of "Luminous Plain."[12]

Liombruno, an Italian romance of the fourteenth century in which can be seen folktale type 400 (The man on a quest for his lost wife) tells how, in the form of an eagle, the Lady Aquilina kidnapped the hero when he was an adolescent, and educated and married him. One day he asked to go see his parents. She gave him her permission but demanded he return in a year and four days at the very latest. He lost track of the time and had to set off in search of his wife. After various adventures, he found her again in a castle sitting atop a high mountain.[13]

2. By sending a ship: this is the case in *Partonopeu de Blois*.

3. By leaving a trail of clues: in *Seifried de Ardemont*[14] by Albrecht von Scharfenberg (thirteenth century), the fairy scattered objects on the road that led to her. The road crossed through a moor, from which there soon emerged a mountain of impressive size.

> Once they had reached the foot of it, Seifried and his faithful squire Waldin discovered that it was surrounded by thick thorny bushes. No path crossed through them, and it was swarming with wild animals of all sorts, snakes, dragons, and lions. They scaled the mountain and discovered a magnificent meadow on the other side, upon which splendid tents had been erected. "If this is not the kingdom of heaven, at the very least it is paradise!" cried Seifried.

The medieval authors introduce or suggest another world in three different ways: through the framework of the adventure; through the obstacles that are encountered; and by the place names. It is a constant feature in medieval romances, and even in medieval epics, that the landscape and action of the story are closely linked. The hero crosses through a wild area, either a forest (for example, the *Gaste Forêt aventureuse* and the *Forêt desvoiable* in *Lancelot*), a moor, a mountain, or a swamp. All these elements are not employed haphazardly; they are combined to form sites and serve as so many signals aimed at the listeners/readers that punctuate the hero's journey. The verbal designation of the landscapes encountered is a kind of anticipation of what is going to happen. A person crosses through a no-man's-land extending between nature and culture, and immediately one is plunged into an adventure. Let us consider one example. Poytislier has set out to hunt the white stag in the forest; his hunting dog bounds away in pursuit of the animal, and the hero follows him through a grove of fir trees. He becomes lost, camps out in a field, spots the stag "on a moor," loses it again, and discovers "a delectable house in a meadow" to which he is welcomed by two maidens. The path he follows is designated as the "unknown way." The text provokes no apprehension for the reader because, after crossing through the border forest, Poytislier has entered the territory of faery, guided by the stag.[15]

In the lay of *Tydorel,* a fay knight wins the love of the queen and brings her to the edge of a lake, into which he then disappears. When he returns, he tells her that he leaves his land and comes and goes by this path whenever he pleases (ll. 425–27). The queen becomes pregnant and gives birth to Tydorel. One day she reveals to him who his father is. The lad makes his way to the lake on horseback and enters it. Never is he seen again: "He stayed there and never more returned."

> *Illec remest, en tel manière*
> *Que puis ne retourna arriere* (ll. 487–88)

We may easily deduce from this that he left to rejoin his father and that the lake is the point of passage between the two worlds.

This kind of subaquatic kingdom appears in a variety of forms. In the case of the Lady of the Lake who abducted and raised Lancelot, the water is only phantasmagoria, and a rational explanation is provided for the underwater kingdom. In the *Demantin* by Berthold von Holle (thirteenth century), the adversary of the hero lives beneath the waves thanks to two stones he carries. Demantin slays him, but his wife—a "strong mermaid" (*das starke merewîp*)—attacks the hero. He wounds her and she flees into the water, carrying the body of her husband. At that moment the river vanishes (*daz grôze wazzer dâr vorswant*; l. 2676)[16] and the knight is left wondering about the reality of what he had seen.

Wigamur, the Knight with the Eagle, an anonymous Middle High German romance written down in the thirteenth century,[17] tells how the hero was abducted by a water nymph and raised by a merman (*merwunder*), which is reminiscent of Lancelot's childhood. In *Jaufre,* written toward the end of the twelfth century and the only Arthurian romance written in the language of Occitan (*langue d'oc*),[18] the gateway to the otherworld is a spring:

> Jaufre heard screams and saw a maiden asking for help for her mistress who was drowning in a spring; he leaned over but, pulled by one and pushed by the other, he plunged into the water as his beloved Brunissen mourned his disappearance. Jaufre found himself in a land of delights, and the most gracious of the two women asked him to protect her against Felon d'Auberue, a horrible monster.* He disposed of the threat to the lady, returned to court, and wed his beloved. After the wedding they set off for their lands and spent the night near the spring, out of which emerged knights, maidens, and their sovereign, the faery of Gibel (*la fada de Gibel*; l. 8424).

Gibel[19] (a distortion of Arabic *djebel,* "mountain")—which became the Mongibello in Sicily—is a region that is generally regarded as hell: according to a legend that underwent a heavy Christian influence, this is where King Arthur ended up after his death.[20] Some texts locate it in Sicily, near Catania, which brings to mind Mount Etna. This is,

---

*She says that it has the head of a horse or bull with eyes big as eggs; thick, black lips; and large, crooked teeth sticking out of its mouth, which is bigger than that of a leopard.

therefore, an example of demonization of the otherworld of faery.

Let us now take a look at the place names that serve as so markers signaling the change of worlds. The kingdom of Gorre is described as the "land from which no one returns." The Sarpenic Forest is located at its entrance. The kingdom is surrounded by water, which makes it an island. Access to it is by the *Pont de l'Espee* (Bridge of the Sword), also known as the *Bridge perillous* (Perilous Bridge), a gigantic sword spanning a black and terrifying torrent of water that forms the border with the kingdom of Norgales, and which must be walked on barefoot. There is another Underwater Bridge that allows access. Gorre is also called *Roialme sans Retour* (Kingdom of No Return), which suggests a land of the dead. Meleagant appears in *Lancelot, or The Knight of the Cart* by Chrétien de Troyes. Study has shown that this figure has a variety of names in the romances, such as Maheloas, lord of the Isle of Glass, behind whom we can see Melvas, most likely a sovereign of the Celtic otherworld, or even a king of the dead.

The Bridge of the Sword. Manuscript from the workshop of Evrard d'Espinques, Ahun (ca. 1475).

The "Vale of No Return" (with its evocative name due to the enchantments of Morgana the Fay, which Lancelot reaches after killing two dragons and crossing two rivers), the "Path of No Return," the "Road of the Devil," the "Castle of Death," the "Waste Land," the "adventurous Waste Forest," the "Strange Isle," and the "Black Isle"—all these names indicate that the knight errant has crossed over a border and entered another world.

The Gold Isle, in Renaut de Beaujeu's late twelfth- or early thirteenth-century romance *Le Bel Inconnu* (The Fair Unknown),[21] is the kingdom of the fairy with the White Hands. In *Le Livre d'Artus* (The Book of Arthur) and *Joseph d'Arimathe,* it is a revolving island to which Nascien has been transported by a cloud, and Lancelot withdraws to the Isle of Joy. In *Apollonius von Tyrland* (fourteenth century) by Heinrich von Neustadt, access to the Golden Valley is via a road forming a bridge that rejects anyone setting foot upon it who is not pure of any misdeed; a little farther on, there is a staircase that has the same properties.[22]

SIGNALING THE OTHERWORLD

The authors of the romances multiply the details signaling, for example, that the castle the knight has come to is on the borders of the otherworld. It is dark, surrounded by black waters or a malefic swamp, or a palisade topped with human heads. It can also be sealed off by a wall made of air. A thousand names indicate that a fortress is not what a person might think it is, and it is no accident that crossroads play an important role in the chivalrous adventures that befall a person at the crossing of routes (*homo viator in bivio*). This is related to a very familiar symbology in which the difficult path is an initiation, and often even leads to sovereignty. In addition, there are enchanting spots in which fairies host the heroes: flower-filled meadows, riverbanks in which a tent has been erected, or paradisiacal gardens. But before the heroes can get there, they must overcome so many ordeals! Most often these are trials materialized by the landscape.

Let us start with the adventure of Perceval as told by Gerbert de Montreuil (thirteenth century).[23] The knight is riding on a narrow path full of thorns and brambles and comes to a mountain where he hears "foul and hideous" (*lait et hideus*) cries. He heads in their direction and finds a slab of red marble and sits down on it. He then hears a voice that asks him to free him of his sufferings by pulling out a spike that is stuck through his body. Perceval complies with this request and sees a worm come out, which then vanishes, but the air has filled with flames, thunder, and wind, and he realizes the devil has duped him. But he manages to imprison him back in the stone slab.

In the adventure of Chastel Perilleus (Castle Perilous), the Knight of Papegau (who is the hero of a later romance, *Le Chevalier du Papegau*, written in the fourteenth or fifteenth century), comes to a mountain that is encircled by a wide, deep, dark black river that is spanned by a bridge so narrow it can only be crossed on foot. In the middle of the bridge, an enchanted iron wheel is turning that is as sharp as a razor. At the end of the bridge stands a sculpted tower some thirty rods high, and behind it, a castle. The knight gets past these obstacles and enters a chamber. A maiden dressed half in purple and half in scarlet appears, followed by an entire host of similarly dressed young women. An armored man attacked the knight who slew him and thereby freed the castle of King Bel Nain.* The location of the castle, its name, and the description of its defenses reveal that this adventure is unfolding in the otherworld. Furthermore, the way in which the knight was led to make his way to Castle Perilous is quite revealing. The knight followed a strange animal, which was red as a hot coal and illuminated all around it. Both followed their path until midnight, rested, and the next day they came to a beautiful, green country with delightful footpaths. They come to the ruins of a castle and the knight sees a man white with age and all dressed in white coming toward him. The animal that guided him here is none other than the late Bel Nain, who seems to be living in the antechamber of paradise: "I am living in a charming spot," he says, "and I will remain here until Merlin's prophecy has been fulfilled. After which, I can go to an even more beautiful place that is full of delights, the day when God rewards the righteous."[24] Bel Nain is

---

*[The name translates to "handsome dwarf." —*Trans.*]

therefore a revenant who tried to rid his kingdom of the usurper who occupies his castle.

In *Le Bel Inconnu* (The Fair Unknown),[25] Renaut de Beaujeu's twelfth-century Arthurian poem in which a young knight learns that his name his Guinglain, the story is told of the Cité Gaste (Waste City). The city is protected on one side by a river that crossed by a bridge and on the other by powerful ramparts and a diabolical knight who we discussed earlier. The Cité Gaste is clearly an otherworld, or, at the very least, a between-world.

Renaut de Beaujeu mentions another land, in this case a fay one: the land of the Beauty with the White Hands, a fairy who lives on the Golden Isle. Here, too, the description leaves no doubt about the nature of the place. The city is surrounded by a river spanned by one bridge, a materialization of the border between this world and the otherworld, and the palace diffuses light. Guinglain sees a tent at the end of a road barred by a palisade of sharpened stakes. The head of a knight is stuck on each stake. Malgiers li Gris defends against any passage (l. 1870ff), and the knight kills him in single combat.

Sometimes it is thanks to the landscape that the reader realizes that an adventure is unfolding in the otherworld. One of the best examples is the *Historia Meriadoci regis Cambriae* (Story of Meriadoc, King of Cambria),[26] written by a cleric living in southern Wales around 1280.

While pursuing Saguntius, the chief of King Gundebald's knights who lives on an island beyond the Rhine called the Land From Which No One Returns (because it is swampy and swallows up whoever who sets foot there), Meriadoc and his troop entered a forest that was impenetrable because of its wild animals, "but also because of the countless incredible ghosts (*fantasmata*) that tormented and abused those crossing through the forest." Weary, they all readied themselves to sleep "but barely had they shut their eyes when dawn began to lighten the sky." The guards awoke Meriadoc, who was amazed to learn the night had been so short. They resumed their journey, arriving at a plain where Meriadoc had often come to hunt with the emperor, and he was stupefied to see there immense buildings girded by a deep moat and a steep curtain wall. In a state of surprise, he and his companions entered the royal hall where a lady greeted him who knew both his face and name. "Do not marvel, Meriodoc, if I have called you by your name. For a long time indeed you have been known to me by face and name," she said, though he had never seen her before. Then she stated: "This little place has existed since ancient times. Neither is this where you suppose it to be, nor has it been in this place except as it is."

The hero, therefore, has traveled into the otherworld.

A feast was served in complete silence; Meriadoc sought to learn who his fellow guests were, but the seneschal only grimaced in response. Meriodoc wished to leave the table, but the lady rebuffed her seneschal with an enigmatic sentence: "Stop, stop, you should not give insult to this noble man, otherwise he would be capable of noticing that our court has been struck with villainy," which suggests that a charm or a taboo weighs over this court. Struck by this, Meriodoc fled with his men.

Without mentioning the otherworld or the land of faery, the author has multiplied the clues reflecting it: the woodland phantasmagoria, the bizarre flow of time, the buildings that had been until now invisible, the total silence at the table, the seneschal's grimaces.

Another equally fantastic adventure also takes place in the story:

So Meriodoc and his companions fled, and darkness enveloped them shortly afterward. Men and horses were stricken with panic and the troop scattered in the forest. In the morning they found themselves in the waves of a river and, leaving it, went back to wandering at random in the forest. There a terrifying storm caught them by surprise. Meriadoc asked his companions if they knew a shelter, and one of them replied that there was "in the vicinity a very large castle but no one that has ever entered has left without shame." A group led by Valdomer entered first and Meriadoc joined them shortly afterward and found them frozen with fear. He explored the castle, entered a chamber where a maiden was sitting on a bed, he took the food he found there and left, and ran into a man of tall stature who accused him of theft and struck him. Meriadoc lost his sword, which was soon returned to him. He took a lance and a sword and made his way to the kitchens where he discovered, close to the fire, a sleeping man whose body was immense (*immensis corporis*) and beardless and whose head was shaved. Meriodoc was noisy when taking more food and the giant rushed at him, but the knight tossed him down a well. A second giant attacked him and killed two men. He got free of him, but all his companions had fled taking with them his charger and his arms. A maiden gave them back to him, and Meriadoc made it back to our world directly.

The concatenation of descriptive elements allows us a glimpse of the topography of the otherworld. Its entrance is the forest full of ghosts, which represents a trial to be overcome. Next, the plain and the buildings depict the center of the faery kingdom that belongs, of course, to a maiden or a lady, a fairy, which explains how she knows the name and face of Meriadoc. This is a characteristic of this kind of supernatural being. Consider *Lanval,* for example. Even if the author made liberal use of the stock elements of the genre, he employed them in a meaningful way. But what did the reader—and not the listener, since this tale was written in Latin—make of a text like this? I think that he was fully capable of deciphering the codes and understanding what underlay all these motifs, thanks to their arrangement, likely because they reminded him of similar adventures that are found in other texts. By means of intertextuality, he should have been able to grasp the quintessence of the narrative.

In *Diu Crône* (The Crown), Heinrich von dem Türlin shows that the mountain is another form of frontier. In the land of the giant Assiles stands a crystal mountain, slippery and sharp, and surrounded by impassable lands; beyond it stretches a beautiful country (ll. 10025ff). In this same Arthurian romance, it is said that the magician Gansguoter built a glass castle that turns on its axis and is surrounded by a deep moat. All of the turrets except one are adorned with severed heads (ll. 12944ff).[27] He built another castle, Saliê, intended for Igerne, when he left King Arthur's court. Its description again shows us we are at a frontier: the castle stands atop a high mountain surrounded by fertile lands, and is defended by automatic crossbows placed in the windows (ll. 20102ff)

WATER AND FORESTS

The reader of our ancient texts cannot help but be struck by the recurrence of two constituent motifs of fairy tales: water and forests. Pierre Gallais devoted a study to these motifs some time ago, based on a very large body of work including the literature, tales, and legends of various nations.[28]

Around the year 1000, Burchard, the bishop of Worms, was the first to mention the ladies of the wood:

> Have you believed what some are accustomed to believe, that there are rustic women called *sylvaticas* ("sylvatics"), whom they say have bodies and when they wish they reveal themselves to their lovers, and they say that they have lain with them, and likewise when they wish they remove themselves and vanish?[29]

Everything is stated in a few words: these supernatural women are connected with forests, they are three-dimensional beings capable of loving mortals, and they can appear and disappear at will. Burchard is furnishing us with what is practically a fact sheet on these creatures, and it corresponds fully with what we can read in the work of Marie de France, the lays, and in the chivalric romances.

It is in a forest that Gerbert d'Aurillac meets the fairy Meridiana; Guingamor crosses through a forest, the border of the faery kingdom; Graelent flushes out a white hind in a grove and she leads him to the fairy; Désiré meets the fairy in a forest; and it is after crossing through a forest full of phantasmagorical phenomena that Meriadoc finds his way to the otherworld.

But the forest is always competing with water. A sermon by Geoffroy of Auxerre,[30] written between 1187 and 1188, tells how a young man bathing in the sea captured a woman whom he wed. She remained mute to all his questions, however. One day, at the urging of a prelate, he demanded his wife to reveal her origins and threatened to kill the son she had given him:

> "Woe to you, unlucky wretch!" she cried. "You are losing a wife devoted to your service at the moment you force me to talk. I was happy with you, and it was a good thing for you, so long as you allowed me to keep the silence imposed on me. I am speaking to you as you demanded, but you will never again see the one who is speaking to you." With these words, the woman vanished immediately. The boy who remained there grew up although he was left all alone. He survived on the food he received from the kindness of others. However, he began practicing swimming in the sea quite often, there where his mother had been found, until one day when, in the presence of many people, this otherworldy woman kidnapped him, as the people there swear, pulling the child swimming toward her beneath the waves, from which he was never to return.

Geoffroy tells another story in the same sermon—it is a story in which water and woods are associated, and the supernatural woman is a foreshadowing of Melusine. A man discovers a well-clad woman in the most remote thickets of the forest. He abducts her, marries her, and they have children. This woman's greatest pleasure is bathing. One day a servant woman spies on her in the bath and sees "not a woman, but a snake writhing in sinuous spirals." Alerted to this, the husband breaks down the door, but his wife has vanished forever.

In his twelfth-century work *De nugis curialium* (Courtiers' Trifles), the Welsh cleric Walter Map compiled various legends that feature the union of fairies and mortals subjected to the power of a taboo. Henno with the Big Teeth (*Henno cum dentibus*) meets a fairy in a forest close to the sea,[31] Edric the Savage meets one in a woodland house,[32] and Wastinus Wastiniauc meets one near a lake in which water nymphs dwell.[33] In *Florimont,* which Aimon of Varennes wrote in 1188, the fairy comes from the Ylle Celee and she has crossed the sea because she loves the hero.[34] Many more such examples can be found.

So we have three specific cases: (1) water in the form of a river, a spring, a lake, or the sea; (2) the forest; and (3) water and woods. Clerical literature can be distinguished from romance literature because it never combines one of these elements with the others. Burchard of Worms, for example, only mentions the forest, whereas Geoffroy of Auxerre sticks to water. The fusion of the two elements apparently took place during the eleventh and twelfth century. In the work of Johannes de Alta Silva,[35] whose *Dolopathos* was written between 1180 and 1212, a young man goes hunting in the forest and sees "a spring and a nymph in it holding a golden chain in her hand" (*fontem repperit nimphamque in eo virginem cathenam auream tenentem manu*). As far as I am aware, the *Dolopathos* and the lay of *Lanval* by Marie de France are the first literary works that connect the forest and the fountain in this regard.

Once the encounter with the fairy has been situated near a forest or flowing water, we can see how we are being confronted by two different traditions that reflect, on the one hand, the Germanic civilization (with the associations it had regarding the forest),[36] and, on the other hand, the Celtic civilization (with the associations it had regarding water). In fact, water is omnipresent in Celtic tradition and the otherworld is reached by sailing there or by crossing over a river.

However, these elements that we perceive as stereotypes are, in reality, mythemes, and behind the springs and groves are conceled the more recent representations of gods, which have been degraded to the level of place-spirits and invested with a new identity: that of fairies from the otherworld. Concerning the Fountain of Barenton, Philippe Walter perceptively notes: "The very etymology of the name Barenton appears to be connected with this bubbling or boiling. . . . The Gaulish god Borvo seems to have been primarily honored near bubbling springs (springs with sparkling water), and he has left his trace in numerous place names."[37]

One question that arises then is: who are the fairies? Burchard called the mysterious women *agrestes* and *sylvaticae*, words that in the tenth century were glossed as "dryads" and "wandering spirits, souls in torment." All the glosses make it possible to see that the being designated is a woodland and ghostly creature, which corresponds exactly to Burchard's description: these creatures appear and disappear quickly.

According to the Latin texts, the fairy is given a variety of denominations, which can be divided into four main groups:

1. She is called a fairy: a *fada, mulier fatata, Bona res, geniciales feminae,* names that have an association with fate by way of an etymology that was well known during the Middle Ages (and appears earlier in the work of Varro, cited by Aulus Gellius [*Noctes Atticae*, III, 16, 10]) and which claimed "Parca"* came from *parere,* "to give birth."
2. She is simply a noble and beautiful woman, a lady: a *mulier et nobilia foemina, puella speciosissima, domina, puella,* or *matrona,* this last term referring to the mother goddesses.
3. Under the influence of the Church, the fairy was demonized and transformed into a phantom, demon, and imaginary being, a *fantasia, fantasma, daemonium in specie mulieris, dea phantastica, mulier phantastica, pestilencia, larva,* or *lamia.*
4. She is a nymph or a dryad: *nympha, dea, adriades, Jana.* This last name is a corruption of Diana and has survived in all the romance languages with sometimes diametrically opposed meanings. In old Provençal, *jana* refers to a nymph of the springs; in Asturias, Xana designates a kind of fairy; in the Algarve, *jâna* is applied to otherworldly nocturnal spinners; in Spain, the term *jana* is synonymous with *fada.*[38]

According to Martin of Braga (sixth century), the Lamiae are aquatic spirits:

[M]any of those demons that have been expelled from heaven have their seat in the sea or in rivers or in springs or in woods and in the same way men ignorant of God worship as gods and offer them

---

*[In ancient Roman mythology and religion, Parca referred one of the three Fates (pl. Parcae), the female divinities that governed the destiny of gods and humans. —*Ed.*]

sacrifices. They are called: in the sea, Neptune; in rivers, Lamiae; and in springs, Nymphs.[39]

For Hincmar of Reims (died 882) they were supernatural women who presided over births (*geniciales foeminae*)[40] and, as a result, were associated with the goddesses of fate and later with the fairies, about whom the same thing was said.

According to Gervais of Tilbury (1152–1218), the Lamiae burst into homes at night and snatched children from their cradles, and were related to witches and nightmares.[41] William of Auvergne (1180–1249)[42] also shared this opinion, which reflects the clerical viewpoint of this era.

If we turn our attention to ancient Celtic literature, we will see that the Lamia was regarded as the goddess Mórrígan (Morrígu). The *Thesaurus Paleohibernicus* gives the following gloss: "Lamia monstrum in femine figura. i. *morrígain*" (Lamia, a monster in female form: Mórrígan).[43] As it happens, the Mórrígan became the fairy Morgue (Morgan, Morgana) in the French texts, and Philippe Walter has pointed out that one of the etymologies suggested for her name is "born of the sea" (**mori-genos*).[44]

If my hypothesis is correct, Germanic fairies are therefore women of the woods, while fairies of Celtic origin are water dryads or nymphs.

SAILING TO THE OTHERWORLD

Sailing is the oldest form of travel in the beyond. It would subsequently become the most common mode of transport in the otherworld.

In Scandinavia, the dead were entombed in a boat that was then burned, but in the account of the funeral of Baldr, Odin's son, the boat was simply pushed out into the open sea. In ancient Russia there existed a boat coffin (*koloda*) carved from a tree trunk. In 922, the Arab traveler Ibn Fadlan described the funeral of a Rus chieftain (in other words, a Swedish chieftain). The dead man was accompanied by slaves, a dog, a rooster, a hen, and two cows intended for his life in the beyond. We should also note the Scandinavian burial sites that used an arrangement of stones in the shape of a boat viewed from above (Danish *skibssætning*, "ship formation").

The otherworld often consists of islands that the hero discovers during the course of a wondrous journey. Celtic literature has a wealth of stories of this type, called *Imrama* (voyages), which are heavily influenced by the apocryphal gospels and the visions of saints. The best known is *The Voyage of Saint Brendan*.

Saint Brendan and his companions (Irish art).

The *Echtra Condla Chaim* (Adventure of Conla the Red), which most likely dates from the eighth century, recounts the following:

A woman appeared to Conla and told him that she was from the land of the living. He alone could see her; the other people present could only hear her words. She said that her country did not know death or old age. "I have come from the country of the living where there is no death, nor sin, nor transgression. . . . We live in the large *síd* and are called the people of the *síd* (*áes síde*)." In love with Conla, she invited him to follow her into her glass boat (*long glano*), and he vanished with her forever.[45]

The most singular of the voyages to the otherworld is that of Máel Dúin (*Imram Curaig Máile Dúin*):

To find and slay his father's murderer, Máel Dúin set sail with seventeen companions who were joined by his three brothers. He found the murderers on an island, but a tempest pushed him back into the sea before he could give them their punishment. From that time, his journey went from one island to another: one with enormous ants; one with monstrous horses; one with demons; one with the house of salmon; one with marvelous fruits; one with the beast; one with the battles of horses; one with fire beasts and gold apples; one with the castle guarded by a cat; one that changed color; one with gigantic pigs and monstrous calves; one with a terrifying mill; one with black mourners; and one that was divided into four by palisades, the first of gold, the second of silver, the third of copper, and the last one of glass. There was also the isle of the magic bridge and the beautiful hostess; the one with the singing birds; the one of the solitary pilgrim; the one with the wondrous fountain that gave whey or water on Wednesdays and Fridays, but good milk on Sundays and the feast days of martyrs; and the island of the terrible smiths. They sailed upon a crystal sea, then upon one of clouds at the bottom of which they could see a beautiful countryside and castles. They encountered fearful islanders and discovered the rainbow river: "a large stream rose out of the bank of the island and crossed it like a rainbow and descended on the other side. . . . From Sunday to Monday afternoon, this river did not flow." They saw a silver pillar in the middle of the ocean, then an island on a pedestal, and they then came to the island of the queen with seventeen daughters. The sovereign told them: "Remain here and you will never grow any older than you are right now; you will have eternal life." After spending three months in the place, they managed to escape and next discovered an island of intoxicating fruits and another with a hermit and a wondrous spring: whoever bathed in it and drank its water would stay in perfect health until their death, without ever losing a hair or a tooth. The sailors then made their way to the isle of laughers, and another surrounded by a rampart of fire, and then they came across a naked man on a rock before sailing home to Ireland.

This travel tale is quite rich in mythemes, like the apples that sate the appetite for forty days and that are a herald of the Isle of Avalon, "the Apple Orchard"; the burning river that consumes any sword stuck into it; a bronze fortress that is entered by means of a glass bridge; and then the country beneath the waves, which brings to mind the legends of drowned cities transformed into underwater kingdoms.

It is the isle of sheep cut in half by a palisade that I find most intriguing. When a white sheep is thrown to the other side, it turns black, and vice-versa. The palisade is the border between two worlds, but which worlds? An answer may have been provided by *Peredur*, a Welsh romance of the eleventh or twelfth century, in which we read:

He headed toward the valley irrigated by a river. Its contours were wooded, but on both sides of the river there stretched two unvarying plains. On one side there were white sheep and on the other, a herd of black sheep. A large tree stood on the river's edge. One half of the tree was burning from top to bottom, the other half bore green foliage.[46]

The presence of the river is more explicit than the palisade: it marks the border of the otherworld and, even more, separates the world of the living from the world of the dead, which is suggested by the change of the sheep's color and more especially by the tree whose green side represents life while its burning side symbolizes death. In Russia, the myth of Buyan Island (*Bujan-ostrov*) indicates there is a magic oak there that is not leafless in the winter or completely covered with leaves in the summer: "On one side it is flowering, on the other it is losing its leaves, on the third side fruits are ripening, and on the fourth the branches are withering." With the island it forms an *axis mundi*, whose roots touch the world underground and whose top reaches heaven. A beautiful young woman lives there, "who stitches up bloody wounds."[47]

The Voyage of Bran[48] tells of a sea voyage that leads the half-sleeping hero toward an island held up by four pillars where joy is permanent and where music steals all death and old age away. A fairy invites him to follow her to the Land of Women (*Tír na mBan*) and disappears. Bran sets sail with twenty-seven companions, stopping first at the Isle of Joy and then at the Land of Women, where all disembark and remain. In the grip of nostalgia, one of the companions makes Bran decide to return to Ireland. When they get there and Bran states his name, the inhabitants reply that this person is dead, but that the tales of his voyage were handed down after him. One of his companions leaps down to the ground and collapses into a pile of ashes[49] "as if he had been buried in the ground for centuries." Bran then realizes that time did not exist on the island.[50]

We should note, incidentally, that some distinguishing characteristics of the Celtic otherworld are music, as evidenced in *The Wooing of Étaín*,[51] as well as bright radiance, nobility, and the absence of lies and injustice, as we see in the *Serglige Con Culainn* (Wasting Sickness of Cú Chulainn; §34):

> *I have seen a land noble and bright*
> *Where none spoke lies or injustice.*[52]

The Book of Fermoy, compiled by Adam Ó Cianáin in 1373, tells the story of Conn of the Hundred Battles (*Cétchathach*) and deserves our attention because it offers two journeys into the otherworld:

> Eithne's widower, Conn of the Hundred Battles, took as his wife Bé Chuma, a woman of the Land of Promise (*Tír Tairngire*), the otherworld, who had been banished by the gods (Tuatha Dé Danaan) for bad behavior. But she was in love with Conn's son Art and demanded that his father exile him from Tara, the kingdom's capital. Because she carried a curse, Bé Chuma caused a blight that destroyed half the milk and wheat of Ireland and the druids announced that it would be necessary to sacrifice the son of a couple without sin and mix his blood with the dirt from Tara. Conn set off in a currach* to find this boy. He came to a strange island filled with fragrant apple trees and fountains of wine surrounded by hazel trees, where he saw a beautiful mansion whose roof was made from the wings of white, yellow, and blue birds. He made his way there. The door posts were bronze and the door panels were crystal. Rígru Rosclethan (of the large eyes) gave him welcome. Conn saw Rígru's son Ségda Sáerlabraid sitting on a crystal chair. He told them the purpose of his journey and Ségda agreed to follow him to Tara.
>
> Just as Ségda was about to be sacrificed, his mother arrived with a cow that was killed in the boy's place. Rígru then advised Conn to get rid of Bé Chuma, who had been driven out of the Land of Promise, but that was impossible.
>
> Winning a game of *fidchell*,[†] Art imposed a *geis*[‡] on Bé Chuma: she had to bring back the magic wand of Cú Roí mac Dáiri to him. She looked for a fairy mound (*síd*) and was eventually granted entry to that of Eógabal while her milk sister Áine helped her obtain the wand. She returned to Tara and gave the wand to Art.

---

*A currach or coracle (Welsh *cwrwgl*) is a boat made of greased cowhides stretched over a willow frame.

†An ancient Celtic board game similar to chess.

‡A *geis* is an obligation that a person cannot set aside. It is part of a system of taboos that surround the hero and form part of the codified relationship between our world and the otherworld.

Art and Bé Chuma played another game of *fidchell,* but the folk of Eógabal's *síd* stole away with the young man's game pieces and she won the match. She then commanded Art to bring back Delbcháem, who lived on Morgán's island. Art set sail and landed on a beautiful strange island filled with apples and charming birds. A house with a roof thatched of white and purple birdwings stood in the middle of the island. This was the home of some beautiful women, one of whom, Créide Fírálaind, informed him of the dangers that awaited him. He stayed there for forty-five days before resuming his journey at sea. He disembarked at a new island inhabited by the *coincuilind* [a type of beast] and some witches. He defeated them, made his way to a frozen and poisonous mountain, entered a valley full of toads . . . crossed a frozen river on a bridge of ice guarded by a giant that he slew, and then confronted Ailill Dubdétach (of the black teeth), the son of Morgán that no weapon could wound, and managed to kill him. He then found Morgán's wife, Coinchenn Cennfhata, daughter of the king of the Coinchend, whom the druids had predicted would die when someone courted her daughter. She therefore made sure to kill all potential suitors and multiplied the obstacles on Art's path: a bath of molten lead prepared by her witches, the giant guarding the bridge, the forest with the *coincuilind,* and so forth. Art introduced himself and saw Morgán's daughter Delbcháem in an arbor at the top of a pillar and entered it. Coinchenn arrived with two women, bearing a chalice of wine and a chalice of poison. Coinchenn challenged Art and they fought. Art slew her and placed her head on the empty stake in front of the fortress. Art and Delbcháem lived together until the arrival of Morgán, king of the Land of Wonders (*Tír na nIngnad*). Art defeated him and took possession of all that country's riches and gave them to his lover, and brought her back to Ireland. He then banished Bé Chuma from Ireland.[53]

The sea voyages of Conn and his son thus illustrate that the otherworld for the Celts was composed of islands. Among the recurring themes we have apples, crystal, and ice. One detail is striking: the names Coinchenn, Coinchend, and *coincuilind* are all derived from *cú* (genitive form: *con*),* meaning "dog" (cf. Ancient Greek κύων). This gives me license to venture the hypothesis that we are seeing a vestige of totemism here, although this is not the only possible interpretation, as we shall see.

Conn and his descendants seem to have been predestined to wander in the otherworld. His grandson Cormac was the hero of a story titled "How Cormac mac Airt Got His Branch." Although it is adorned with Christian morality, the text features the appearance of the god Manannán mac Lir, which triggers the hero's crossing into an imprecise elsewhere:

> Cormac and Eithne lived in Tara and had a boy and a girl. One morning Cormac saw a strange youth holding a fairy branch with apples in his hand; when he shook it, wonderful music uttered from it: anyone who was ill or injured that heard it would fall into a restorative slumber and wake up healed. Cormac desired to own this branch, and it was given to him in exchange for three promises. The stranger asked for Cormac's wife Eithne, his son Cairbre, and his daughter Ailbhe, and he left with them. After a year had passed, Cormac went off in search of them. He followed the track the youth had taken, but a dark mist arose and, once it had dissipated, Cormac found himself alone on a marvelous plain. He saw a house with men on the roof trying to cover it with bird feathers, but the wind kept carrying them away. Cormac then came upon a youth taking down a large tree and feeding it to a fire, and a well with three streams flowing in and out of it. He made his way to a large house where a young warrior and a beautiful woman bade him welcome. They invited him to eat some pork with them and explained that it was a magical pig that would be whole again the following day. But the pig would not cook unless four true stories were spoken over it.

Cú was used to coin many human names (cf. Dottin, *Manuel pour servir à l'étude de l'Antiquité celtique,* 111). The most famous is Cú Chulainn, "Culann's Hound," a name that was permanently given to Sétanta after his victory over the dog of the smith Culann.

While they were waiting for the meal, the young warrior explained to Cormac the meaning of what he had seen in the Land of Promise. The men covering the roof were people who had only worked during their lives to seek wealth. The youth who tore down the tree was someone who "distributes food while everyone else is being served and enjoying the profit thereof," and the well with the streams represented different types of men.

The young warrior was named Manannán Mac Lir and he brought the branch to Cormac to test him because he wanted to bring him here to learn wisdom. He then returned Cormac's wife and children to him. Before he left, he gave him a goblet that would break into four pieces if a lie was spoken before it, the wonderful branch, and a magical table-cloth. Cormac and family then went to sleep, when they awoke the next morning they were back in their own land of Liathdruim (Tara).[54]

Jan de Vries notes that the lord of the Land of Promise (Tír Tairngire) is Tethra and that "the plain of Tethra" refers to the sea. He goes on to say:

> Now as Tethra is finally called Lord of Mag Mell in the *Echtrae Conli*, it is probably permissible to deduce from this that he was also the sovereign of the "Elysian Fields" that people thought were far away on the Ocean and perhaps even at the bottom of the sea.
>
> It is obvious that, if the ancient gods and souls of the dead cohabited in the *síd,* this was also the case in this remote island of the blessed.[55]

These considerations throw new light on the background of Art's adventures. It is possible that he brought Delbcháem out of the empire of the dead, like Orpheus. The following elements support this hypothesis:

✳ The names coined from *cú,* "dog," are frequently associated with hell or the underworld.

✳ When Creide described the dangers that lay in wait for Art during his quest for a wife, she mentioned "a great ocean and dark between thee and deadly and hostile is the way there."

✳ The obstacles he encountered: river border, bridge, mountain, supernatural antagonists.

✳ A crystal arbor on the top of a pillar, obviously an ecotype of the Mountain of Glass.

If we accept that the stories of Conn, Art, and Cormac are only variations of the same, single myth—as the kinship of the motifs would suggest—the union of Art and Delbcháem represents that of the king of Ireland with a nature goddess—look at the arbor and green clothing that the maiden wears, which causes or restores the fruitfulness of the earth (the kingdom was suffering a shortage of wheat and milk), compromised by the arrival of Bé Chuma, whom the Tuatha Dé Danaan had banished "into the vast sea and its depths." If they acted this way, it was because they hated the Gaels who had defeated them and forced them to seek refuge underground and become the people of the *síd*. The myth that underlies the three stories could be reconstructed as follows:

> As revenge against men (the Gaels), the gods killed a nature goddess, which created a "waste land." After having received the information he needed for his quest, a hero sets off on it, descends into the underworld, symbolized by the Dog Heads and the obstacles, vanquishes its rulers (Ailill of the Black Teeth, Coinchenn, and Morgán), retrieves the goddess from hell and brings her back to Ireland, whose prosperity is restored.

Let us now depart from Ireland and return to France. In *The High Book of the Graal*, Perlesvaux sails toward the Isle of Abundance, which bears the Castle of Four Horns (*Chastel de.IIII. araines*), so called because four trumpets sound at its four corners. When he arrives, the sea draws back, and the gallant knight can cross without getting his feet wet. Everything is splendid in this place. There are some disturbing details: he first sees two men whose hair and beards are whiter than snow although their faces appear quite young, and then there is a cask that looks like it made of glass and contains a living knight inside. Men dressed in white open a wide and horrible trench from which emerge mournful cries; these are the cries of the kings of the Isle of Abundance who proved unworthy of their position.[56] This pit is therefore linked with a place of punishment that the author of the romance calls the Isle of Penury, which we can view as a version of purgatory.

> Continuing his journey, Perlesvaux saw a castle in flames, and a hermit told him that it had been burning since the son of King Pelles had killed his mother, and that it is from this place and one other that the fire that brings an end to the world will come. Continuing his voyage, he sailed past devastated and deserted islands, and stopped on another island where twelve hermits were guarding twelve graves, and eventually reached the Forest of the Black Hermit—a hideous place with no leaves or greenery or the song of any birds—whereupon he came to a castle surrounded by a dreadful river. Riding a black steed, the Black Hermit attacked the knight, who cut him down. Then the people present opened a wide trench, from which instantly arose an atrocious stench, and, grabbing the vanquished knight, tossed him into it.[57]

The stench implicitly refers to hell. Moreover, the text says: "The Black Hermit is Lucifer, who is lord of hell, as he wished to be that of paradise."

> *Li Noirs Hermite es Lucifers,*
> *Qui autresi est sire d'enfer*
> *Come il vout estre de paradis.*[58]

Partonopeus de Blois, a courtly romance written before 1188 and translated into German by Konrad von Würzburg (thirteenth century), a medieval version of *Cupid and Psyche,* tells how the eponymous hero of the book becomes lost in the forest of Ardennes while pursuing a wild boar. This forest is enchanted and infested with dragons, elephants, snakes and guivres. It stretches to the sea and plays the role of a no-man's-land before the sea, which represents the border of the otherworld. Partonopeus reaches the littoral and finds a beautiful ship, which is empty. He sets sail in it with his horse and falls asleep. This means of transport—a boat without any crew or pilot—is, by all evidence, sent by a supernatural being who wants to meet the knight. When he awakes, Partonopeus sees a bright light coming toward the ship; there is a city and a castle there, at the foot of which he disembarks. The city and the castle are deserted. He enters the castle and finds something to eat, and then, led by two torches, enters a bedchamber. Two invisible servants help him disrobe. When Partonopeus lies down to go to sleep, the two torches disappear. A woman, Melior, a fairy who has been given a rational identity, joins him in the middle of the night and convinces him to swear to never attempt to see her. He spends an entire year there, but then longs to go see his family again. Because of the intervention of an adversary,[59] he loses Melior, but after many trials he finds her again.

In *Toerecke,* an anonymous romance written in Middle Dutch that has been dated to around 1262, there is a Ship of Adventures (*Scip van Aventuren*) that is white as snow. Whoever climbs aboard will never return (l. 22890ff). Once the knight had set sail in the ship, it set off at top speed and brought him to a wonderful castle. The lord of this castle led him to the Chamber of Wisdom (*die Camere van Wijsheiden*). Vagueness is the rule here, and we are not sure if we are still in our world or that of the fairies.

With regard to the types of fay boats, there are basically four types: a boat without a pilot or crew (as in *Partonopeus de Blois*); a boat without sails or rudder (as in Marie de France's lay of *Guigemar*); a boat with a mysterious helmsman (as in *Perlesvaus*); and a boat pulled by a swan (as in *Lohengrin*).

Finally, islands are omnipresent in the romances. *La Vengeance Raguidel* (The Vengeance of Raguidel), a romance written by Raoul de Houdenc around 1200–1210, features Lingernote, a maiden who is expert in magic and had the Castle of No Name built on a floating island.[60] And we have seen that *Diu Crône* by Heinrich von dem Türlin, an Arthurian romance from the beginning of the thirteenth century, mentions the Isle of Women, access to which is reserved for the elect, and to Levenet, its queen.[61] In this same romance, the crystal palace of Lady Fortune (*Frau Sælde*) is surrounded by a lake; this place is only accessible to the elect, and sight of it will heal the ill.[62]

EIGHT

THE OTHERWORLD IN FOLKTALES AND SONGS

A number of researchers have detected the proximity of folktales with myths. Of course, myth and tale are perpetuating the same wondrous imaginal realm:

> The imaginary realm of the marvelous could not have been preserved for so many millennia if it did not contain lasting and immortal values of existence and of universal consciousness. People only hold on to and pass on from generation to generation what they love.[1]

The folktale is not a derivative of myth and has its proper place in the oral tradition. However, as Philippe Walter has said, the myth and the tale are both the sum of all their variations. They contain a dual expression and should be read on two axes: one that reveals a structure (the syntagmatic axis), and the other, the variation (the paradigmatic axis).

FROM MYTH TO STORY

There were two traditions relating to the myth of Orpheus and Eurydice during the Middle Ages: one tradition was known by all; the other was largely unknown. The Byzantine poet John Tzetzes tells how Orpheus

Orpheus before Hades and Persephone,
Palazzo del Te (sixteenth century), Mantua.

pulled Eurydice out of a swoon with music, and adds that at the very moment Eurydice was about to die from the bite of a serpent, Orpheus brought her back to life "by means of the magic spells that he had gotten from the muse, his innate intelligence, and his vast erudition."[2] Orpheus would therefore be a mage or a sorcerer; Greek tradition makes him a shaman-like figure.[3]

Sir Orfeo,[4] written in Middle English around 1325 (and based on a French lay that we only know of due to its being mentioned in several works),[5] recounts the following story. King Orfeo of Winchester was the husband of Heurodis, who fell asleep under a tree one day and was carried off onto the otherworld by the fairy king. After a long period of wandering, he follows a group of women to his wife's location:

> Thro' a cleft in the rock lies the Fairy way
> And the king he follows as best he may;

Thro' the heart of the rock he needs must go,
Three miles and more, I would have ye know,
Till a country fair before him lay,
Bright with the sun of a summer's day;
Nor hill nor valley might there be seen
But level lands, and pastures green
And the towers of a castle met his eye,
Rich and royal, and wondrous high.
The outer wall of that burg, I ween,
Was clear and shining, as crystal sheen.

He then finds himself facing the dead:

With that the porter made no ado,
But gladly he let Sir Orfeo through.
The king looked round him, to left, to right,
And in sooth he beheld a fearsome sight;
For here lay folk whom men mourned as dead,
Who were hither brought when their lives were sped;
E'en as they passed so he saw them stand,
Headless, and limbless, on either hand.
There were bodies pierced by a javelin cast,
There were raving madmen fettered fast,
. . .
Some floated, drowned, in the water's flow,
Shrivelled were some in the flame's fierce glow.[6]

We can see that this fairyland is actually the beyond, the afterlife; the torments that are mentioned and the appearance of the people he sees (injured and mutilated) leave no doubt about this. *Sir Orfeo* is an important testament to the transformation of myth into story under the influence of Celtic traditions, several features of which we find here: the kingdom of faery and the description of the enchanted land (*locus amoenus*).

The king of the underworld returns Heurodias to Orfeo:

The king said: "Since it is so	Þe king seyd: Seþþen it is so,
Take her by the hand and go."	Take hir bi þe hond and go.

(ll. 467–68).

His wife he took by the hand,	His wiif het ok bi þe hond
And got himself swiftly out of that land,	And dede him swiþe out of þat lond
And went out of that kingdom	And went him out of þat þede,
Just the same way as he had come.	Riȝt as he come þe way he ȝede.

(ll. 471–74).

In the nineteenth century, Scottish folklorist Biot Edmonston collected a ballad on the Isle of Unst (Shetland) that was directly inspired by *Sir Orfeo*. The heroine's name was Lady Isabel, and Orfeo played the bagpipes, a fine example of an ecotype. At the end of the ballad, the king of faery declares: "Take your lady and return home" (*Yees tak your lady, an yees gaeng hame*).[7]

Let us note that the myth has undergone quite a few transformations. For example, Boethius (died 524) gave a particular end for the hero in his *Consolation of Philosophy*.[8] The king of Hades, full of pity, cries out:

Take your bride with you,	*Donamus comitem viro*
Bought by your song;	*Emptam carmine coniugem.*
But one condition binds our gift:	*Sed lex dona coerceat:*
Till she has left these dark abodes,	*Ne, dum Tartara liquerit,*
Turn not your eyes upon her.	*Fas sit lumina flectere,*
Alas! at the very bounds of darkness	*Heu, noctis prope terminos*
Orpheus looked upon his Eurydice;	*Orpheus Eurydicen suam*
Looked, and lost her, and was lost himself.	*Vidit, perdidit, occidit.*

Fulgentius (468–533), who was called the Mythographer, suggested the following etymologies for the names of this couple: Orpheus would be *oreafone*, which is to say, "best voice," while Eurydice means "profound judgment."[9]

The myth of Orpheus can be found in North America in a Cherokee story. The law of ecotypes comes into play here, of course, but the structure is unchanged. The dead woman remains a prisoner of the underworld because a prohibition has been violated:

> The Mother of the Sun's daughter died from a rattlesnake bite. The Sun no longer showed itself, and the Little Men announced that if people wanted to see it again, they must bring the dead woman back from the kingdom of the spirits (Tsusginai), and they gave each of the seven envoys a sourwood rod and a box. They told them they would find the spirits in the midst of dancing and that they should stay outside of their circle, but that when the dead girl began to dance, they should each strike her with their rod. She would fall to the ground, then they must put her in the box. They should then bring it to her mother without opening it under any pretext whatsoever. The seven men followed these instructions to the letter and took the path home. But through trickery the young woman forced them to open the box, something flew out of it, and when they arrived at the home of the Sun's Mother, the box was empty.[10]

SURVIVALS OF THE BEYOND

During the Middle Ages, visions described a journey to the beyond. But what part of these visions derived from collective memory and beliefs? The beginning of an answer is provided to us by folktales, which are extremely rich in this area and present heroes and heroines making roundtrip visits to the otherworld. This is also an initiatory jouney: the protagonists return as different people from who they were before they were forced to confront the unknown, fear, and a wide variety of adversaries. This is also basically what the visions relate: the trance-journeyer, because of what he learned during his trip, is no longer the same on his return, which is most often revealed by a radical change of behavior.

Through narratives which are only known to specialists, it is possible to show the persistence of certain mindsets or mentalities. When we approach fundamental anthropological questions that relate to life, death, and dreams, it is clear these questions will continue to arise as long as there are people. Generally, in tales and legends the beyond gives way to the otherworld, and we must go to little-known collections to find descriptions of them.

The richest harvest of such material is found in Gypsy tales.[11] The otherworld is located on a mountain, in a cave, or inside a hollow mountain where it is guarded by nine white dogs. The deceased starts attempting to make their way there when their body starts to decompose, and this painful and terrible journey lasts for nine years. The deceased has to travel through seven mountains that clash together (which is reminiscent of the Greek Symplegades); face a snake that blocks the road and demands a gift of milk and honey; give meat to the nine dogs; and, finally, cross through a dozen deserts swept by a glacial wind that is as sharp as a knife. This is why the close relatives of the deceased burn the latter's clothing and bedding to provide them with a little heat. They also give them milk for this journey; otherwise they are at risk of being stuck between the two worlds. Lastly, the deceased lead a life in the beyond that corresponds to the life they led when still alive, and they retain all their characteristic features: a blind man will remain blind, a cripple remains crippled. But humans cannot make their way to the beyond if their body has not been washed, nor can they do so if, while alive, they neglected to burn and dispose of their cut hairs and nails.

The beyond is also represented by the Mountain of Cats, so named because hundreds of souls transformed into cats live there, people who committed many sins when they were alive. Here they must remain for many years before being able to go to the kingdom of the dead (*them mulengre*). The mountain is girded by a wall of fire that only goes out on the night of Saint John. Heinrich von Wlislocki collected several tales based on these beliefs.[12]

Gypsies also believe that the dead sinners are changed into black crows and have to live in this form for a long time before they are allowed to enter the otherworld. While waiting, they form three distinct groups: the drowned, whose souls belong to the water spirits who imprison them in pots; the murdered, whose souls go into wild animals and remain there as long as their murderer has not died and had his soul move into an animal, where it will remain for centuries before going on into the beyond; and one last group composed of the souls of those who passed away in their cabin or tent (*tan, tanya*) and wander about the earth, entering and leaving their bodies (*trupos*) as long as they have not decomposed.

We should recall that in one of Grimm's tales (nr. 29, type AT 431), it was necessary to cross a river before finding the entrance to hell, which was entirely black and full of soot.

In folk traditions, the journey into the beyond does not take place in a dream or ecstatic vision, but physically, in life itself. Here is one example. Drawing from Estonian folk songs, the writer and doctor Friedrich Reinhold Kreutzwald (1803–1882) wrote the *Kalevipoeg,* a reconstructed epic that retraces the tragic life of the son of Kalev.[13] In songs XVIII and XIX, the story includes a descent into the otherworld, a enclosed space whose doors open onto a precipice, from which arise clouds of smoke:

> With possession of a small magical bell, Kalevipoeg succeeded at overcoming all obstacles. He came to a dark cavern that lit up when he jingled his bell, but this was not "the light of day or that of the moon." A net of silver and metal cables stopped him, yet he pulled free of it and then tried to cross a river but started to sink. He got out of his predicament although "a deceptive, pale light illuminated the area" and a fog made of "a myriad of black flies and mosquitoes" invaded the path. The devils fled at the hero's approach, who this time now came to a river of flaming pitch and resin traversed by a steel bridge on which three hordes of demons were waiting for him. He forced his way through and reached the gate to hell. He smashed through the door and entered a room holding the liquid of life and the potion of death, as well as the Horned One's mother. Kalevipoeg spotted a hidden door, which opened before an army of Hell's best warriors. He cut them all down and then confronted the Horned One in a duel. He eventually bound him with iron shackles that he

attached to a rock wall before sealing off the gate with a huge boulder. He took all the riches that he found then and left.

This episode of Kalevipoeg's life contains the essential elements of a trip into the beyond: fire, river, smoke, darkness, and demons, in addition to another detail, the suspension of the flow of time:

> *Time had no measure*
> *The days had no border*
> *In the bosom of the depths,*
> *The sun could not shine*
> *The moon could not gleam,*
> *Not stars indicate the time* (XVIII, ll. 258–63).

It is obvious that a substantial number of the motifs present in the vision are quite archaic and predate Christianity, as the folk traditions demonstrate. We must also take into account the ongoing exchange that took place between paganism and Christianity, and even elements of syncretic blending.

We can explore this area in greater detail by making use of three reference works: Thompson's *Motif-Index of Folk-Literature* (cited as "motif"),[14] Aarne and Thompson's *The Types of the Folktale* (cited as "AT"),[15] and Tubach's *Index Exemplorum* (cited as "TU").[16]

HELL, PURGATORY, AND PARADISE

A very large number of folktales speak about the beyond, and we will have to content ourselves with some representative examples. We may start with hell, leaving aside the tales of fooling the devils and pranks. The hero enters hell to save three young girls (AT 466**), to heat the furnace (AT 475), to bring back three hairs from the devil's beard (type AT 461), to obtain the receipt of a disputed payment (AT 756C*),[17] to free his bewitched wife (AT 425J), or to recover the contract signed with the devil (AT 756B). A pastor sees all his parishioners in hell (AT 1738B) or in boiling cauldrons (motif E755.2.1),[18] which is the theme of "Curé de Cucugnan" in Alphonse Daudet's short-story collection *Lettres de mon moulin* (Letters from My Mill).

"Spadonia," a Sicilian story collected by Laura Gonzenbach (1842–1878) and published in 1870, tells of an excursion into the beyond:[19]

> "Once upon a time there was a pious king who was particularly devoted to the souls in purgatory. Every morning he had an oven full of freshly cooked bread for them, and each morning the Lord sent him a donkey carrying two baskets made of raffia, in which the sovereign placed the bread and the donkey brought it to the souls in purgatory." On the king's death, his son, who was doing the same thing, wondered if this was good or evil, and ordered his servant Peppe to climb on the donkey's back to learn where he went, and then come back and tell him everything he had seen and heard. On his way, Peppe saw some strange sights—a lovely verdant meadow where the most beautiful grass was growing, but the cows that grazed upon it were thin and miserable; and a prairie on which the grass grew sparsely and it was poor and dried out, but the cows grazing there were splendid and quite fat;[20] a river of blood and another of milk; and so on—an explanation for which he received from the mouth of God.

In 1873, François-Marie Luzel (1821–1895) collected the following legend from the mouth of Barbe Tassel, of Ploaret:

> The lord contested the claim of Kerloho, his tenant, that he had paid his rent, so the tenant consulted a holy man who sent him to the house of his brother, a brigand, so that he could show him the way to hell. The robber advised he bring with him a bottle of holy water, a cruet of milk from a mother nursing her first child, and a leather whip. Once this was done, the brigand ordered his servant, who was as ugly and black as a demon, to take the farmer to hell.
>
> The servant led Kerloho up to the entrance of a cave in the woods, gave a whistle, and two devils came out asking, "How may

we serve you?" One of the devils took the visitor on his back and, after running for several hours, the tenant saw a light. They came to "an immense room filled with fire and flames, and hideous devils that were keeping the fires going under an infinite number of kettles and silver and gold seats. . . . All around him were groans and horrible cries extracted by pain." Kerloho eventually recovered his quittance and the devils led him back to the entrance of the cave.[21]

"The Devil's Stoker," a folktale with twenty versions[22] that was studied by Marie Louise Ténèze, features a boy whose father gave him to a demon. He entered into the devil's service. The devil gave him the keys to hell before leaving on a trip and forbid him from entering a cave that held a retort filled with the blood of the damned. Of course, the boy violated the prohibition and discovered the retort and a huge pot over the fire. He took off the lid and glimpsed the head of his grandmother, who advised him to ask for "a full basket of souls" as his salary. On the devil's return, the boy asked to leave and demanded his due; he got the basket. When he passed by a stream, he washed the souls and they became "white as snow." He gave them back to God, who asked him if he wanted to go to heaven and the boy assented. "Well, go say goodbye to your parents, I am only giving you eight days." At the end of this time, the boy died and went to heaven.

Heaven is reserved for those who behave well and whose actions are not motivated by a profit in cash, "The Three Children," a heavily Christianized tale from Gascony, essentially relates the following:

A widow had three sons. In succession, each met a gentleman who gave them a letter to take to their mother and a switch with which to strike the sea when they got there. The two older brothers were happy to toss the letter into the water and pocket their reward, forty crowns, while the youngest brother followed the instructions of the man who offered him a horse for his journey. The sea parted in two and the boy ran a long time before reaching the home of the Holy Virgin. He fell asleep; she woke him up after seven years and gave him a missive for her son. He gave it to Jesus, who invited him to dine at the child's mother's house. Once there, he sent the two older boys to hell and the youngest to paradise.

The horse-psychopomp can be seen in another folktale, as noted by Paul Sébillot:

Two friends swore an oath that they would invite one another to their wedding, whether living or dead. One of them died and returned to attend his friend's wedding, but only the bridal couple saw him. Some time afterward, the dead man invited his friend and requested he come meet him in the alleyway that ran alongside the cemetery. At the appointed time, a white mare carried the living person into the beyond. After the wedding, the mare returned him to this world, but all of his relatives were long dead, as three hundred years had passed.[23]

One of the folktalkes collected by Afanasyev, "The Magical Wife" (nr. 167) tells how an idiot goes to hell. Following a ball of yarn, he comes to a lake that opens up and reveals a path; after he has taken a few steps on it, he finds himself in hell. He sees the old king with a load of wood on his back and demons armed with iron whips who drive him to the furnace.

Reflecting the theme of *refrigerium,** which is attested in the literature of revelations, a legend from Alagna Val Sesia in the Italian Alps situates purgatory on the glaciers:

A man met a woman near the glacier of Bers and asked her where she was going: "She said she was going to the glaciers in order to hack out some steps so that the soul of her mother, who had died recently, could get there more easily."[24]

---

*[The concept of *refrigerium* (Latin: "[meal of] refreshment"), which originally referred to a commemorative meal held near a gravesite for the dead in pre-Christian Roman culture, was adopted and modified by early Christian writers in figurative way to designate a beatific state enjoyed by the blessed souls while awaiting final entry into heaven after the Last Judgment. —*Ed.*]

Maria Salvi-Lopez noted how the women of Alagna believed that, before ascending to heaven, the soul of a deceased person was obliged to purge itself of minor sins by spending some time in the glaciers of Mount Rosa; family and friends could shorten the time of that punishment by prayer. In Nendaz (Switzerland) in the 1980s, the elderly people still believed that souls in torment lived in the glaciers. Numerous accounts along the same lines have been recorded in the cantons of Grisons, Uri, Vaud, and Bern.[25]

Paradise is rarely mentioned. In the tale type "The man in heaven" (AT 809), it is the reward for a person's good deeds. The story of "The Talking Skull" offers the following narrative:

By following a skull that rolled in front of him, a man witnessed spectacles that were beyond his comprehension: two crows fighting together, a priest drawing water with a bottomless pail, and a house where birds flew out every time the door was opened. He then came to a castle full of lights. "Those are the lights of life: for as long as a person lives, he has his little light, and when he dies, it goes out," his guide told him, and the man realized that his was almost entirely consumed. Then the skull explained to him what he had seen: the crows were two brothers who never stopped quarreling; the priest was overly enamored of temporal riches; and the birds that flew out of the house were poor souls who had found redemption. The man then learned that he had been following the skull for three hundred years. He went back to his village and told people his name; no one knew him. The town hall records were searched and traces of his family were found: they had not been there for three hundred years. They went to the church and said a Mass for the man, then "a white dove was seen fluttering around the altar. The stranger was kneeling, motionless and fixed in place, and when he was touched, he fell into ashes and dust.

The tale, which is built upon the Christianized mythemes of a journey to the beyond, evokes purgatory by means of the crows, the priest, and the birds leaving the house. The little lights that are symbols of life stand out as elements from the pagan background. Furthermore, the notion of a different time can be traced back to an old archetype. The fact that the man's guide is a skull is a clear indication that this is a euphemism of the traveler's death. Nicole Belmont underscores this:

> The tale is formed of successive figures that are organized into dramatizations and suggest mental images to the listeners. They receive them, decipher them, and formulate them in the deepest levels of their unconscious. These figurations are never ornamental, they constitute the very substance of the narrative.[26]

Another folktale, "The Girl Who Married a Dead Man" (AT 471), places the afterlife in a grove, beneath a large rock cliff. When someone knocks on this rock with a white wand, it opens. A magnificent castle stands in the depths of the earth. One day, when the brother was paying his sister a visit, his brother-in-law brought him to an arid moor upon which fat cows were grazing, and then to a beautiful field where there were standing two thin cows;[27] next, they came across two goats fighting each other, and finally a church in ruins. The thin cows were in purgatory, and the fat cows had been upstanding men who gave alms. As for the church, "it was full of people, but they were all dead and nothing remained of them but shadows"; all had been delivered: "It was said by God that they would remain in the state in which you saw them until a person came by who was not dead and took pity on them."[28]

In the Grimms' *Fairy Tales* we find several mentions of a journey to heaven, but this is, in fact, a remnant of pious legends. In "Mary's Child" (nr. 3), the Virgin Mary brings a young girl to paradise to visit the abodes of the twelve apostles. She then opens a door and the young girl sees the Trinity. She spent eleven years in this place before being expelled for an unconfessed sin. In "Master Pfriem" (nr. 178) the visit takes place in a dream. "The Peasant in Heaven" (nr. 167) is the only story in which the visitor is a dead person.

On the other hand, paradise is very much present in the Christian legends from Lower Brittany as collected by François-Marie Luzel in *Les Légendes chrétiennes de Basse-Bretagne*. In "The Shepherd Boy Who Brought a Letter to Heaven,"[29] paradise is located on a mountaintop; it is a beautiful castle with walls of gold and precious stones, standing in the middle of a large prairie filled with aromatic flowers and chirping birds.

A small shepherd met an old man, who asked him to carry a letter to paradise and described to him the way there: "Listen, first take the narrow path you see over there—and he showed him the path on the right. The road is difficult, uneven, stony, and filled with brambles and nettles, and brambles and thorns; there are also vipers, toads, deaf creatures, and all sorts of venomous and hideous reptiles . . . . Keep walking with courage and you will soon come to a stone fence that bars the road; you will cross through this fence. But do not look back before you have crossed it, whatever you might hear, or else you are lost. Once you have passed this barrier, you will find yourself at the foot of a tall mountain, and you must climb to the top of this mountain, through the nettles, the brambles, and the thorns. . . . If you can reach the top of the mountain, you will see there a beautiful castle, whose walls all of gold and jewels will dazzle you. But you need only knock at the door of this splendid castle and Saint Peter will immediately open it, for this is heaven."

The shepherd boy set off on this path; he tore his feet and legs amid the brambles and he was threatened by serpents. He crossed over the stone fence and cast a glance back. He saw the road was full of fire, demons, and horrible and menacing monsters. He reached the foot of the mountain and made the painful ascent, whereupon he saw a castle shining with light in the middle of a flower-filled prairie surrounded by a silver wall with one door. He knocked, Saint Peter opened it for him, the Good Lord showed him heaven and informed him that he had left home one hundred years ago.

When he returned to the old man, he gave him a letter from God and described what he had seen. With that, the old man carried him off to heaven for it was God himself.[30]

This tale is also found in Cordoba (Argentina) with a few differences: the boy must cross three rivers and, as a reward for carrying the letter, the Virgin Mary gives him a coat covered with silver.[31]

A Norwegian tale, "The Ladder to Heaven,"[32] blends the theme of the swan women with Christian elements; and the otherworld takes the form of a quite singular paradise:

> By taking possession of the feathered garment of a dove woman, "a bird of paradise," a boy began to live with her. Before marrying her, she told him not to invite Per the Black to the wedding because he was a curser and if he cursed him back, he would lose her. He violated the prohibition and she had to part, but before leaving him she gave him half of her gold ring. He set off to find her and eventually arrived at the home of a very old woman who told him how to find the ladder to heaven. "Go to the large lake, which you must cross. Here is a spool of thread that you will push in front of you on the water; it will weave a bridge beneath your feet. You will then come to the bridge to heaven. It is standing up against an immense mountain wall. One of its uprights is made of gold and the other is silver. . . . Once you start to scale the ladder, it is very important that you don't look down, otherwise you will fall and you will sleep for seven years at the foot of the ladder. If you manage to climb all the way to the top, you will be in heaven." After a setback, he succeeded, was recognized by his beloved thanks to the half ring, and their wedding was prepared.[33]

Several other tales from the Asbjørnsen and Moe collection follow the same thematic, that of the man in search of his vanished wife and that of the princesses abducted by beings from the otherworld.[34]

In Sicily, Laura Gonzenbach noted a tale (nr. 20) with a very odd narrative sequence in which Saint Francis of Paola carries a little girl to the otherworld:

> A little girl met a young monk, who told her: "Dear Pauline, ask your mother if it is better to suffer in your youth or in your old age, and bring me her answer." The next day, he took her to a deserted region, into a tower that had no door and only one window. There, he educated her.

CROSSING INTO THE OTHERWORLD

Arnold van Gennep offered evidence that "the journey to the otherworld and entering it includes a series of rites of passage whose detail depends on the distance and topography of this world,"[35] and he drew a distinction between rites of separation, rites of liminality, and rites of incorporation. This is a "division" we likewise find in the tales. In his analysis of folktales, Max Lüthi made a distinction between marine, subterranean, aerial, and faraway worlds.[36] The latter are those whose nature is revealed by their extreme distance from the domicile of the hero.

The otherworld of folktales includes two facets. The one that is positive is fairyland, the land of eternal youth, often an island (motif 134), like that of Avalon for the Celts; a hollow mountain (motif F131); a kingdom under the sea (AT 1889H); or even the country of immortals from the tale types of "The magic flight" (AT 313) and "Friends in life and death" (AT 470). The other facet, which is negative, is the land of ogres and demons: consider the relevant tale types (AT 462) and "The ogre's (devil's) heart in the egg" (AT 302), and the land of the dead (motif E481) that was reached by crossing a bridge (motif E481.2.1.). These worlds take the place of hell as it appears in the medieval vision accounts, but, contrary to the *exempla* (TU 2517–18), they do not involve scenes of torture. Nicole Belmont notes that "the heroes or heroines don't seem to distinguish this world from the otherworld, any more than they distinguish between the individuals encountered on this side or the other side. The frontier is not perceived by them, and they do not seem to notice the ontological otherness of the figures in the otherworld."[37] This is already the case in medieval romances.

Let us take a moment to consider the well-known motif of the bridge. In Russia, the living built a symbolic bridge to help the deceased reach the beyond. In Romania, after death, the souls of the dead had to travel a long path before reaching their destination safe and sound. This road is full of ambushes and obstacles, and all the measures taken at death aim at facilitating the final journey of the deceased.[38] As in the Christian literature of visions and revelations, the geography of the beyond is characterized by a very uneven terrain, with steep mountains that give way to narrow valleys, and the soul is forced to take paths covered with brambles, and cross thorny heaths, precipices, ravines, rivers, and so forth. Darkness is omnipresent, which is why people should offer candles and tapers to the dead. The soul eventually reaches a divide (a torrent, a river, etc.) that cannot be crossed without a bridge—this is a fundamental difference with the classic bridge to the afterlife that all souls take and that causes the souls of evil men to tumble off into hell. It is here that Romanian beliefs are particularly interesting: all souls can only get past this obstacle by means of their own bridge; there is only one per individual, and each is guarded by an angel (or a demon) who forbids anyone who is not its intended individual from crossing it. It is therefore necessary for everyone during their lifetime to build a bridge—no matter how rudimentary, even two planks thrown over a ditch, for example—to cross after they die. If a person has not constructed one, it is up to his close friends and family to do this immediately after the death, for the soul will not leave the body right away after death—an idea we find among many Indo-European peoples.[39]

In Sweden, the runic inscription on the Ramsund stone, erected around 1030 near Eskilstuna in Södermanland says this: "Si(g)rid, Alrik's mother, Orm's daughter, made this bridge for the soul of Holmgeir, her husband, father of Si(g)rod." The bridge was, in fact, a causeway that made it possible to travel through the surrounding marshland.[40]

According to Russian beliefs, the soul of the dead person performed a series of roundtrips between heaven and earth before being directed to heaven or hell. "The first two trips take place immediately following death, and then at the end of forty days. The other 'transfers' vary based on the qualities of the deceased." The crossing can be made thanks to a rainbow or the Milky Way, which also has the name "path of the dead heading toward their eternal rest." The motif of ascension is found in southern Russia, where a ladder is made from dough baked in an oven at certain times of the year, and consisting of three to twenty-four rungs.[41]

In folktales, the ascent to heaven can be made by means of a plant, such as a tree or a cabbage stalk (AT 1960G). The Grimm Brothers' tale "The Threshing-Flail from Heaven" (nr. 112) tells of the ascension up a tree of a peasant who has decided to go see what the angels are doing. In Afanasyev's Russian folktale collection, "The Vixen Healer" (*Lisa-lekarka,* nr. 11), "The Old Man Climbs to Heaven" (*Starik na njebe,* nr. 12), and "The Mourning Vixen" (*Lisa-placeja,* nr. 13) offer the same plot, but it involves a cabbage that is growing in the *isba* [a Russian log cabin]. We should note that crossing over into the otherworld by climbing a tree is a feature of shamanism.[42]

People go to the otherworld to fill a need, find a remedy, and so forth. The tale types "The man on a quest for his lost wife" (AT 400) and "The search for the lost husband" (AT 425) are those where the protagonist's quest leads most often to the otherworld.[43] On the way, a number of people are encountered who serve as guides: old women, the Virgin Mary, the devil, a saint, the Evening Star, or animals (such as a fox, wolf, or toad). Sometimes is it an adversary who, despite himself, plays the role of guide: he flees, the hero follows in pursuit and reaches the otherworld.[44]

Magic makes it possible to cross into the otherworld. In 1959, Henri Noël recorded the following folktale from Nicaragua:

A man was contemplating suicide because he had lost his wife, but his cousin dissuaded him and brought him to the home of a magician, who told him what he needed to do to rejoin her and bring her back from the beyond: "Follow this stream until you come to a lake with one island. There you will find a tree trunk on the ground. Climb aboard it and go to the island. There you will see a hole that will allow you to climb down to the kingdom of the dead. Once you have found your wife, leave, cross back over the lake on the trunk, and come see me. I will take care of the rest." The magician ordered him to disrobe, drew several circles on the ground and inscribed letters and signs inside them with ashes. With a piece of charcoal, he drew strange letters on the man's forehead, chest, and back, and then he entered the circle, played the flute and danced. The man felt like he was growing lighter, as if he was being carried, and came to the stream. Following the magician's instructions, he entered the beyond. He came out of the hole

into a clearing where the sun was shining and then reached a village where he saw many people that he knew, mainly his parents
and his great-grandparents, who led him to his wife. He kissed her
and the symbols written on his chest vanished without him noticing. His wife agreed to follow him, but not until the next day. He
gave no further thought to returning until three days later when
he saw his reflection with the symbol on his forehead in the water
of the stream. He realized that he had to go home to his children
and went back the way he had come, followed by his wife. But he
forgot to visit the magician, wiped the last symbol off his face, and
his wife vanished. He hardly recognized anyone in the village, his
children were now seventeen or eighteen, and his own hair had
turned gray. He searched everywhere for his wife, and then disappeared. It was said he had gone back to the home of the dead.[45]

I would like to compare this tale with a curious story from the
Nahuatl Indians of Mexico, whose otherworld is located on an island:

A man dies, stands up, takes a bag with provisions and makes his way
to the edge of the sea where a seal is waiting for him. He climbs on
its back and it carries him to the Isle of the Dead, where he arrives
at sunrise. Just as day is breaking, the seal transforms into his late
father, who invites him into the village where he sees his first wife
again. During a feast, the supreme chief of the community informs
the man that he should not be there because the taboo he violated
and which caused his death was not the right one, and he told him
that the lethal taboo weighing on him was the prohibition of sneezing while urinating. A bird brought the man back to his bed. In the
morning, the man told his wife of his adventure, and she said it was
just a dream. But he showed her his three-week-old beard, because in
the land of the dead there are no razors.[46]

We see here the omnipotent nature of a curse that causes death, but
the chief of the community, in whom can be recognized a face of the
Grim Reaper, restores the deceased man to life. There is no search for

a lost loved one. The life in the afterlife is then identical to the life in this world. As is the case in ancient Scandinavian belief, one finds one's family again, one eats, drinks, and celebrates: here we are a long way off from the afterlife of the religions of the Book. In Transylvania, a folktale collected by Franz Obert (1828–1908) introduces some supernatural figures specific to Romanian beliefs and places the afterlife in an imprecise elsewhere:

A father promised his son Iuon who was weeping all the time, to bring him back Rujălina, "the milk-white maiden who made the forest green and who casued the fruit trees to flower," whose name means "Beautiful as a Rose." Once he grew up, Iuon reminded his father of his promise, and the latter set off on the road but did not find her. Iuon left, too, and questioned Mother Saturday (Sâmbătă), then Mother Sunday (Duminică), from where a bee carried him "beyond the lands and the seas," up to a castle where he was made gooseherd. He married Rujălina. Visiting his castle, he found a cask, inside of which a *zmeu** was imprisoned. He gave it something to drink, and the *zmeu* freed itself and asked: "Which would you prefer: to leave and abandon Rujălina, or to stay and die? Choose! You are in my power." Iuon abandoned his wife, found a sword, and saved some eaglets that were about to be devoured by a dragon. The grateful eagle furnished him with a magical horse, thanks to which he was able to wrest his wife free of the *zmeu*'s claws and win back his castle.[47]

In the Gypsy tale "The King of the Eagles and the Three Brothers," the otherworld is located at the heart of a mountain:

An eagle demanded a piece of a roast that the brothers were cooking, but one of them became angry and stabbed the bird's foot with a stake. The youngest brother tried to pull it out, but the eagle flew

---

*The *zmeu* is a fantastical creature that is sometimes human and sometimes a dragon; it corresponds to the Greek *drakos*.

off and carried away the boy holding onto the stake. He flew far, very far with him and eventually reached an immense mountain in which there was a large hollow. The eagle landed and entered the hole, and they came to a beautiful prairie where the sun was shining and in which stood a large golden dwelling. The eagle then said: "Because you tried to help me, I brought you here. Here, you will have all you desire and live eternally. Your sole task is to comb my wife every day and you can do whatever you please with all the rest of your time." Every morning the eagle went back to the human world and only came back in the evening. The hero learned that he had abducted the woman, a princess, one day when she was bathing. He got the eagle drunk, then pulled a feather from his left wing, which he used to carry them back to our world.

When a ball of yarn shows the way, it is an old woman who performs her actions through this intermediary. The hero is going to encounter guardians of the otherworld, savage and terrifying beasts like the dragon, which is often associated with the underwater worlds. The journey includes one or more qualifying trials (such as tests of strength, generosity, or intelligence), because the otherworld is only accessible to one who is worthy, the chosen one.

Water and the sea play an important role as a border. In one of the folktales collected by Afanasyev ("The Sensible Wife" [*Mudraja zena*] nr. 167), the hero follows a ball of yarn until he reaches the sea, where he discovers a path that he follows all the way to hell. Another story[48] talks of a boy searching for his fiancée. He comes to a lake, turns his back to it and starts walking backward; hardly has he begun when he finds himself under the waves in a white stone castle. In "Elena the Wise" (*Elena-premudraja*, nr. 181), a soldier frees an unclean spirit, who invites him to his place and entrusts him with the task of keeping watch over his three daughters. He brings the lad into a place "beyond the three-times-ninth country, in the thirtieth kingdom" a recurring expression referring to the beyond in Russian folktales. In another folktale, Ivan Son of Bull (*Ivan Bykovič*, nr. 101) sails with his companions in search of a princess with golden hair: "They arrive at an invisible kingdom, the nonexistent country . . ."—how could the notion of an otherworld be expressed any better!

In the "Tsar-Maiden" (*Car'-devica,* nr. 177), Ivan, the son of a merchant, sets off for the thirtieth kingdom in search of his beloved. On the way he encounters three Baba Yagas, and then the firebird carries him up to the sea. He finds a cottage in which a woman is living who questions him, and he informs her of the purpose of his quest. She reveals to him that the young queen was her daughter, that she no longer loves him, and that his love is hidden. Thanks to a ruse, Ivan wins back his belle and returns home with her.

If we decipher this story, two details show that the heroine is dead and held captive in the beyond. Ivan cannot cross the sea, and it is said that the young girl's love is "at the edge of the ocean. There is an oak; in the oak, a chest; in the chest, a hare; in the hare, a duck; in the duck, an egg, and in the egg, the love of the young girl queen." Ivan finds the egg and brings his beloved back to life. The story's plot seems to be modeled on that of Orpheus. The supernatural woman is in several instances connected to the aquatic element. In "The Sea King and Vasilisa the Wise" (*Morkoj car' i Vasilisa Premudraja,* nr. 169), the supernatural wife of the hero is the daughter of the "Sea King" (*morskoj car'*) or "king of the waters" (*vodjanoj car'*), or even simply called "water spirit" (*vodjanoj*). If we examine the other versions of the story (nr. 170), we learn that the castle of the Sea King "is surrounded by a high palisade ten versts long, and a head is stuck on each stake." Furious that Vasilisa fled with Ivan Tsarevich, the Sea King changes her into a river for three years. Once this time period has elapsed, when Ivan is on the verge of getting married, a serving woman sees a young woman in the water of the well; it is Vasilisa, of course, and the well is the passageway from one world to the other.[49]

In another tale collected by Afanasyev, the access to the "three kingdoms" (*Tri carstva,* nr. 91 and nr. 93), one of the names for the otherworld,* is found beneath a stone:

---

*We know that this is the otherworld because its location is always described with a formulaic expression: "beyond three-times-nine countries (*za tridevjat' zemel'*), in the three-times-tenth kingdom (*tridesjatoje tsarstvo*)."

Three brothers, who left in search of a fiancée, encountered in turn a snake that pointed out the path to take and led them to a large stone while telling them: "Turn this stone over and you will find below what you are seeking."

The otherworld is therefore explicitly presented as the place connected with the wife.

The youngest brother climbed down the hole and arrived in the kingdom of copper, then that of silver, and finally that of gold. After having helped the three girls climb up to the human world, the hero, betrayed by his two older brothers, has to find another way to get back to his world. He therefore goes "beyond the thirty lakes," to the home of Baba Yaga, who owns an eagle that can bring him back "to Russia."

The motif of the flight that makes it possible to go from one world to the other expresses the immense distance separating them. Another version of this story (nr. 92) locates the three kingdoms at the top of a mountain:

The hero meets an old man who gives him a little ball that he must roll before him and which leads him to the foot of high mountains. He breaks open the door of the cavern he finds there, and the iron claws that he discovers attach themselves to his hands and feet of their own accord, an undeniable sign that he has been chosen.

The rest of the story describes how it took a month for him to climb to the top of the mountain. These claws echo Slavic folk beliefs, according to which the deceased must scale a mountain to reach the beyond—something also seen in the Russian expression *otpravit'sa na gorku,* literally "go to the hill," which means "to die."

Still, in the tales collected by Afanasyev, we see in "The Mink Beast" (*Norka-zver',* nr. 95), an animal that has devasted the king's hunting reserve. Ivan, the son of the king, confronts the beast but it escapes though wounded. It lifted up a white stone and traveled into the otherworld after having told Ivan that he could only be defeated there. Ivan had a leather rope made that was long enough to reach the otherworld. Once he had made his way there, he met a beautiful lass who chose him for her husband, and she told him how the Mink Beast was her brother who lived in a silver palace. She gave him a magic sword, a flask of strengthening water, and informed him that he had to decapitate the monster with a single stroke. Ivan made his way to the blue sea, saw him sleeping on an island, and slew him.

So people are no longer carried into these otherworlds by an angel or a saint, but by pursuing an animal (motif N774); it is sometimes a bird that attracts the man there (motif B151.2.02) or abducts him and takes him there (AT 537). In the Russian folktales collected by Afanasyev, a little spool of string indicates the path to the otherworld to the hero (nr. 167). The voyage sometimes takes place in dream (motif F1). In contrast with the medieval visions, people go there physically and not only in spirit, *in corpore* and not *in spiritu*. The frontier of the otherworld is indicated by one or more rivers (motif F162.2) and a bridge (motif E481.2.1), and it also by this way that one enters the land of the dead (motif F171). In this world beyond, time is suspended or slowed down, and years seem like days (motif D2011), but it is extremely important not to stay there too long (motif C712). Going back after one has been there obliges a person to respect a prohibition: ingesting a certain food, or getting down from a horse (motif F116), otherwise time will reclaim its rights and the person will die. In fact, this metaphorically means that one never really returns from these lands. The tales provide euphemisms for death, and two tale types (AT 313* and AT 470) call this territory the land of the dead or the immortals. Here there is a big difference with the literature of revelation in which the comatose visionaries come back to life.

One enters the otherworld through a cave, a well (AT 480), a lake, a pond, a river, a gate, a trapdoor, a spring, a forest, a crossroads, or a cemetery by climbing a tree (AT 468). But access may also be gained by wishing to bring back the golden apples of the beyond (AT 514) or the water of life (AT 551), or by setting off in search of the supernatural woman whom one has lost by violating a taboo (AT 400B)—this is the story of Cupid and Psyche—or for having revealed the existence of the fairy, which is the theme of *Lanval* (AT 400A), or by scaling the Mountain of Glass or Crystal (AT 400C, 471, 530). We encountered this latter representation earlier in the twelfth century in Urich von Zatikhoven's *Lanzelet,* in which a fairy (*merfeine, merminne*) abducts Lanzelet and brings him to her land that is only inhabited by women where everything flowers all year long. Her castle is built on a crystal mound that is as round as a ball and has a door made of diamond.[50]

One notable difference between the ealier visions of the beyond and the imagery in the folktales is that, as the narrative perspective has changed since the Middle Ages, it is no longer a question of sinners being punished: there are no more evocations of tortures and no more warnings. It is easily felt that there is a common backdrop to tales and visions, which is well illustrated by the story of Godescalc. In fact, we find here legendary elements like the river of terror, which has been borrowed from Germanic mythology:[51] "its entire surface was in fact covered by various sharp steel weapons, so intertwined and so dense that no one could cross it without cutting themselves." During this journey, Godescalc comes to a linden tree: "all the branches of the tree were covered by an infinite number of shoes."* The explanation for this follows when he comes to a field:

> "The entire surface of the field was planted with a kind of thorn that was as sharp and cutting as needles, and as stiff and dense as pig bristles. This field of horrors stretched on for about two miles. So those who wore shoes could cross it in complete safety without incurring any injuries, but it is hard to say what kind of torment and pain would be endured by those who went barefoot."

This is a reflection of the Germanic belief of the "hel-shoes" (*helskór*) that were put on the feet of the deceased before they were buried. This ritual passed down into folk traditions. In Austria, Johann Adolf Heyo (1849–1927) collected the following account:

---

*This is the first time that this motif appeared in medieval literature.

A generous young woman once gave her only pair of shoes to a poor person. When she died, she was compelled over the course of her journey to the beyond to cross barefoot over a thorn-covered heath. But look, there on a thorn bush are hanging the shoes that she had given away, which she can now put on.[52]

An Argentine tale collected in Mendoza, presents a mirror as the access to the otherworld, and a precise ritual must be respected:

A woman lost her husband. An elderly wet nurse, whom the couple house because she was poor and homeless, told her this: "In my village people say that if on a night of the full moon you stand in front of a mirror with a lit candle held in your left hand, you will see the dead person you are mourning appear. They also say that you can go join that person through the mirror, but I don't know if you can come back or have to stay on the other side forever." The woman followed this advice, saw a door open in the depths of the mirror, and then her husband came in. "Give me the candle, close your eyes, and walk straight ahead," he ordered her. She obeyed and rejoined her husband, crossed through the door and walked through a long, dark corridor, came to a second door that opened onto a large park where there was a bridge crossing a stream. On the other side was the little house where they were going to live together. The woman became pregnant and had to return to earth. Her husband accompanied her. She crossed through the door and found herself again in her living room. The wet nurse told her that she had been absent for three months.[53]

The grave is also a form of the otherworld, and a Sardinian tale offers the following image:

Walking in front of the tomb of an anonymous stranger, a man with no family and suffering from loneliness invited the deceased to come visit him.[54] One evening the dead man arrived, and they both cooked, ate, drank, and spent some pleasant hours together.

The late stranger invited the man to visit him in return. A short time later, the latter went to the grave where his host was waiting. Near the sepulcher there was a trapdoor that, when opened, revealed a pit in which there was a ladder leading to a small house containing a kitchen, living room, and bedroom. They had dinner and then returned to the surface. The stranger then said, "When I come see you again, I will bring a horse and carriage because the walk will be hard for you, and you will come to live here as there is room enough for two. The man went back home but his limbs felt heavy and he thought he had had too much to drink, however, when he looked in a mirror, he saw that his hair was white. The villagers told him that he had been gone for twenty years. One day, he disappeared and no one knew what happened.[55]

The reader cannot help but be struck by this depiction of the otherworld that is in some way an antechamber of the beyond. As in numerous medieval texts, the dead lead the same lives they had when they were alive. The tale oddly places the entry of the deceased's home next to his tomb, which suggests that the grave is only a temporary dwelling before the big departure, a journey whose length is suggested by the use of a cart.

Because the story of "The Seven Crows" (AT 451) enables us to see the way in which folk traditions have adopted ancient elements, we will spend a bit of time with it.

Following their father's curse, seven brothers were changed into crows and flew far away. Their sister set off in search of them and made her way to the ends of the earth, where she met the sun, the moon, and the stars. The Evening Star gave her knucklebone and told her: "Without this little bone, you will not be able to open the glass mountain, and that is where your brothers are." She then came to the border of the otherworld, which here takes the form of a glass mountain. She found the door but, because she had lost the knucklebone on her way, she unlocked it with her little finger after she cut it off. A dwarf came to her and served her a meal that she devoured without waiting for her brothers to return. When they sat down at the table, they asked who had been drinking from their cups and eating from their plates. "If God could make it so our little sister was here," said the seventh brother, "then we would be freed." The little girl came out from her hiding place (she was listening from behind the door), and the crows reassumed their human shapes and returned home.[56]

Which are the elements here that would suggest this tale is, in fact, one about making a journey into the afterlife that has been adapted into a journey to the otherworld? At least since Gregory the Great, the bird has been seen as an epiphany of the soul, which allows us to interpret the transformation of the brothers as a death, and the raven is most often seen as a herald of death. The brothers were removed from the world of humans. Since classical antiquity, the far end of the world has been regarded as the site of the afterlife—recall the legend of Alexander the Great that situates it beyond the Land of Darkness. The glass mountain clearly indicates the change of world, and it can only be entered by sacrificing a piece of yourself. The little girl's journey closely resembles that of a shaman looking for a dead person, as in the myth of Orpheus.

One of the Grimms' fairy tales, "Frau Holle" (nr. 24; AT 480) takes us into another, subterranean world:

A little girl dropped her spindle down a well and jumped in after it to get it back. She lost consciousness and, once she had recovered her senses, she found herself in a sunny, flower-filled meadow. After a variety of encounters, she made her way to a tiny house where Frau Holle lived, whose name means "the gracious one." She entered her service, but then became nostalgic for her family, and asked if she could leave. Frau Holle granted it to her, opened a gate, and the little girl found herself above, on the earth, not far from where her mother lived.

In "The Story of Fata Morgana," a Sicilian tale recorded by Laura Gonzenbach,[57] the otherworld can be reached through a very deep pit that comes out to a beautiful garden where the hero finds three maidens who are prisoners of a giant that he slays. His brothers help the maidens climb out, but they attempt to kill him, and the hero remains stuck in the world below. In the giant's palace, he finds a marvelous steed who tells him one day that his father has lost his sight and can only recover it thanks to the water of Fata Morgana, the horse's sister. By taking the horse's advice, the hero gains possession of the water and eventually marries the fairy.

When the otherworld is far away, the road leading there travels through the kingdoms of copper, of silver, and of gold, or by the homes of the wind, the moon, the sun, or even those belonging to the days of the week (AT 468). In the tale type "The danced-out shoes" (AT 306A), the hero must cross through an iron forest, and a lake or rivers, and in the tale type "The sons on a quest for a wonderful remedy for their father" (AT 551) the miraculous remedy, which is the goal of the hero's quest, is in a castle that closes itself off at noon.

Numerous Russian tales evoke an otherworld that is underwater, which is almost an exact copy of our own, and by comparing Grimms' fairy tales with those of Afanasyev, Natacha Rimasson-Fertin revealed how predominant this motif is in the world of the latter. The tale "The Firebird and Princess Vasilisa" (*Zar-Ptica i Vasilisa-carevena*; Afanasyev nr. 132) describes a world like this: "Down there, everything is like it is in our world: the light is the same, there are fields, meadows, green thickets, and the sun is shining there," a description that is confirmed by another story: "There were nothing but green plains, gardens, and thickets." In "The Czar of the Wave and Vasilisa the Magical" (Afanasyev nr. 170), Ivan Tsarevich finds his way there: "Over there, all is like it is here at home; the light is the same, there are fields, meadows, green thickets, and the sun is shining there." This description is confirmed by "The Reckless Words" (Afanasyev nr. 174), in which the hero walks backward into a lake and immediately finds himself in the devil's white stone palace.

In a Transylvanian tale, a spirit of the spring leads a boy into his underwater kingdom:

A man and woman had a boy, but they were so poor that even the ashes in their hearth did not belong to them! Once he was grown, their son told them, "I want to find a position so I can feed all three of us." His parents agreed, and his father accompanied him to the end of the path where there was spring full of clear water. They sat down there to have lunch and say their farewells. The father began choking on a small piece of cake that his wife had cooked for her son's upcoming journey; he had a good deal of difficulty swallowing it and all he could say was: "Hai! Hai!" Hardly had these two words left his mouth when the fountain began bubbling and a spirit came out. He offered to hire the boy. The father gave his consent and the spirit disappeared into the eddies of the spring with the lad.[58]

Metals play an important role in the tale type "Quest for a vanished princess" (AT 301A) and mark out the hero's journey. At the same time, they symbolize the three places of the afterlife: steel metaphorically reflects hell; silver, purgatory; and gold, paradise.

While pursuing a bird that came to steal a gold pear from a marvelous tree every night, a boy found his way into the otherworld by climbing down a well, where he met an old woman who revealed that the bird—an eagle—was her son, and that he was a great magician. The boy arrived at a steel castle and found a maiden held captive there by the magician. She told him that her two other sisters were also prisoners: one in the silver castle and the other in the gold castle. If he could succeed in slaying the eagle, he would free them.

In the third castle, the young woman being held prisoner there gave him an enchanted sword in which the magician's strength was kept (a variation on the external soul) and told him what he had to do. He killed the eagle, went back to the well, and his elder brothers hoisted the three sisters back to the surface, but he kept one of each girl's slippers. One was steel, one was silver, and one was gold. The elder brothers wanted to marry the sisters, but the latter each refused until they had a slipper identical to the one they had lost.

Following his brothers' betrayal, the youngest brother remained underground. The old woman then advised him: "Give my son back his sword and he will bring you back"; and this is exactly what happened. The youngest brother then had three more slippers forged and presented them to the king. The three brothers then married the three sisters, and the youngest brother abandoned all thoughts of revenge.[59]

I should point out that, in the majority of these tales that involve brothers, it is always the youngest brother who displays the generosity and altruism needed to fulfill the quest. He shares his bread with a starving animal, provides a dead person a grave, and so forth.

The hero in the tales appears as a kind of intermediary between the two worlds—the trials that he undergoes and gets through betray a method of election and grant him the right to access the otherworld.

NINE

IN SEARCH OF
THE LOST SPOUSE

The structure of the folktale that concerns the search for the lost spouse (AT 425A) hinges on the following elements: union of a supernatural being with a mortal subject to a prohibition—violation of that prohibition–separation–pilgrimage–tasks to accomplish–reunion of the couple; in the mythological tales, there is ascension to the world of the gods and to immortality. The most ancient example of this type of tale can be found in the Sanskrit literature long before our time:

The nymph Urvaśī (उर्वशी) decided to stay in the mortal world for a while and came down from the heavens. She met the handsome prince Purūravas (पुरूरवस्) and they fell madly in love with each other. She agreed to become his wife on three conditions: that he never separate her from her two rams, which she loved as if they were her children; that he make sure she never saw him undressed; and that he was to give her only clarified butter for food. They lived together, but the Asparas (nymphs), Gandharvas (celestial musicians), and the Siddhas (Perfected Masters) grew bored in heaven with her being away. They caused her prohibition to be violated and Urvaśī disappeared. Purūravas traveled the world over looking for her, found her, and they saw each other once a year. She gave him five sons. The Gandharvas then granted the prince the favor of living with Urvaśī forever and welcomed him into their world.[1]

In the eleventh century, the Kashmiri writer Somadeva, author of *Kathāsaritsāgara* (The Ocean of Story), clearly shows the evolution of the mythological tale toward the theme of the animal spouse (AT 425A):

Nur-Singh, a poor woodcutter, had a daughter, Tulisa, who one day heard a voice coming from a ruined spring in the forest that asked her to be his wife. Her father eventually agreed. The voice commanded him to place on his daughter's finger a ring that was floating in the air, and then Tulisa was carried off to a palace where she lived happily with her husband, who she only saw at night. It was forbidden for her to leave the palace, where servants kept her entertained with music. Following the bad advice of three old women she saw out a window one after the other, she asked the name of her husband, who had made her swear not to ask him that. He went to the edge of a river and, as she persisted, entered the water and revealed his name, Basnak Dau, and a snake's head appeared at the surface of the water before diving out of sight. The palace vanished and Tulisa and her father found themselves as poor as they had been before.

One day she heard two squirrels talking who informed her that her husband's mother had lost all her sovereign authority because her son had become king of the snakes. So she had become allied with Sarkasukis, the king of the vultures, who, changed into an old woman, had prompted Tulisa to ask her husband his name. One of the squirrels let her know that she could save Basnak Dau: she would have to walk into the east, swim across a reptile-filled river, look for the egg of the Huma (Hooma) bird on the other side, and place it in her lap until it hatched. She then returned to her mother-in-law's palace and entered her employment, but the woman imposed difficult tasks upon her. If she was unable to complete them, serpents would devour her. They included collecting the aromas of a thousand flowers in a crystal glass, and creating a splendid piece of jewelry worthy of a princess out of a jar of sand—the woodcutter's daughter emerged successfully from several other similar trials.

Once the egg had hatched, Huma stabbed out the eyes of the green snake that the queen wore around her neck, which made it possible for Basnak Dau to recover his kingdom and reconcile with his wife. Tulisa succeeded, found her husband again and became queen and wife of one of those powerful genies that, under certain conditions, govern the invisible kingdoms.[2]

The kinship of the two tales is obvious. In both cases, we have the union of a supernatural being and a human, but the sexes have been reversed. Winning back the husband (or wife) involves passing some trials, which, once overcome, make it possible to gain access to the world of gods or genies. Somadeva's introduction of helpful animals—the squirrels—moves the story toward the realm of the fairy tale.

In the *Metamorphoses,** written between 160 and 180 CE, Apuleius of Madaurus tells the story of Cupid and Psyche, which is based on the same structure as the preceding tales: taboo, transgression, separation, quest, reunion.

Doomed to a dire fate, Psyche was carried off by Zephyr, who brought her to a beautiful castle. She ate there, served by invisible beings; she then went to sleep in a beautiful room. Over the course of the night she was joined by Cupid, who asked her to never seek to see him. The young woman's two sisters paid her a visit, brought there by Zephyr, and consumed by jealousy, encouraged Psyche to discover her lover's identity. One night she lit a lamp and discovered a sleeping god by her side. Alas, a drop of burning oil fell on Cupid's shoulder, waking him up, and he vanished back to the home of his mother, Venus, who kept him captive there. In despair, Psyche set off in search for him after a vain attempt at suicide. She thereby made her way into the otherworld, where Venus imposed various tasks or trials on her. For each of them she received assistance from a variety of helpers: ants, a reed, and Jupiter's eagle. For her final task she was

---

*[More commonly known as *The Golden Ass* (*Asinus Aureus*), as Augustine had referred to it. —*Ed.*]

ordered to collect in a box a piece of Proserpina's beauty. But just as she was about to kill herself by jumping from the top of a tower, she was told what she needed to do to successfully pass this trial. Psyche succeeded, but, a victim of her own curiosity, she opened the box and fell into a deathlike sleep. Meanwhile, Cupid has freed himself and brought his beloved back to life. They wed and the gods permit the young woman to drink the ambrosia that confers immortality.

There are many variants of this story. For example, there are the legends of Melusine, from which the motifs of the quest and the reunion have disappeared. The third task Venus imposes is to bring back a flask of a particular water, an ambiguous episode because of the description of the place and the nature of said water:

"Do you see the top of the steep mountain overlooking that towering bluff, from which the dark waters of a black spring flows down, where it spills into the cleft of the neighboring valley and then waters the marshes of Styx and feed the harsh streams of Cocytus? Go there at once to draw me some of its icy waters from the very bottom of the spring where it gushes out most deeply and bring it to me at once in this flask,"[3] Venus ordered Psyche.

Here two beliefs show through: that of the otherworld as a mountain, and that of the water of life that the tales often place in or on a mountain. Psyche has to truly venture into the beyond, which is indicated by what she encounters there: dragons, and waters that never stop shrieking and threatening her with death, but thanks to the intervention of Jupiter's eagle, she brings back the flask. This is when the supreme test is imposed, a descent into the underworld:

Take this pyxis* and go at once to the palace of Orcus in the Underworld. Give this pyxis to Proserpina and tell her: "Venus asks

---

*[A small cylindrical box with a lid, used for cosmetics or jewelry by women in the classical world. —*Ed.*]

that you send her a little of your beauty (*modicum de tu mitttas el formonsitate*), even if only enough for one short day. For she has used up all that she had caring for her ailing son."

So what is this "beauty?" That it is certainly a balm—the ancients kept their balms in a pyxis—with dual properties, embellishment and healing, clearly emerges from the words of Venus. The balm is simply another form of the water of life. Psyche is therefore given the responsibility of bringing remedies intended for Cupid from the otherworld.

In a state of despair, her thoughts turned to suicide and she climbed to the top of a tower to throw herself off, hoping to make her way to Tartarus this way, but the tower began speaking to her and advised her on what she needed to do: find the Tainaron* hidden close to Lacedaemon. "There you will the Pluto's back door and through the gaping entrance a difficult path will appear." Once she crossed the threshold, she made her way to the Palace of Orcus, but she had to bring cake for Cerberus and carry two coins in her mouth to pay Charon. She should neither answer the requests of those she met nor touch them, for these were traps set by Venus. Once she was through them she would arrive at the home of Proserpine. Psyche succeeded to get the pyxis from her and started the trip back home, but once she had left the underworld, she opened it. "But inside there was no beauty at all but only a sleep like death, a Stygian slumber that, once it was freed by the removal of lid, took possession of her and filled all limbs with a fog of thick lethargy, and she fell down where she stood on the path, prey to its power. She lay there motionless, no more than a sleepy corpse."[4] Cupid restored her to life then went in search of Jupiter who summoned the gods, granted immortality to the young woman, and ordered Mercury to bring her up to heaven.

---

*The ancients located the entrance to Hades in a cave near Cape Tenarion (cf. Virgil, *Georgics,* IV, 467).

While Apuleius was likely inspired by a Greek novel that Photios summarized in his *Bibliotheca* (Βιβλιοθήκη),* written around 843, we should not overlook the fact that he lived in Madauros in Numidia (which is the Algerian city of M'daourouch today) and had been educated in two cultures. I am going to examine a Berber story as it is reflective of the cultural environment of Apuleius:

A man had four daughters; before leaving on a trip he asked them what they wanted for a gift. The youngest one answered: "A pigeon dancing on a roof all by itself." The man eventually spotted one, but a voice forbade him from capturing it. In terror he begged the voice to identify itself and he was told: "Asphor'ulehóa," the name of the son of a Teryel, an ogress. The man agreed to give him his daughter's hand in exchange for the pigeon, and Asphor'ulehóa said: "One day I will come in the shape of a camel. May your daughter climb upon my back with her pigeon and she will be happy." The man became ill and he called his four daughters to his deathbed to tell them: "One day a camel will come that will bring good luck if each of you sit on it, starting with the eldest. You, my youngest daughter, will be the last and bring the pigeon with you." A year later the camel came for her and brought her to a large farm where there was not a living soul. That evening, someone knocked on the door of her room and a voice ordered her to extinguish the oil lamp. She obeyed, and a being lay down next to her and went to sleep. When she woke up, her nighttime visitor had vanished, and this happened every night.

One day her sisters paid her a visit. When she told them of her situation, they replied: "Don't be stupid and try to find out what kind of monster your husband is. . . . You just need not obey his command: don't put the oil lamp out, but cover it with a pot. Once he is sleeping, take it off and you will see what kind of creature he is." The young woman followed this advice and discovered that Asphor'ulehóa was magnificently handsome and his body

---

*Lucian of Samosata is also said to have written a *Golden Ass,* which was recast by a Lucius of Patras.

was covered with tiny children busy spinning a tunic for his wife. When the latter spoke, Asphor'ulehóa woke up and left. His wife followed him with great difficulty and came to a farm belonging to her mother-in-law. The old Teryel imposed four tests on her; if she failed, then she would eat her. She had to clean the yard without leaving a speck of dust; fetch a sack filled with bird feathers, one from each bird, and then return to each bird its feather; and she had to separate the water from milk in a pitcher. Thanks to the help of Asphor'ulehóa and his magic powers, the young woman succeeded in completing the first three trials. The Teryel tried to devour her but Asphor'ulehóa rescued his wife, and burned the Teryel and her sisters in their farm, and brought his wife back home.[5]

If what we have here is an ecotype of the story of Cupid and Psyche that simply shows a tale of this type was circulating in Numidia in ancient times, many motifs remain mysterious. First there is the gift that the youngest daughter requests and nothing explains, then the false selection of the chosen one by the camel: she is the only one with the wonderful pigeon. Other details are never explained. For example, when the sisters set off in search of their youngest sibling, they know her husband's name. How did they learn it? But the most intriguing detail is that Asphor'ulehóa's body is covered with cherubs (Arabic *malaika*) spinning a tunic he has chosen. Contrary to the tale type "The search for the lost husband" (AT 425), no separation results from the violation of the prohibition.

Asphor'ulehóa is obviously a god whose commands have the force of law; he commands, he causes water to gush from a wall to clean the yard; compels the obedience of a palm tree, in the branches of which he hides his wife; and orders the earth to open up and the deep pit that appears there to be filled with fat and fire. This is the pit that swallows up his mother and her sisters, the ogresses (*teryel/teryalin*).

Among the variations of this tale, there are two that are worth citing because they attest perfectly to the alterations that the paradigms of a story undergo without changing the syntagmas.

Domenico Comparetti collected a tale in Monferrato (Piedmont) worth looking at:

> While pursuing a hare, an eighteen-year-old prince came to a palace; the tables were set. He was hungry so he ate and then went off to rest. At midnight he heard someone enter, undress, and lie down. He felt around but could not feel anything (*toca, toca, non sente nulla*). In the morning the person left. The next day he went home to his parents and explained the reason for his absence to his mother. "How silly you are," she replied. "Why didn't you take a flint and a fuse to light a lamp so you could see who it is!" Despite the pleas of his mother, he left again and, once night had fallen, lit a candle when he felt a presence next to him. He then saw a young woman "beautiful as an eye of the sun" (*e vide una raguzza che pareva un occhio di sole*). A drop of wax fell on her and she woke up. "Poor boy," she cried, "if you had slept one more night beside me, I would have revealed myself to you," and she vanished. He left in search of her and one year and three days later came to an inn at the edge of the Red Sea. The innkeeper's daughter fell in love with him, but he told her he already had a wife. Furious, she mixed a sleeping potion (*una polverina da far dormire*) into his meal. When Bella of the Sun (*Bella del Sole*) arrived, she waited for one hour, set a gold chest next to him and then left, but a hermit had seen everything and took the object. The next day, the same incident, but a ship came with Bella of the Sun accompanied by three young girls. She tried to wake the boy up, but in vain. She then slipped a ring onto his finger and went away. On the third visit, she left a lock of her hair. The hermit returned the three gifts to the young man, who climbed aboard the boat abandoned by his visitors. He crossed the sea and wandered in a forest, "hairy as a bear" (*peloso como un orsa*), and his clothing turned into rags. Bella of the Sun's father was hunting in the woods and found the prince, whom he brought back with him. One day a contest was arranged to determine who would wed the daughter of the Sun (*la figlia des Sole*). The prince was victorious and made himself known thanks to the presents he had been given. He washed and

shaved himself, then sent someone to fetch his parents and introduced his wife to them.[6]

The text, which is also fairly enigmatic, lets it be known that the
hare was none other than the animal shape* assumed by Bella of the
Sun, but nothing explains why she imposed a prohibition, whereas, in
similar stories, it involves a process of freeing a person who has been
bewitched. It will be noted that the sex of the supernatural being varies
in accordance with the country and the time period, which seems to
correspond to a patriarchal or matriarchal society. Another alteration
is that the antagonist is no longer a mother-in-law but a young woman
disappointed by the prince's indifference to her.

We can attempt to outline the evolution of the tale with the help of
structuralist methods. The paradigmatic axis is that of the multiplicity
of the variants. The syntagmatic axis is that of the synchrony.

Paradigms	Man or Woman.
	God, goddess, or unspecified supernatural being.
	Prohibition (from one to three).
	Antagonist(s): sisters, mother-in-law, jealous woman.
	Separation / no separation of the lovers.
	Impossible tasks: three or four / none.
	They are accomplished with the help of a supernatural being.
	One task remains unfinished.
	Reunion, marriage.
	Welcome in the otherworld (that of gods or that of genies).

Syntagm: Quest for the spouse after transgression.

Over the course of the narratives, we can see a slow process of
demythologization. From a nymph who comes from the world of the

---

*In the medieval texts, as we have seen, the animal guide is a stag or wild boar.

Gandharvas or a god come down from Olympus (Cupid), we come to a Basnak Dau, the serpent king, to the multiform Asphor'ulehóa, and a young woman under an enchantment, Bella of the Sun. The one major constant of this narrative is the prohibition on seeing the supernatural being, in other words, learning his or her identity such as we see in Basnak Dau's concealing of his name. There is a typological connection between the texts cited—the genetic link cannot be proven—that strongly suggests they all reflect an archetypal idea: essentially, this says that the union between individuals belonging to different worlds is possible under certain conditions.

The deep structure of these texts reveals that the trials undergone by the hero or heroine are qualifying in nature and make it possible to detect if he or she is worthy of moving up to a higher world. In this sense, the trials are a kind of initiation. I can therefore suggest the following schematic outline: the protagonist of this type of tale dies and then is reborn into eternal life,[7] as is quite legible in the story of Urvaśī and that of Psyche, and then this pattern is gradually effaced as the human societies evolve.

However, these two women do not represent isolated cases, and there are at least two good attestations that are reminiscent of Psyche's story. First, there is that of *Prometheus Bound* by Aeschylus (circa 526–456 BCE), which tells the story of Io, beloved by Zeus, and presents another form of the tale type "The search for the lost husband" (AT 425):

Dreams besieged Io, the priestess of Hera, at night that encouraged her to give up her virginity. She shared them with her father, who consulted the oracles of Delphi and Dodona. The answer was that he should drive his daughter away, which he did. Having almost caught the lovers by surprise, Hera changed her rival [Io] into a heifer: "Immediately my form and mind were distorted, and with horns, as you see, upon my forehead, stung by a sharp-fanged gadfly I rushed with frantic bounds to Cerchnea's sweet stream." Then, hidden from Hera, Zeus changed into a bull and coupled with Io. Hera sent a gadfly charged with stinging Io without respite, and this was the beginning of many tribulations for her, until she was freed from her state and become a goddess worshipped in Egypt, Isis.[8]

In the second century, Apollodorus of Athens recorded the story of Semele, also loved by Zeus. Jealous, Hera assumed the form of Beroe, the young woman's nanny, who suggested to her that she ask her divine lover to appear in all his glory. When Zeus appeared in a blaze of thunder and lightning, Semele was incinerated and died. Once he had been deified for his deeds, her son Dionysus went down into Hades and brought her back, whereupon she was admitted to Olympus.

Finally, the tale type "The search for the lost husband" features a hierogamy whose reward is immortality. Recall Guingamor and Lanval disappearing into the faery kingdom, and Graelant barely escaping death when the time of this world reclaimed its rights.

TEN

FOLKTALES
AND SHAMANISM

"The folktale is the repository of a spiritual legacy; it is a transformed residue of ancient beliefs and traditions that are like those of shamanic origin,"[1] emphasizes Philippe Walter. In fact, folktales reveal numerous traces of shamanism, certainly not as a "technique of ecstasy" (to borrow a phrase from Mircea Eliade),[2] but as themes and motifs that are scattered throughout the texts and make it possible to better grasp what is hidden behind the tales, which at first glance seem so simple. We should remember that, according to shamanism, the world is divided into planes connected by an axis and that travel (a cosmic journey) between these different levels can be made through trance. Here are the most noteworthy themes of shamanism:

* The external soul: a distinguishing feature of shamanism is its belief in several souls located at different places in the body, notably the bones.[3] In general, three souls are described.

* The bone ladder.

* Going in search of someone in the otherworld: soul retrieval.

* Rebirth from one's bones after dismemberment. This dismemberment is an initiatory ordeal.

* The language of animals; the shaman knows the secrets of nature.

❋ The tree or plant that grows to heaven. This is the cosmic tree, the *axis mundi,* represented by the post with seven or nine notches in the shaman's hut.

❋ Becoming a bird or being accompanied by a bird to undertake a journey, while living, into the heavens and the beyond.

❋ The cosmic mountain; the journey beyond the grave.

We will address most of these themes individually below.

The External Soul
This is seen in the tale type "The ogre's (devil's) heart in the egg" (AT 302, 302A, 400C, and 468). This is not truly a soul, but the life force that is located outside of the body inside an egg, or a series of containers. It is also present in the tale type "The singing bone" (AT 780), in which a flute made from a bone reveals the identity of the murderer of the person the bone originally belonged to.

The Bone Ladder
This appears in the tale types "The girl as helper in the hero's flight" (AT 313) and "The maiden who seeks her brothers" (AT 451).

Folklorist Theodor Vernaleken (1812–1907), an Austrian counterpart to the Brothers Grimm, tells how the Master of the Winds ate a chicken and gave its bones to a little girl who had left home to find her brothers. She came to a glass castle that had no doors or windows. Sticking the bones in the smooth surface of the wall, she used them like a ladder and managed to free her brothers.[4]

Going in Search of Someone in the Otherworld
One of the shaman's special skills is the magic healing that consists of bringing the spirit or soul of a person that has been stolen by the demon of an illness back from the beyond. To do this, the shaman takes a trance journey with the assistance of his spirit helpers. We find this in "The man on a quest for his lost wife" (AT 400) and "The search for the lost husband" (AT 425). The hero travels into the otherworld and, after various trials and ordeals, comes back with the object of his search.

The archetype here is the story of Orpheus, which, in contrast to the fairy tales, ends badly.

"The Green Mountain," a folktale collected in Brière (France) by Geneviève Massignon, tells the story of a young man who loses his father's fortune playing cards and decides to drown himself:

> Having lost his father's fortune at cards, a young man decided he would end his life by drowning himself. When he reached the river's edge, he saw a man there walking on the water who prevented him from committing suicide and who asked him why he was doing it. Once he learned the young man's reasons, the man offered him double the sum he had lost on condition that he come find him on the Green Mountain* at the end of a year and a day. The boy therefore made his way to this place and the devil imposed three tasks upon him that the hero successfully completed thanks to the help of the devil's daughter. For the last task—collecting three dove eggs from the top of the Green Mountain—the young girl had to be cut up into pieces, boiled in a stew pot, and her bones pulled free from her flesh to be used as a ladder. The boy took the eggs, collected the bones of the dead girl in a cloth, and boiled them again in a pot to put them back together, but he had left a fingernail back on the mountain. It was this clue that allowed him to recognize his beloved when the devil offered him one of his daughters to wed.
>
> The devil still wished to kill his son-in-law, and the young couple fled.[5] The devil's daughter built a castle not far from her husband's home, and she gave him fair warning: he must not let anyone kiss him, otherwise he would forget her. His godmother surprised him with a kiss on one occasion and he forgot all about his wife, but he got her back a short time later.

In an article entitled "Orphée dans le miroir du conte merveilleux" (Orpheus in the Mirror of the Fairy Tale), Nicole Belmont has compared the story of the myth of Orpheus with the fairy tale of "The

---

*Variants of a Green Mountain in other versions of the tale include a Black Mountain, a Black Forest, a Castle of the Golden Mountains, or a Castle of Thunder.

Devil's Daughter." The latter tells the story of a single boy who goes to the otherworld and brings back "to earth" a woman whom he marries after forgetting her for a certain period of time, whereas the myth of Orpheus tells the story of a married man who, when his wife dies, goes to find her in the afterlife, fails to bring her back, and dies "single."

Orpheus and Eurydice	The Devil's Daughter
Married man	Young single man
who has lost his wife	who has lost his own self
sets off into the beyond	heads off into the beyond
the master of the underworld	the devil
returns his wife to him	gives him a wife
during his return	during the return
he must not look back	he must look back
does not succeed in bringing his wife back	is brought back by his wife
lives as a "bachelor"	lives "as a bachelor"
fleeing all women	seeking good fortune
because he clings to the memory	or remarries
of his wife	because he has forgotten his wife
in the icy solitude of Thrace	in his country and his family
he is torn to pieces by the Bacchantes	he recovers his memory and his wife
and dies a bachelor.	and henceforth lives married.[6]

Belmont notes the convergences and reversals between the two stories:

> The reversal of the general narrative scheme is accompanied by reversals but also similarities in the episodes and motifs. The story stresses the bachelorhood of the hero, a boy living with his parents and who, when he leaves his family, finds amusement with friends his own age playing cards, or who, according to one version, refuses to even consider moving out of his parents' home. For his part, Orpheus is married to Eurydice. The young man loses his

self—metaphorically or literally—while Orpheus loses his wife, who was bitten by a snake. Both head off into the beyond. This afterlife does not have the same narrative definition in both stories. While there can be no doubt in the story of Orpheus that it is the underworld of ancient Greek religion and mythology, the afterlife of the fairy tale is, as has been noted, more difficult to pin down. It is neither the pagan underworld nor the Christian hell, although it is a domain of the devil; it is, however, an "other world."

In addition to the journey into the afterlife, "The Devil's Daughter" has retained a fundamental element of shamanic beliefs: the dismemberment of the body into pieces. In the Greek myth, Orpheus is torn to pieces by the Bacchantes, who then scatter his body parts; in the fairy tale, the woman is cut up by a man who then reassembles the pieces of her body and brings her back to life.

Rebirth from One's Bones after Dismemberment
This theme appears in the Middle Ages in *The Beguiling of Gylfi*, the second part of the *Prose Edda* by Snorri Sturlusson (1179–1241), in which the following episode from the life of the god Thor is recounted:

Thor was traveling with Loki in his chariot drawn by goats. In the evening they arrived at a peasant's house and were given a night's lodging there. During the evening Thor took his goats and slaughtered them both. After this they were skinned and put in the pot. Everyone ate. Then Thor placed the goatskins on the other side of the fire and instructed the peasant and his household to throw the bones onto the goatskins. Thjalfi, the peasant's son, took hold of the goat's ham-bone and split it open with his knife and broke it to get at the marrow. . . . In the morning, Thor took his hammer Mjolnir, raised it, and blessed the goat hides. Then the goats got up and one of them was lame in the hind leg.[7]

Josef Haltrich (1822–1886) tells a story collected in Transylvania that is quite similar. A pastor kills his lamb to feed Jesus and Saint Peter.

Once the meal is over, Christ advises him to gather all the bones together and place them on the animal's hide. The next day the animal was completely restored to life.[8]

Humans go through the same treatment in the tale type "My mother slew me; my father ate me" (AT 720): after being dismembered, the hero comes back to life once his bones have been collected and reorganized properly. In "The Green Mountain," as we saw earlier, there is a young girl who has to be cut into pieces and boiled in a stewpot until her bones come loose from her skin so they can be used to make a ladder. The boy gathers all her bones together in a towel and then boils them in the pot again so that she can be made whole once more.[9]

A tale collected by Georg Schambach and Wilhelm Müller in Lower Saxony is worth mentioning because of the hallucinatory process it depicts:

An enchanted princess could only be freed by a prince who has become lost while hunting in the forest, is twenty years of age, and will agree to allow the spirits to dismember him for three nights in a row.* "The next day a stag will appear, holding a flask of oil in its mouth," the princess informs him; "it will gather together all the bones of your body and rearrange them as they should be. He will then anoint them and they will go back into their proper place and be covered with flesh. Once this has been done, you will come back to life." The spirits—some twelve of them—decapitate him, dismember him, and then devour his flesh. The stag then comes to fulfill its duty.[10]

The prince thus succeeds in passing this trial, but he fails another one. The princess then vanishes, and he has to set off in search of her. Thanks to the help of animals, he crosses the red sea, the white sea, and the black sea—obviously borders of the otherworld—and finds his beloved again, who by all evidence is no mere mortal.

Another folktale that is akin to the preceeding one is much less explicit and contains no more than a mere trace of shamanism:

---

*The plurality of the conditions here is notable.

A soldier met a princess who had been magically changed into a snake in a castle, and she said to him: "You can free me, if you like, and I will then be yours along with all my treasures." He agreed and she explained to him: "At midnight for three nights in a row,[11] a king and all his soldiers will come to the castle. They will look in every nook and cranny until they find you. They will then lead you before their sovereign who will do whatever he possibly can to make you talk. Don't allow yourself to be impressed by this, and do not speak a single word. Summon all your courage and, despite all their promises and threats, remain as silent as the grave, for if even the smallest syllable falls from your mouth, both of us are lost. You will be mistreated and brutalized, but don't utter a single word. Whatever they do to torture you, the next morning you will feel even better than you do today, and all these sufferings will be to your benefit. On the third night, they will cut off your head, but the next morning you will be fresh and fit. If you are persistent in not speaking, I will be freed and we will both find happiness." During the third night, the soldier was decapitated and he fell into such a deep sleep that he did not wake until the following day. His first gesture was to put his hands to his head to see if it was still there.[12]

The helper that restores life (the stag), the flask of oil, and the requisite conditions have disappeared from this Zingerle folktale with the title "The Bewitched Princess." Torture has replaced the dismemberment, and only the decapitation and the sleep offer a glimpse of the shamanic background of the text. These elements gradually faded away, as is shown by a folktale that Pauline Schullerus collected in the Harbach Valley (Valea Hârtbaciului, Transylvania) at the end of the nineteenth century:

Frederick made his way to the "Black World" to free an enchanted king as well as his wife and daughter; he had to sit next to a totally black woman in a silk cradle, without speaking. From midnight to two o'clock in the morning, demons came out who wished to mistreat him. If he could manage to stay there for three nights, the spell would be broken.[13] Because he had a talisman (the sword of God!),* he did not suffer any harm.

Finally, the last account we will consider in this respect comes from the Brothers Grimm:

> A young man found a bewitched young girl in a castle who had been cursed to be a snake. She asked him to free her. "How can I do this?" the boy asked. "Tonight twelve black men laden with chains will come. They will ask you what you are doing here, but say nothing, do not answer them and let them do whatever they please to you. The will torment you, beat you, and stab you, but let them do it and say nothing. At midnight they will have to go away again. And on the second night twelve others will come; and on the third night, twenty-four others who will cut off your head. But at midnight they will no longer have any power, and if you have held firm without saying the slightest word, I will be free. I will come find you and I will have a flask with the water of life in it. I will smear it on you and you will come back to life and be as healthy as you were before."

The kinship of these four texts is obvious, despite the variations, and the table below gives us a good overview of them:

Lower Saxony	Tyrol	Romania	Germany
Princess	Snake	Black princess	Snake
Forbidden to speak	Forbidden to speak	Forbidden to speak	Forbidden to speak
Twelve spirits	King + soldiers	Demons	Twelve black men
Three nights in a row	Three nights in a row	Three nights in a row	Three nights in a row
Decapitation + dismemberment	Maltreatment + decapitation	Torments from midnight to 2 a.m.	Torments until midnight + decapitation
Stag + flask	Slumber		Water of life
Resurrection	Resurrection		Resurrection

---

*This is reminiscent of another version of the Grimms' tale nr. 92 ("The King of the Golden Mountain"), in which the hero protects himself from the demon thanks to a magic circle and the Bible. During one of the nights of tests, ghosts use him as a bowling ball.

Through the four examples just cited and that represent a narrative sequence of the tale type "The man on a quest for his lost wife" (AT 400), we are witness to the slow process of deterioration of a belief as ancient as the world. Severed from its roots at the heart of a civilization, it collapses, leaving nothing but a few stray remnants that have become incomprehensible and tumble into the category of mere fantastical motifs, which are the hallmark of fairy tales. Historical evolution, religious shifts, and time have done their work, yet the collection of such shattered remnants allows us to get a good glimpse at what is hidden behind these motifs.

The death of the hero is often euphemized, and it is an animal that is slaughtered in his stead. One detail reveals all the underlying facts here, however: because he can understand the language of the birds, a boy tells his father that one day he will have to kneel before him. The father decides to have the son killed and orders a woodcutter to execute him and bring him his eyes, stomach, and index finger as proof. Once they are in the forest, the woodcutter hesitates and the boy tells him: "Kill in my place the pig I fattened up for you; take his eyes and his stomach, then cut off my index finger, and take it all back to my father."[14]

The Language of Animals

"The Serpent's Secret" precisely reveals the background of the acquisition of the language of animals. The reptile gives a ring to the hero and tells him: "As long as you wear this ring and never reveal its secret to anyone, you will be the wisest man in all the world. You will be able to talk with all the animals, and you will see all the treasures hidden in the depths of the earth, the bottom of the sea, and in the heavens."[15] We should recall the close ties Orpheus maintained with animals.[16]

The Tree or Plant That Grows to Heaven

The theme of the tree or plant that grows all the way to the sky[17] is best known by the story of "Jack and the Beanstalk" (AT 328),[18] but is also evident in "The Fox Healer" (Afanasyev, nr. 11), and the tale types "The fisherman and his wife" (AT 555, of which there are French versions) and "The princess of the sky-tree" (AT 468). This is a variation on the cosmic mountain that gives access to the otherworld when scaled or when one goes deep within it. This narrative configuration features a paradoxical passage. Among the North American Indians (Arapahos, Chilcotins), the sky can be reached by climbing a tree that sometimes grows taller as someone ascends it.[19]

Becoming a Bird

Becoming a bird or being accompanied by a bird appears in the tale types "The three stolen princesses" (AT 301) and "The flight with the eagle" (AT 537). Here, and in other tale types where helpers are a key feature, we find the last trace of the shaman's helper spirits. The hero of these tales receives aid and/or advice from animals (often grateful) or individuals, and it is thanks to their help that he brings his quest to an end. The eagle and the horse appear most frequently and assume the duties of a psychopomp.[20] Let us consider as an example the tale of "The Three Deserters" collected by the Zingerle brothers:

After freeing three princesses who had been held captive in the otherworld, the hero is betrayed by his companions and remains trapped underground. He asks a dwarf for help, who tells him: "I am going to help you right away. I can change into whatever I like. I am going to change into an eagle and carry you, but flying will be very exhausting, so you must quickly kill a lamb and cut it into three portions. You have to give me a piece every time I shout for one, otherwise we will fall and you will die." The dwarf immediately fulfilled his promise, and the eagle carried the young man holding the meat in its claws. Three times the eagle, who was flying like the wind, had asked for meat, and they were still a long way from the surface when the eagle demanded meat for the fourth time. The lamb had all been eaten. What could be done? Seeing no other solution, the soldier quickly sliced off a piece of his calf and gave it to the eagle. Several moments later, they emerged into the open air.[21]

The return to this world calls for a sacrifice; the notion this implies is that no one can come back from the beyond without making some form of compensation.

The folktales need to be deciphered because the shamanism is never overt. "The Three Brothers and the Three Sisters" (AT 304), an Albanian tale, wonderfully illustrates how it can be hidden within a story:

A prince set off in pursuit of his wife's abductor, known as Half-Man Half-Iron. A falcon carried the prince up to a high mountain "that people called the other world." The meat carried by the prince to feed the bird was not enough, and he had to slice a piece off of each of his thighs. Once they reached the top of the mountain, the falcon regurgitated the pieces he had swallowed and the prince put them back in their rightful place and was healed. He found his wife, who hid him, but Half-Man Half-Iron found him, killed him, drank his blood, and "as for the skin and bones, he tossed them in front of his house." The falcon saw them, flew to two mountains that opened and closed, went in, filled his beak with swallow's milk, and returned to revive the prince. The prince then persuaded his wife to pretend to be sick so her abductor would reveal where the seat of his strength was located. Eventually, she learned its location: "My power is in such-and-such mountain, where lives a wild boar," Half-Man Half-Iron told her. "He has a silver tusk; in that tusk there is a hare, and the hare has three pigeons in its belly. That's where my strength lives." Once the prince slew the pigeons, the abductor died, and the falcon brought the couple back home.[22]

The external soul—disguised here as power—the resurrection of the prince thanks to swallow's milk(!), and the journeys on the back of the falcon, who plays the role of a shaman's helper spirit, are all motifs of shamanic origin.

We have to turn our attention to countries that are far from Europe to find texts in which shamanism is more obvious. Henri Noël's collection contains the story I am summarizing here, which he recorded in

Mexico during the 1950s. It provides us with two shamanic sessions:

1. With the devil's help, a prince wished to abduct the king's daughter, with whom he had fallen in love. The demon led him into a cave in the forest and told him to go through it into the otherworld. How was he to do that? the prince wondered. The devil answered him: "Take this box, this drum, and this flute. Go into the cave and rub the balm on yourself, beat the drum with your left hand, and play the flute with your right hand. Once you have done that long enough, you will transform into a jaguar. Go to the royal park next to the forest, pretend that your lower limbs are paralyzed and allow yourself to be captured. You will be imprisoned in a courtyard. Pretend you are sleeping; they will want to show the sleeping jaguar to the princess. Seize her, cross through the park and the forest, then enter the otherworld through the cave." Following this advice, the prince was able to abduct the princess.

2. Another individual in love with the princess fell into great despair at her abduction. One day he gave alms to a poor woman and told her of his misfortune. She offered to help him and brought him to an ancient temple in the forest that was half in ruins. The beggar lit candles and incense: "Stand in the middle," she ordered him, "and breathe the smoke in deeply, and when you hear me singing, start singing along with me." For a long time they sang this monotonous chant:

> *Eli, Beli,*
> *Subtraheli,*
> *Oro, doro,*
> *Ut tu soro.*

Several hours later, an angel appeared, and the man felt wings growing from his back. The angel brought him to a mountain where they entered a cave and found themselves in the otherworld. Taking advantage of the jaguar-man's slumber, they abducted his captive and returned to the royal palace, whereupon the angel disappeared.[23]

If we leave aside the Christian elements of this story (the devil, the angel), what we see here is a trance-inducing session of the shamanic type with the drum, flute, and the balm that presumably contains a hallucinogen. The transformation into an animal is in response to its intended purpose: the abduction of the princess. The second session, which is more heavily Christianized—it takes place in a chapel "of ancient times"—is essentially brought about through the chanting and the smoke that the would-be lover must inhale. In both cases, the journey into the otherworld requires an "expert," represented by the devil and the poor woman who are the result of acculturation and have been substituted for the shaman of stories that very likely far predate the time in which Henri Noël collected them.

Among the Tlingits, a coastal native people of the Pacific Northwest in North America, "The Chain of Arrows" tells a story of a journey to the beyond to bring back a boy who had disappeared after offending the moon:

The son of a village chieftain was shooting arrows at a star, and they eventually transformed into a ladder that he scaled for two days before reaching the sky. He met his grandmother, who pointed out the house of Moon, in which he could find the boy he was looking for. She gave him a pine cone, a columbine flower, a piece of thorny wood, and a fragment of a sharpening stone. He went to the Moon's house, where he heard the sorrowful weeping of his comrade. He helped him get out and left the pine cone in his place, urging it to imitate the boy's wails, then both boys took flight. They came to the grandmother, who ordered her grandson: "Go and rest at the place where you were the first time you came. Think about nothing except the playground you had at your disposal." They obeyed her and returned to the foot of the ladder. They heard a drum in the village chieftain's house, where a funeral feast had been organized for them, and then they returned to their respective families.[24]

In his analysis of this folktale, Alsace Yen discerned the following structure: loss, journey into the afterlife, sleep, helper (the grandmother), deliverance, return (magical escape).[25] The evidence suggests that this story is based on typical shamanic beliefs, but the death of the body has been euphemized as a kidnapping. Nevertheless, the funeral feast indicates his death.

Let us now go to Greenland. The great explorer of the North Pole, Knud Rasmussen (1879–1933), collected a number of Inuit (Eskimo) tales. As the hero, several of these tales feature the shaman Avggo, who visits the beyond:

> After visiting all the places frequented by the great shamans, Avggo decided to go the "the celestial land of the dead." He invoked his guardian spirits and his drum entered into the action before he was done with his incantations. Once his spirits had gathered together, he began his trance journey, flying toward the horizon to where earth and heaven met. There he came to a staircase that he climbed with some difficulty and reached the great celestial meadow. A crowd rushed up to him and his spirits, among whom he saw his father, who gave him a good deal of information about this world of the dead, and when he saw that the night was drawing to a close, added: "Now you must make haste to return before daybreak; otherwise you must remain here for all eternity."[26]

On another occasion, Avggo decided to visit the land of the dead beneath the surface of the earth. His soul went off with his guardian spirits into the depths of the sea. They came upon a kind of path and went deeper and deeper, until they finally touched upon a frontier between the earth and the sea, formed by a river of foam that could only be crossed by jumping on the stones jutting out of the water. The soul crossed, climbed a very slippery cliff "where the dead had a habit of wandering during their journey between the earth and the underworld," and it was welcomed by a large crowd of people. Avggo discovered all the wonders of the abysses, and then came back.[27] In the medieval visions discussed earlier we have already encountered some of these elements, such as the river and the bridge, which is represented here by the stones.

How did this gradual slide from shamanism into the fairy tale come about? This is what "The Ancestor Who Visited the Land of the Dead" tells us:

> Having plummeted into despair by the death of her two sons, a woman lost consciousness at the end of two days and everyone thought she was dead. She then saw that she was on the road to the land of the departed, spotted a huge hole in the celestial vault, snuck there by crawling, came to a large revolving stone, and heard a voice asking: "Is that a dead person who has just arrived?" She then saw her grandmother, who shouted to her: "You must answer that I am not dead but a living person who just got here." The question was repeated a little farther on and she gave the same response. She then entered a house where she found her sons trapped in ice up to their legs because she had mourned their deaths too strongly. "Those are your tears that covered our feet and turned into ice," they told her. The grandmother invited her to go home and she reluctantly agreed. She passed again by the now motionless stone and reached the opening leading into the sky. Here she met a young man from her country who was crawling into the sky. She pushed him before her, despite his resistance, and made him return home. Through the window she saw the man's body had been laid out on the ground and that people believed him to be dead. But because she had brought his soul back, his body came back to life. The woman's soul next reentered her body and she came back to life.[28]

Without the text stating so explicitly, the woman behaves like a shaman and brings a soul back from the beyond. The primitive belief is masked, and a story motif is introduced into the text, one known to folklorists as "A child returns from the dead" (AT 769), in which a dead child bowed down under the weight of a heavy pitcher appears to his mother and explains to her that the pitcher contains the tears she has spilled because of him, tears that are causing his suffering. Among the corpus of old Scandinavian ballads, "Fæstemanden i Graven (Aage og Else)" (The Betrothed in the Grave [Aage and Else]) features a dead man who comes back to ask his fiancée to stop weeping for him:

Every time you weep for me,
and you are troubled in mind:
my coffin is soon filled
with clotted blood.

. . .

Every time you sing to me
and you are joyous in mind:
then my tomb is hung about
with rosy leaves.[29]

From this short overview of the traces of shamanism in folktale traditions, we can see that the otherworld has replaced the beyond, that it borders our own world, that the hero needs help and advice, and that animals play an important role there, either as means of transport—a magical horse, an eagle—or as counselors. The hero understands the language of the animals, which is already a sign of being chosen.

ELEVEN

THE EXPERIENCE OF IMMINENT DEATH (NDE, OBE)

From the perspective of contemporary science, visions are considered as the product of disassociative states or OBEs (out-of-body experiences),[1] which occur when consciousness is nullified by sleep, a fainting spell, a coma or a catatonic state, or as a consequence of an NDE (near-death experience).[2] In 1943, George Tyrrell[3] saw in these OBEs—he created the concept—the proof of life after death. In the Middle Ages, if we eliminate the narratives that arise from the mystics,* the OBEs were caused by illness. The psychiatrist Philippe Wallon has noted:

> In a general manner, it has been observed that if the subject is near death, in a state of anoxia (with an absence of oxygen), the data are verified, whereas if it is a simple reduction of consciousness obtained with the help of meditation techniques, the results are often false. The information appears to be more accurate the deeper the state of unconsciousness.[4]

According to psychoanalysis, a vision is a projection of mental content outside our system of spatial reference. But in the neurosciences, the brain is capable of electrical activity organized during the course of

---

*The mystics obtain their visions through fasting, mortification, and ascetic practices.

the early phase of clinical death,[5] which would explain the autoscopic hallucinations and discorporations.

Let us take note, in passing, of an interesting linguistic detail: in the case of accident victims and other injured people in similar situations, a team of intensive-care specialists known as *réanimateurs* (resuscitators)* will step in. It so happens that the sixteenth-century verb *ranimer* was replaced later by *réanimer* with the meaning "to restore vital functions and bring back to consciousness." The latter term, *réanimer,* was coined from *re* (back, return, etc.) + *anima* (soul), which gives this word its full depth and can be understood as meaning "to bring the soul back into the body," to bring back to life, to resuscitate.

At the present time, science would explain visions of an otherworldly journey as the product of a disassociative state of consciousness, but the case of Godescalc (see page 46) does not fall into the context that describes, unless it also acknowledges the (psychosomatic) effect of the mind over the physical body, which is completely possible. This is shown by the various examples of people bearing stigmata: from the thirteenth century to the present day, "the names of over 350 people bearing stigmata have been recorded, the majority of whom were women."[6]

The sensation of leaving the body has been attested to in numerous accounts. For example, Ernest Hemingway, who was wounded by a shell during World War One, had the impression of leaving his body. He described his experience in his semi-autobiographical novel *A Farewell to Arms:* "I tried to breathe but my breath would not come and I felt myself rush bodily out of myself and out and out and out and all the time bodily in the wind. I went out swiftly, all of myself and I knew I was dead and that it had all been a mistake to think you just died. Then I floated, and instead of going on I felt myself slide back. I breathed and I was back."[7]

Of the many accounts of this phenomenon, I would like to cite Kristel Cahanin-Caillaud, who tells of her impression after a car

---

*[The French term *réanimateurs* could be more literally analyzed as "reanimators." —*Trans.*]

accident of seeing herself located above her body. From a second coma that lasted four weeks, she retained the memory of leaving her body again, during which time she had a sensation of fullness and an absence of suffering. She was at the edge of a luminous tunnel that was drawing her to it, but she was connected to a cord and had the choice of holding on to it and returning to her body, or of letting go of it and leaving.[8]

RAYMOND MOODY'S RESEARCH

Since the appearance of Raymond Moody's very successful book *Life After Life*, many people have studied the phenomena connected to illness and accidents, essentially when such situations have caused a catatonic state or coma, during which accident victims see themselves outside of their body or even heading for the afterlife. From a corpus comprised of three hundred accounts, Moody has extracted the essential elements of these narratives: the person affected hears an unpleasant noise and then quickly passes through a tunnel, which for some people becomes darker and for others is luminous. A being of light appears that is often identified as an angel. The accident victims see their entire life flash before their eyes, and then a demarcation line seems to appear that separates their life on earth from the one to follow, but they are—quite reluctantly—compelled to go back into their body. None of this is new, and quite a large number of medieval texts offer remarkable parallels.

The NDE specialists who know this, or who have integrated it into their research, are quite rare, however, since a diachronic perspective is not their primary concern. Their books seek to show that death is not an end and allow their readers to soothe themselves with a gentle hope. But even as early as the twelfth century in Iceland, the dead had the good fortune of returning to their families and feasting with them. An identical thought underlies these concepts.

Raymond Moody sees the near-death experience as presenting the following structure:

A man is dying and, as he reaches the point of greatest physical distress, he hears himself pronounced dead by his doctor. He begins to hear an uncomfortable noise, a loud ringing or buzzing, and at the same time feels himself moving very rapidly through a long dark tunnel. After this, he suddenly finds himself outside of his own physical body, but still in the immediate physical environment, and he sees his own body from a distance, as though he is a spectator. He watches the resuscitation attempt from this unusual vantage point and is in a state of emotional upheaval.

. . . Others come to meet and to help him. He glimpses the spirits of relatives and friends who have already died. . . . At some point, he finds himself approaching some sort of barrier or border, apparently representing the limit between earthly life and the next life. Yet, he finds that he must go back to the earth, that the time for his death has not yet come. At this point he resists, for by now he is taken up with his experiences in the afterlife and does not want to return. . . .

Later he tries to tell others, but he has trouble doing so. In the first place, he can find no human words adequate to describe the unearthly episodes. He also finds that others scoff, so he stops telling other people. Still, the experience affects his life profoundly, especially his views about death and its relationship to life.[9]

Medievalists reading Moody would not be surprised because they would recognize themselves to be in a very familiar terrain, that of the literature of revelations and visions. During the Middle Ages the term *visio* did not have its current meaning. It meant a state of *ecstasy* (from the Greek ἐκ, "on the outside," + ἵστημι, "to stand, to be outside oneself"), in other words, an exit of the soul from the body (*raptus extra corpus*), and, simultaneously, a state of revelation.[10] The soul of the visionary is carried away by a bird (as in the visions of Alberic, Baldarius, and the Monk of Vaucelles) or by an angel or archangel, and the texts state explicitly *in extasi raptus* (carried away in ecstasy), *raptus in spiritu* (carried away in spirit), and that his soul hovered over his body. In the *Book of Visions*, Otloh of Sankt Emmeram put these words in the mouth of someone possessed by trance: "I felt myself acting not in flesh but in spirit" (*non carnaliter sed spiritualiter agi sentirem*).[11]

Moody and his successors have thus recognized a certain number of motifs, such as those mentioned above, which call to mind the journeys into the region beyond this world. But these researchers did not take the medieval visions into consideration—Moody was only familiar with the vision of Dryhthelm. However, the correspondence between the motifs of these visions and near-death experiences shows that the visions cannot be reduced to narratives from religious literature, and that they are not simply a collection of descriptions borrowed from the Bible and the apocryphal texts, but are also the ancestors of contemporary accounts of NDEs. In this regard, they cannot be considered as inventions, and they deserve to be taken into account by the science of thanatology and that of clinical psychology.

THE INVESTIGATION BY KARL OSIS AND ERLENDUR HARALDSSON

Karl Osis and Erlendur Haraldsson conducted an investigation into NDEs[12] using a corpus of three hundred accounts collected by doctors and nurses from North America and India. Both of them devoted themselves to a statistical study that is interesting in several respects, which I will summarize below:

❋ 80 percent of these individuals had visions of the afterlife.

❋ 18 percent had apparitions of the dead or of religious figures.

❋ Out of one hundred patients, eighteen saw living individuals, forty-seven saw dead people, and thirty-five saw religious figures.

With regard to the apparitions of the dead, 90 percent of these were people close to the person experiencing the NDE, that is, family members or friends; 65 percent of the time their purpose was to bring the patient into the afterlife. The patient's reaction to this was positive 72 percent of the time and negative 28 percent of the time. When the reaction was positive, the comatose individual resisted the return of his spirit into the body. Those who objected to returning were essentially Indians, as in the following case: an Indian who had some university education was recovering from mastoiditis and was scheduled to be discharged from the hospital that day. Suddenly he shouted, "Here is someone dressed in white! I will not go with him!" But five minutes later, he was pronounced dead.[13]

On the other hand, a little girl suffering from a congenital heart disease who was experiencing a crisis told how she had seen her mother, who brought her a beautiful white dress, similar to the one she had. She was happy and begged her to get up and come with her because she was ready to take her on her journey. This vision made the girl extremely happy and calm until her death, which occurred four hours later.[14]

The fact that the religion of the person who experiences an NDE is a decisive factor is revealed in many accounts. A man that was afflicted with severe head trauma described this to his pastor:

> I was with the Lord. I rode in a heavenly vehicle through space toward a bright light. The light got brighter and brighter as the craft got closer. I stopped at the gate to a magnificent city with an indescribable beauty. I was surrounded by angels and loved ones. . . . Just as I was about to be ushered through the pearly gates, two heavenly beings stopped me. "You can't go through," they said, "You must return."[15]

The vision of the city brings to mind the description of Heavenly Jerusalem, and the account precisely reflects the patient's Christian upbringing. Ralph Wilkerson's report of the testimony of a Christian carpenter who fell victim to a heart attack and was mistakenly pronounced dead also mentions a brilliant city and a resplendent light emanating from the right side of Jesus's throne. The patient then stated:

> Then a strange thing happened. My attention was attracted to the hospital, and I could see my body lying upon the bed. . . . I asked Jesus what I should do. His answer was a question: "What do you want to do?" I replied that I preferred to stay with Him, but that if He would be with me and give me the fulfillment of a ministry I had never gained, I would elect to go back to Earth.[16]

The comparison between Americans and Indians therefore shows that each person sees deities corresponding to their religion, which reflects the influence of the cultural and religious environment, as well as the subject's personal history.

The parallels that can be found between the visions and NDEs (OBEs) at the time of death are quite surprising:

✻ Separation of body and soul.

✻ The soul leaves this world, often by crossing through darkness into the light.

✻ It enters a world that contains one or more spaces.

✻ It meets individuals, some of whom have haloes.

✻ The meeting gives it great joy.

✻ The soul cannot stay in this infra-world.

✻ It reluctantly returns to its body.

Myriad other details are often added, such as:

✻ The soul hears magnificent music.

✻ It sees a river.

✻ It is serene.

✻ Time is suspended.

✻ The experience is ineffable.

✻ The narrator encounters skepticism from witnesses.[17]

The essential differences between the medieval visions and the NDEs should not be overlooked. These differences are simply a reflection of the evolution of mindsets or mentalities over time. Today, images such as the weighing of souls, hell, purgatory, demons, and torture[18] have vanished because religion has lost its influence, and, since the time of the Enlightenment, theology has become increasingly indifferent about punishments in the afterlife, whereas the latter were a major concern in medieval sermons and exempla. Individuality and autonomy have become much more pronounced, and this is how the person on death's threshold can travel by himself from darkness into light, whereas in the medieval visions a guide was needed. One final difference is that in modern OBEs and NDEs the victims of accidents and other patients see their whole lives flash before their eyes in a fraction of a second. This was never the case in the Middle Ages.

The comparison of the results of near-death-experience studies with the medieval literature of revelations tends to show that we are facing the same phenomenon, but one that is perceived differently due to the centuries of evolving mentalities that separate the two ends of the chain of transmission. Each era has recorded in its own way the type of experiences that were undergone. Here the law of ecotypes presents a temporal variant, as opposed to a spatial (geographical) one.

The kinship between the experiences undergone by these visionaries *in hora mortis* [at the hour of death] and the narratives of the Middle Ages is undeniable and shows—as if this were necessary—the unity of the human mind, or "unity of the psychic" as Max Wundt described it.* God's image has gradually changed, and it is a God of kindness and mercy who has come forward, to the detriment of the God whose wrath struck down those who violated his law. Nowadays, an appeal is made to other sentiments, especially that of hope. Through a curious reversal, we find pagan concepts returning: the otherworld is not a dreadful place, it is only the transition from one form of life to another, where we find again those we loved and who live in the beyond according to ancestral beliefs (attested to by the stories of revenants and the offerings of food and drink made on graves). We could say that we have gone back to the times when the archetypes gave shape to memories, something that would hardly surprise those researchers who speak here of atavistic and even genetic memory.

---

*[Wilhelm Max Wundt (1832–1920) was a leading figure in the establishment of several areas of modern psychology, including experimental psychology. —*Ed.*]

THE INVESTIGATION OF HUBERT KNOBLAUCH

By concentrating on Germany and by taking into consideration the ancient opposition between East and West along with other parameters, Hubert Knoblauch based his work on a large corpus of accounts and showed that the structure of these narratives about the NDE vary and are subject to cultural and social factors. He charted the results of his investigation in the following way:

Motifs	Region		Sex		Religion		Total
	West	East	Male	Female	Church member	non-member	
Wonderful Sensations	59.5	40.0	43.9	56.1	56.7	46.2	50.0
Life Recap	42.9	45.0	48.8	39.0	43.3	44.2	43.9
Horrible World	16.7	10.0	17.1	9.8	16.7	11.5	13.4
Tunnel	31.0	45.0	39.0	36.6	53.3	28.8	37.8
Full Awareness	66.7	62.5	61.0	68.3	63.3	65.4	64.6
Leaving the Body	38.1	22.5	34.1	26.8	23.3	34.6	30.5
Light	50.0	30.0	31.7	48.8	40.0	40.4	40.2
Heavenly World	45.2	30.0	29.3	46.3	40.0	36.5	37.8
Horrible Sensations	28.6	60.0	48.8	39.0	50.0	40.4	43.9
Feeling of Being Dead	28.6	22.5	19.5	31.7	26.7	25.0	25.6
Entering Another World	54.8	40.0	43.9	51.2	46.7	48.1	47.6
Contact with the Dead	11.9	20.0	17.1	14.6	20.0	13.5	15.9
Meeting with the Living	31.0	32.5	31.7	31.7	33.3	30.8	31.7
Meeting with Nonhumans	11.9	10.0	9.8	12.2	10.0	11.5	11.0
Total n	42	40	41	41	30	52	82

What this table reveals is that the NDEs were experienced as positive in the West (59 percent felt wonderful sensations) and negative in the East (60 percent felt horrible sensations). Religion also played a role, albeit a modest one: the faith of 22 percent of the people who had an

NDE became stronger, but 28 percent were of the opinion that nothing survives after death.

Researchers have ventured a scientific interpretation, which the French philosopher Edgar Morin has mentioned in an interview.[19] One NDE study[20] notes that 20 percent of heart attack victims have this kind of experience. A sociologist cites an experiment performed on rats by researchers at the University of Michigan during the thirty seconds that separates cardiac arrest from brain death. They found that the brain experienced more intense activity than in the waking state, with an increase of "gamma waves," brain frequencies associated with heightened levels of consciousness, showing that the brain is capable of highly organized electrical activity during the phase preceding clinical death.

This observation can offer an explanation for what the victims of NDEs see: the replay of their lives and meeting family members. This electrical activity seems to permit a liberation of the unconscious that projects its own concerns, hence the importance of religious elements and their differences based on culture.

We may mention one final detail: visions and NDEs are supported in fact by a particular conception of the soul or spirit as an entity that can escape out of the body. A very similar notion is also found in shamanism or trance.

In short, what science defines as "non-ordinary states of consciousness,"[21] and which replace the illness of the visions and the coma of NDEs, would allow for the occurrence of an out-of-body journey to the beyond or into another world. There is a study waiting to be undertaken here, the foundations for which have already been laid by Saint Anne Hospital in Paris, in collaboration with the Ethnological Institute at the University of Strasbourg in its degree program "Anthropology of the Trance." This touches on a variety of different phenomena: appearances of the Virgin Mary, appearances of saints or ghosts, abduction by aliens, poltergeists, precognition, dual-personality experiences, NDEs, meetings with "little people," meetings with incubi or succubi, and so on—in other words, the entire palette of the visions.

CONCLUSION

Now that we have reached the end of this investigation—which has taken us from classical antiquity to the present day, and allowed us to gather some revealing testimonies—we may draw some conclusions.

Whether they concern journeys into the afterlife by visionaries or near-death phenomena, the texts all state that the afterlife is not the only otherworld, that the human beings can go there in spirit or in body, and that death is not an end. This notion is condensed in the folktales and in the legends, even though the former often use euphemisms for death, whereas the latter transcribe "reality" as it is perceived and interpreted by its witnesses. And then word of mouth comes into play and has its effects: the narratives lose or gain elements, and move closer to—or further away from—mythology and religion.

The durability and longevity of the underlying thought is staggering, and I have already noted the similarities between the experiences of those who were in a trance and those who were victims of an accident. The neurosciences, psychiatry, and psychology are all well positioned to shed new light on these phenomena.

The beliefs brought to light in this study are partially explained by the (crazy?) idea that death is merely the change of a state or world, and not a journey into nothingness. These texts are therefore bearing a message of hope, and this hope is reflected wonderfully in the medieval lays and the folktales: the man who has been wronged, injured, or abandoned receives assistance from supernatural beings that represent a form of belief in transcendence. This assistance may come from God, angels, saints, or—in a secularized variant—from fairies. In this way the literature tells us that man is not alone and should never despair of his fate because resignation is the worst of evils.

The texts I have cited (with no claim at being exhaustive) have their contemporary extensions in novels, heroic fantasy, and films. Novelists and filmmakers alike have latched on to NDEs, thereby helping to give greater popularity to these phenomena. In 2009 Gayle Forman published the novel *If I Stay*, which tells the story of a young woman suffering a coma in the wake of an accident that took the lives of her parents and brother. She then leaves her body and watches her family and friends. She has to face a dilemma: join her parents and brother in the afterlife, or come back to life to be with her other close friends.

In Bernard Werber's *Les Thanotonautes* (The Thanatonauts; 1994), the story starts with an out-of-body experience. Michael, a man who suffered an accident, soars out of his body and then falls back. The issue is then to draw up a map of the beyond. Jean Bresson gets past the somatic wall, a blue territory and another that is black; a second thanotonaut succeeds in getting over the red wall, and so on. The explorers of the beyond overcome trials and ordeals, and their quest for knowledge is punctuated with dangers. In *The Lord of the Rings*, J. R. R. Tolkien stages the battle of the Hobbits (men) of Middle Earth (Miðgarðr!) against the absolute evil embodied by Sauron, whose henchmen are monstrous creatures: it brings to mind Dante's *Inferno*.

La Porte des enfers (The Gate to Hell) by Laurent Gaudé, a very original novel inspired by Virgil, essentially recounts the following:

To retrieve his dead son, Matteo descends into the underworld with the guidance of an old, ailing priest, Don Mazerotti. A *professore* tells them where an entrance can be found in Naples, and the two men set off. After an hour's walk in darkness, they reach a room in which a pale light is floating. The continue on and enter a forest— the "Howling Wood"—whose thorn-covered trees scratch them as they pass. They then hear cries and are attacked by disembodied entities. They come out of the forest and find themselves in front of a giant portal, the Gate to Below. The old priest dies; his double leaves his body and guides Matteo farther into a meadow "covered with black grass." They reach and cross the River of Tears, after which they scale a hill of slag where they see the dead. The shade of Don Mazerotti leads Matteo to a rocky wall into which a door has been carved. On the other side they find the Bloody Bushes, which they cross through to reach the hall of the dead to come.

When they leave it, they find themselves on a terrace overlooking an immense valley. In its center they see the citadel of the dead on a promontory. A growing noise captures their attention; it is made by the dead, among whom Matteo spots his son. He grabs him and retraces his steps, but his strength is failing. Don Mazerotti then explains to him: "[Death] will not let you leave again. You stole a shade from him; he wants a life in exchange." The priest crosses through the gate with the child and comes back to life, and the door shuts on Matteo.[1]

The reader will easily recognize the similarity of this novel with the medieval visions: river, valley, mountain, the same countryside, and the Howling Wood with the sharp thorns are reminiscent of the field that Godescalc has to cross. This is the way depictions of the afterlife are transmitted by way of a thousand channels. Is it necessary to underscore again the obvious kinship of the fictional backdrop with shamanism? And isn't the search and rescue of a soul in hell the storyline of the myth of Orpheus?

Randall Wallace dealt with the theme of near death in his film *Heaven Is for Real* (2014). Following surgery, a pastor's son says he saw heaven and Christ, and that he met family members he had never heard mentioned before.

Kazumi Yumoto's novel *Journey to the Shore* inspired the 2015 film of the same name by Kiyoshi Kurosawa, the plot of which is as follows. A dead fisherman returns to see his wife and tells her how he traveled throughout Japan after his death and sympathized with both the living and the dead. He asks her to come with him so she can see what he saw. The dead can therefore leave the beyond and come find those who had been close to them, which brings us back to a detail that is common to many near-death experiences. The tone is much darker than in Kurosawa's film *Real* (2013), which retells the story of Orpheus and Eurydice with a reversal of roles—it is the heroine, Koichi, who brings her comatose husband back to life.

What we see is the same ancient and ceaselessly updated set of beliefs that have been adapted to the local culture, but whose structure remains strictly the same—only the paradigms vary. This is how a new mythology is continuously created that attests to the fascination exerted upon human beings by the unknown—an unknown whose most beautiful illustration remains death.

INDEX OF SIGNS, SYMBOLS, AND OMENS

In the mentalities of earlier epochs, everything was a sign: the meeting of a person (priest, prostitute, and so on), birds (*aves ominales*), an animal (fox, wolf . . .), the call of a bird, untimely phenomena (thunder in winter or during Christmas), a dream, sneezing, and so forth. Philippe Walter notes: "Even when illiterate, people possess their own system for decoding the world. It only works through observation. At the basis of everything, the people believe there is a generalized system of analogies at work in the universe. . . . Beliefs are therefore based on an analogical code."[1] John of Salisbury (d. 1180) speaks of this at length in his *Polycraticus*. In a letter (*Epistola* 65) Pierre de Blois (d. ca. 1200) provides a list of unpropitious (*infaustus*) omens (dreams, meeting a hare, a woman with disheveled hair, a hunchback, etc.), and the preacher Berthold of Regensberg (d. 1272) writes: "There are those who believe in ill omens: meeting a wolf would be a good omen, even though this beast does harm to the whole world. . . . On the other hand, meeting a priest who has received the orders would be a bad omen."[2]

Announcing the Deceased

A person has to announce the death of the master or mistress of the house to the horses by jingling their keys; the same is done for the bees and other animals; otherwise they will die, the trees will wither, and the bees will disappear or leave (Lithuania; Grimm, *DM,* III, 492).

When someone in a house dies, those who keep honeybees must

definitely make sure to announce the recent unfortunate event at each hive, and then attach a small piece of black cloth to it, else they will soon perish (France).

When the master of the house dies, the person who takes his place must introduce himself to the bees (Germany).[3]

Barley Grain

On Christmas morning a barley grain can be found beneath the table at each place where during the eve someone was eating Christmas porridge. If one of the grains is hollow, it announces the death within the year of the person who was sitting there (Norway; Liebrecht, *Volkskunde*, 326).

The person who finds a hollow barley grain in his food will soon die (Norway; Liebrecht, *Volkskunde*, 326).

Bed

If the bed is placed so the feet of the person sleeping in it are pointing toward the door, he will die (Harz, Germany).

The person who lies on a bed he has inherited cannot die (Germany).

If you stand at the foot of the deathbed, you make the individual's agony more painful (Germany).

The feet of the bed should not face the door, because the bodies of the dead are carried out feet first (France; Mozzani, *Livre*, 1,000).

Bell, Clock

When the bells produce a dull sound, or they echo again after being rung, a person will die soon after (Germany).

If the bells sound dully, a death will follow (Schmidt, *Rockenphilosophie*, IV, 5).

If the sound of the bell continues to vibrate long after it has been rung, it is because death is hovering over someone in the parish (Brittany; Le Braz, *Légende*, 10).

If the church bell sounds on Sunday during the Paternoster or the Amen, one of the parishioners present will soon die (Germany).

If the clock chimes during the Christmas meal, a member of the family will pass away (Germany).

If the corpse changes color when the bells are rung, it is because he is inhaling dirt.

If the clocks sound at the same time as the bells ringing to summon people to prayer, someone will die (Schmidt, *Rockenphilosophie*, III, 24).

If two bells of the city sound at the same time, two spouses will die (Germany).

If the castle clock is not functioning properly, a nobleman of the lineage will perish (Pforzheim, Germany; Grimm, *DM*, III, 455).

A clock stopping inexplicably is a portent of death for a person in the family (Wales; Owen, *Welsh Folk-Lore*, 304).

Birthmark

If a pregnant woman remains standing or sitting by the foot of a bed in which someone is dying, the child she is carrying will bear a blue mark above the nose called a *bière*. This means that the child does not have long to live (France; Thiers, *Traité*, IV, 1).

Blood

Three cold drops of blood dripping from your nose is a sure sign that someone close to you is going to die (Scotland; Gregor, *Echo*, 135).

Broom

If someone sweeps the room right after someone's death, he or she will soon die (Germany).

Burial

When one is bearing a dead person to be buried, he must be set on the ground at every crossroads (Tyrol, Austria; Heyl, *Volkssage*, 780).

A Wallachian is never buried in the morning because those close to him want to hasten the departure of the soul with the setting of the sun; they fear that in the morning, when the sun rises, the soul of the dead person will not stray out and thus become victim of a vampire (Wallachia; Schott, *Walachische Märchen*, 302).

A burial should not on any account be looked at from a window. Whoever does so will soon follow the dead person into the grave (Scotland; Gregor, *Notes*, 214).

Burrowing Owl

The burrowing owl comes out of the cemetery to find the person or persons destined to die in the year (Nièvre, France; Mozzani, *Livre*, 438).

If the burrowing owl is flying with its claws in the air above a house, someone is going to die there (Rolland, *Faune*, II, 43–49).

Candle, Taper

The candle on the married couple's table that goes out first will indicate which of them will die before the other (Norway; Liebrecht, *Volkskunde*, 323).

When the candle that was left to burn all night is put out on Christmas morning, its smoke will drift toward the person destined to die in the coming year. If it floats toward the door, a corpse will be taken out through it that year (Norway; Liebrecht, *Volkskunde*, 326).

A candle that goes out on its own in a house is a herald of death (Schmidt, *Rockenphilosophie*, IV, 8. Tyrol; Heyl, *Volkssage*, 780).

One must light and extinguish a consecrated candle near the person dying, and then make a cross above him with the smoking wick; this will keep the spirits from approaching (Tyrol; Heyl, *Volkssage*, 780).

A death is often announced by the candle of death (Scottish: *dead-can'le*) that can be seen moving around the house in which the death will occur, and along the road that will be taken to the grave site (Scotland; Gregor, *Echo*, 133).

Around 1820, when people wanted to know whether an ailing person would live or die, they placed five yellow wax candles on either side of Saint Abilon's altar, five for life and five for death. If the life candles went out, the patient would die (Sébillot, *Folk-lore*, IV, 154).

In the courtyard of Prémorvan-en-Pluduno castle (Cotes-d'Armor), if someone sees a candle burning down to the floor go out, someone in the village will die within twelve hours (Sébillot, *Folk-lore*, IV, 193).

If the candle on the altar goes out of its own accord, the preacher will die within the year (Schmidt, *Rockenphilosophie*, II, 58).

If the candles on one side of a married couple are casting a weaker light, the member of the couple on that side will die first (Prussia, Germany).

The dead man's candle (*canwyll georff:* "corpse candle") is an omen of death. It is a torch with a blue flame that moves forward; sometimes it is held by the ghost of the future deceased (Wales; Owen, *Welsh Folk-Lore*, 298–301).

You should never burn three candles at the same time in one room, otherwise it is a sign that the three candles of death will soon be lit: one for the bedside, another on the table, and the last one in the hearth (Brittany; Le Braz, *Légende,* 9).

A taper that goes out during the *Quarantaine* (the forty days following the death) is a herald of someone's death (France, Metz region; Mozzani, *Livre,* 441). In the country of Wales, this means the pastor's death is imminent.

A flow of wax means a coffin in the house (Wuttke, *Volksaberglaube,* §296).

In the north of England, a shroud is called a "winding sheet," and in Scotland, a "dead pale."

Cat

Coming across a black cat announces a death (Germany).

If cats are grooming themselves in the window of a sick person, death is close (Schmidt, *Rockenphilosophie,* I, 71).

If the cats in the house of a sick person bite one another, he will not be long in passing away (Germany).

Chair

Once the coffin has been picked up, you must turn all the chairs over and leave them upside down until sunset or until people have returned from the burial, otherwise the spirit of the dead person will come back (Scotland; Gregor, *Notes,* 212).

Child

The child that falls asleep during its baptism shall soon pass away (Estonia; Grimm, *DM,* III, 490).

The children who cry during their baptism die soon afterward, or precede their parents to the grave (Germany).

The children who die unbaptized join the Wild Hunt (Württemberg, Germany).

In Lower Normandy it is believed that the little dead children who stick their arms out of their graves are those who raised their hands against their parents (Bosquet, *Normandie,* 263. Germany; Wuttke, *Volksaberglaube,* §307).

When unweaned children die, a bottle of mother's milk is placed in their coffin; their mother will no longer have milk or aching breasts (Germany).

Church
Anyone who falls ill in a church shall perish (Schmidt, *Rockenphilosophie,* III, 89).

Coffin
If the coffin echoes with a dull noise when it is shut, another member of the household shall die (Worms, Germany; Grimm, *DM,* III, 452).

One should not bump the door sill with the end of the coffin, otherwise all the inhabitants of the house shall die (Germany).

Along the path taken by the funeral procession, the front of the coffin should be struck against the pedestal of all the crosses erected on the sides the road (Brittany; Le Braz, *Légende,* I, 295–96).

The coffin of a newborn child should not be nailed shut, otherwise its mother will not have any more children (Ireland; Wilde, *Ancient Legends,* 214).

You must not interrupt the carpenter making the coffin if you want the dead person to rest in peace (Pforzheim, Germany; Grimm, *DM,* III, 455).

Communion
If a sick person takes communion, he or she will die (Schmidt, *Rockenphilosophie,* IV, 78).

Construction
The construction of a house will bring about the death of the owner after a short time (Gregor, "Rites," 173).

When a new house is being built, the step of the threshold has no sooner been installed than the Ankou comes to sit on it to wait and see who will be the first person of the family to cross it; it is necessary to have any kind of domestic animal cross it first, or, to draw him away, give him the life of some animal as tribute (Le Braz, *Légende,* I, 157–58).

The person who moves into a new house must first toss a living creature in it before him—a cat or a dog, because the first to enter the house will die (Chemnitz, Germany; Grimm, *DM,* III, 451).

Contagion

Some launder the linen used by a dead person during his or her illness, to prevent it from causing the death of those who use it after them (France; Thiers, *Traité*, IV, 3).

There are some who maintain that the honeybees which are around the patient's house when extreme unction is being administered, die a short time later (France; Thiers, *Traité*, IX, 7).

When the master of the dwelling has deceased, the hives of the honeybees are covered with a black sheet so they do not die for want of wearing mourning for their master (France; Thiers, *Traité*, IX, 7).

The fire in the fireplace is extinguished and the perishable goods are thrown away because the spirit of the dead person could corrupt them. This is done between the time of death and the funeral (England; Mozzani, *Livre*, 1,156).

When a woman gives birth to a stillborn child, it is necessary to not take the body out of the room through the door but through the window for fear that all the babies the woman will give birth to later will also be stillborn (France; Thiers, *Traité*, IV, 1).

If one cuts a sprig of rosemary and places it on the dead person in his grave, the entire bush will die once that sprig rots (Schmidt, *Rockenphilosophie*, IV, 50).

The death of the master of the house is announced to the horses by jangling his keys, and it is also announced to the other animals, especially to the bees, otherwise the livestock will die, the trees will wither, and the bees will die or leave (Latvia; Grimm, *DM*, III, 492).

When a cadaver passes in front of a house, all the hives should be turned over, otherwise they will be "cursed" (Tyrol; Heyl, 781).

If a pregnant woman passes by a grave, her child will not be long in dying (Schmidt, *Rockenphilosophie*, IV, 15).

A funeral procession should never cross through a field, even if it is fallow (Estonia; Grimm, *DM*, III, 489).

When a couple on their way to get married in church come across a dead person, the husband will be the first to die if the dead person is of the same sex; on the contrary, the bride will be the first to die if the corpse is the same sex as her (France; Thiers, *Traité*, X, 5).

When there is a dead person in the house, the hives must be moved, and the wine and vinegar shaken, otherwise the bees will perish, the wine will turn, and the vinegar spoil (Spire, Germany).

The birdcages, flowers, and hives belonging to a dead person must be moved or covered with cloth, and his casks must be knocked three times (Ansbach, Germany; Grimm, *DM*, III, 458).

At the moment someone dies, the seeds in the granary must be turned over and the wine in the cellar shaken, otherwise the sowed grain will not sprout and the wine will turn (Germany; Grimm, *DM*, III, 467).

At the time someone dies, it is necessary to wake up everyone who is sleeping, particularly children, otherwise they will quickly follow the dead person (Germany).

When there is a death in the house, all the casks must be knocked on, otherwise the wine will turn (Worms; Grimm, *DM*, III, 453).

The coffin of a woman who died in labor should not be carried on the shoulders but with ropes (Germany).

When the death knell is sounding, people shouldn't eat, otherwise they will get a toothache (Schmidt, *Rockenphilosophie*, I, 39).

A child should not be baptized immediately following a burial, otherwise the child will follow the dead person (Grimm, *DM*, III, 489).

The tree on which a man has been hung withers (Germany).

If a grave remains open during a marriage ceremony it may be that they are burying a woman, man, or child. In the first case, the husband will be a widower; in the second, the wife a widow; and in the last case, all the children they raise will die young (Grimm, *DM*, III, 450).

A vehicle used to transport a dead person should not be returned immediately but left outside for some time, if not, several family members will die (Grimm, *DM*, III, 489).

Cricket
Crickets, dogs, and owls announce death with their cries or calls (Pforzheim, Germany; Grimm, *DM*, III, 455).

Cross
If the candle-snuffers have the appearance of a cross, a member of the family or of the household will not be long in dying (Norway; Liebrecht, *Volkskunde*, 326).

A member of the household will die soon if a horse rolls in front of the door and if two wisps of straw or two wood shavings form a cross on the ground; if the top wisp is longer, death will strike a man; if the cross is small, it will be a child (Norway; Liebrecht, *Volkskunde,* 313).

Some people place crosses in the crossroads at the time of a death so that the dead person can find his way back home when he wants to return, or when he goes to the Last Judgment (France; Thiers, *Traité,* IV, 1).

A halt must be made at every crossroads on the way to the cemetery, and small crosses should be placed at each (Brittany; Rio, *Voyage,* 103).

Crow

A crow or raven perched and croaking on a house where someone is ill means that the person is doomed to die (Germany).

Hearing the crow caw twice predicts the death of a man, three times, that of a woman (France; Mozzani, *Livre,* 509).

Crows flying around a house are a herald of discord and death (Tyrol).

When the crow caws near a house in which someone is sick, it is saying: "I am going to get you, I am waiting for you!" (Brittany; Mozzani, *Livre,* 509).

A crow crying around a dwelling announces a corpse, even if it is only that of an animal (Chemnitz, Germany; Grimm, *DM,* III, 450).

Cuckoo

The person who doesn't hear the cuckoo singing will die that same year (Tyrol).

If a cuckoo sings for three nights in a row over a house, there will soon be a death there (Prussia).

Danger

Whoever frees a soul from purgatory does not have long to live (Tyrol; Heyl, 782–83).

If someone steps on a needle that was used to stitch a shroud, there is a risk of being stuck by misfortune and even death (Vosges; Mozzani, *Livre,* 31).

You must never drink from a jar, otherwise you cannot die; if you have done it and your death agony is dragging on for too long, it is necessary for someone to put an upside-down jar on your face (Norway; Liebrecht, *Volkskunde,* 331).

If a piece of cloth or wool is passed in front of the dead person's mouth, a member of his family will pass away (Worms, Germany; Grimm, *DM*, III, 453).

If an article of clothing or cloth brushes the dead person's mouth, one of his relatives will die (Germany).

Someone who spins on Saturday night will come back after her death (Germany).

You must not donate a previously worn shirt for a shroud; otherwise the person who owned it will gradually waste away as it rots in the grave (France).

If the spun thread is not taken off the bobbin and is left on it all night, the next child will be hung one day (Germany).

Divination

On All Saints' Day, an offering of as many pieces of bread as there are members of a family should be made by casting them into water; the one whose piece of bread sinks like a stone will die soon (Brittany; Rio, *Voyage*, 34).

Nine pastry cakes—that represent silver, cradle, bread, ring, skull, old man, old woman, ladder, dish—should be cooked on the night of January 31. They are placed on nine plates, and each person helps themselves three times: whatever a person grabs will happen to them in the coming year (Lithuania).

One should put a pile of salt on the table on Christmas night; if it dissolves over the course of the night, someone will die the following year; if it remains intact, that person will remain alive (Germany; Grimm, *DM*, III, 475).

The first time you bake pastries after the New Year, you must make as many little cakes as there are people in the house. A name should be given to each cake and a hole made in it with your finger. The hole of the person destined to die will disappear when it is cooked, the others will remain (Schmidt, *Rockenphilosophie*).

Little breads for the New Year are cooked on the eve; each bread is given a name and it is believed that the one whose little bread opens when cooking will suffer from a life-threatening illness that year (Germany).

On the night of November 12, the ashes in the hearth should be flattened down; if, in the morning, they show footmarks leading to the door, a family member will die that year (Isle of Man; Rhŷs, *Celtic Folklore*, I, 318).

On the first of the year in some parishes of Finistère in the seventeenth century, offerings of a number of pieces of bread on which the names of family members were inscribed were made to springs; depending on whether the pieces floated or sank, people would know if they were going to die in the coming year (Brittany; Gaidoz, "Superstitions," 485).

To know if a disease was going to be fatal or not, the patient would be placed between two holes—one of life and one of death. Depending on which one he turned his face toward, he would either recover or die (Scotland).

The dead person's straw mattress would be thrown out and burned, and people would study the ashes to see what kind of footsteps appeared in them in order to deduce the imminent death of a man or beast (Grimm, *DM,* III, 489).

The person who puts Saint John's Wort in a beam of the living room—one sprig named for each person in the house—would know in what order these people would die. The plant that dried out first would indicate the person who would be the first to die (Germany).

Every member of the household should drop a penny with a hole in it in a pail of water on Saint Matthew's Day. The person whose penny sank would not live out the year (Germany).

Smooth stones should be taken out of a waterway and thrown over one's right shoulder, then placed in a peat fire for the entire night; if the ill person was not destined to recover, the stones, when knocked together, would make the sound of a bell (Ireland; Wilde, *Ancient Legends,* 206).

On New Year's night, periwinkle leaves would be placed on the stove or on a burning hot shovel. If they shriveled up it was a sign of good fortune; if they caught on fire, it was a sign of death (Germany).

If someone lay down at midnight between gravestones during the twelve days between Christmas and Epiphany, he would see those destined to die over the coming year pass by (Germany).

The clothing of the patient would be thrown into Gwynedd's well to know his or her fate; depending on which side they sank, it would be a prosnostication of death or recovery (Hebrides; Le Braz, *Légende,* I, 82).

The person who, after Midnight Mass, stops outside a cemetery and lets his gaze wander over it will see the dead strolling about and coming out of their graves, as well as those who would die over the coming year. If he saw a coffin, it is he who would die (Germany)

Doe
Whoever sees a doe on the night of Saint Ninoc'h will die on the day of his or her wedding (Brittany; Kérardven, *Guionvac'h*, 9).

Dog
Dogs that bark at night twice are a sign that death is threatening a woman; three times, it is a man (Corsica; Filippi, "Légendes," 466).

If a dog bursts out of the room of a patient, that person will die (Germany).

When dogs bark at night, it is because death is passing over (Germany).

A dog barking with its head lowered toward the ground is a herald of death (Germany; Grimm, *DM*, III, 473).

The side to which a barking dog turns is where the next corpse will come from (Germany; Grimm, *DM*, III, 476).

Door
Three knocks on the door are a herald of death (Brittany); likewise in Ireland if, at midnight, the knocks come three nights in a row. In Scotland the three knocks come at regular intervals, every one or two minutes (Gregor, *Notes*, 203).

The doors of the houses that the funeral procession passes must be shut to prevent the dead person from hiding there (Germany).

The door must be shut behind a dead person and someone must stay to guard the house, otherwise there will soon be another death (Germany).

The house should never be left empty during a burial, otherwise the dead person who is believed to have accompanied his corpse to the cemetery, will remain at the house to guard it (Brittany; Le Braz, *Légende*, I, 298).

When the corpse has left the house, someone knocks on the closed door three times so that the dead person never returns (Germany).

Dragonfly

If a dragonfly strikes someone's forehead, he will die within the year.

We should note that the dragonfly is called *mârte de dyâl*, "Devil's hammer" or *makrê*, "wizard" (Monseur, *Le Folklore wallon*, 14).

Dream

If you dream that the pall is falling down, it is the announcement of an imminent death (Germany).

Dreaming of water, especially murky water, predicts a death (Germany).

Dreaming of fish is a message that an acquaintance or an inhabitant of the house is soon to die. If the dream is of small fish, a child will die; if it is of big fish, it will be an adult (Germany).

Dreaming of horses is a sign of death, unless they are white (Brittany; Le Braz, *Légende*, 10).

When a person dreams about a wedding, it means the death of one of their friends (France).

A dream about a procession or about clergymen is a sign of death (France).

Someone who dreams about a church has to die (Germany).

Dreaming of laundry or water announces the death of relatives or acquaintances (Zinterle, *Sitten*, nr. 396).

Dreaming about a priest in a cassock means that the dreamer will die, or someone close to him, or a member of the household (Germany).

If someone dreams about pigs, a person will die soon (Zingerle, *Sitten*, nr. 398).

When someone dreams about a person carrying a load of dirty linen, it is a sign that one should soon lose someone close to him or her. If there is fresh water or salt water in a dream, it means that a family member is ill; if the water is clear, his or her life will be spared; if it is murky, he or she will surely die (Brittany; Le Braz, *Légende*, 10).

Eating

If the patient asks to eat after communion, he will die; if he asks for a drink, he will live (Chemnitz, Germany).

The person who is the first to take a serving of porridge on a feast day will be the guest that dies first (Norway; Liebrecht, *Volkskunde*, 337).

Encounter

When two night watchmen at either end of a street ring [alarms] together at the same time, an old woman living on that street will pass away (Germany).

If two close friends run into each other without recognizing one another, one of them is doomed to die (*feig*) (Norway; Liebrecht, *Volkskunde*, 337).

Fingernail, Toenail

If someone turns toward the north while cutting their nails or hair, he will die soon (Iceland; Liebrecht, *Volkskunde*, 369).

Fish

If a pregnant woman has a desire for fish, her child will die early or the woman will give birth prematurely (Germany).

Fox

If a fox, sometimes yelping, crosses the path to the cemetery in a single leap, a death is imminent (Norway; Liebrecht, *Volkskunde*, 326).

Frog

If you unexpectedly find a small green frog, which is called *ralet* or *graisse* in some lands, don't name it but hang it around the neck of a feverish person to heal him. If the animal dies soon, it is a sign that the patient will soon be better; but if it doesn't die for a long time, it is a sign that the patient will languish and is even in danger of dying (France; Thiers, *Traité*, V, 4).

Gift

If a woman dies when giving birth, a piece of an almond tree or a book should be placed in her bed, which should be unmade and remade every day, otherwise she will not rest in peace before six weeks have gone by (Schmidt, *Rockenphilosophie*, I, 36).

The peaceful rest of the dead person is dependent upon each of the people standing around his grave throwing three clumps of dirt into it (Ansbach, Germany; Grimm, *DM*, III, 458).

It is necessary to give a woman who has died in labor her scissors and everything needed for sewing (pincushion, thread, needle, thimble), otherwise she will come back to look for them (Pforzheim, Germany; Grimm, *DM,* III, 456).

For the dead person to find rest, he or she should be given a brush, silver, a needle, and thread. Some people brush the dead person's hair and leave the brush near him (Estonia; Grimm, *DM,* III, 489).

When the coffin is lowered into the grave, before it is filled, seven paupers are given an offering of seven kreutzers and seven loaves, with a candle stuck in each of them. It is believed that the soul of the dead person can thus pay for the seven border fees he must cross through to reach heaven. Next, these poor people are served a meal and depending on one's means, they are given a gift (Wallachia; Schott, *Walachische Märchen,* 302).

Money is placed in the mouths of the dead to prevent them from coming back when they have buried a treasure (Schmidt, *Rockenphilosophie,* III, 20).

This notion is the root of tales like "The Dead Man's Treasure" (Le Braz, *Légende,* I, 86–87).

It is believed that people who have buried a treasure have to remain between heaven and earth; they are seen in the form of white spirits.

Some place the largest piece of money they have in the dead person's right hand when the shroud is being put on so that he or she will receive a better welcome to the otherworld (France; Thiers, *Traité,* IV, 1).

A small coin is placed in the dead person's hand (Wallachia; *Walachische Märchen,* 315).

Some imagine that it gives the dead pleasure to have small cords woven with a few knots placed between their hands, or by having them tossed into their grave or tomb (France, Thiers, *Traité,* IV, 1).

So that a dead person does not remain naked in the otherworld, it is necessary to distribute his clothing to friends or to the poor. Those people should only wear these clothes to Mass for three consecutive Sundays; after that, they can wear them as they like (Curtin, *Tales,* 10).

Grave

It is a bad sign if a part of the tomb does not want to be shut (Germany).

If a grave is opened for a woman during a wedding, the husband will be a widower; if it is for a man, the bride will lose her husband; if it is for a child, other children will die (Chemnitz, Germany; Grimm, *DM,* III, 450).

If a pregnant woman walks over the grave of a suicide, the child she is carrying will die (Scotland; Gregor, *Notes,* 208).

If a married woman walks over graves, her child will have a clubfoot (Ireland; Wilde, *Ancient Legends,* 205).

If someone stumbles at a grave and then falls down to the ground, he will die before the year is out (Ireland; Wilde, *Ancient Legends,* 83).

If someone trips over a grave or walks on it, he will not be long in dying (Germany).

The person who fills the first grave will die soon after (Hebrides; MacPhail, "Folklore," 403).

If when digging a grave the dirt does not stop falling back into it, a member of the family or the village will die; the side from which it falls indicates from which direction death will come (Germany).

The gravedigger must only dig the grave on the day of the burial, otherwise the dead person will not leave us in peace (France).

When someone digs a grave in a church, a chapel, or a cemetery on a Sunday to bury someone, several people of the parish will die that same week (France; Thiers, *Traité,* V, 3).

Anyone who jumps over a grave will stop growing (Germany).

Grooming the Dead

The scissors of the tailor sewing the shroud and the razor of the barber shaving the dead man that jingle, announce a death (Germany).

The comb and razor used to groom the dead person should be placed in the coffin, otherwise anyone who uses them will lose their hair (Ansbach, Germany; Grimm, *DM,* III, 458).

Healing

Hanging a dead man's bone taken from a cemetery around the neck of a patient can cure fever (France; Thiers, *Traité,* V, 4).

When a sudden pain or paralysis strikes you, which is called the "grip of the dead" (*Dödmands-greb*), you must rub yourself with the bone of a dead man. If it has been taken from a cemetery, it is better to bring it from there before evening; if that is impossible, one must bring a piece of iron in its place (Norway; Liebrecht, *Volkskunde,* 313).

When a person is ill, the hand of a corpse or mortuary linen should be passed over him. Before placing the latter on the corpse, the edges should be cut, and these bands are then attached around the arms and legs of the dead person, then they are untied a little later and kept to heal the ill by burning them and bathing the individual that is suffering in their smoke (Norway; Liebrecht, *Volkskunde*, 312).

Stick needles in a dead person's shroud in order not to be scared (Thiers, *Traité*, V, 4).

To get rid of warts you must take some dirt from under your right foot at the moment a funeral procession is passing by and throw it in its direction (Ireland).

Hearse

If the hearse stops on its way to the cemetery, there will soon be another death in the household of the person that is being carried for burial (Courtney, *Cornish Feasts*, 168).

Helping the Dead

In the Bocage of the Vendée region, polished stones were placed in coffins, and it was said that the dead man would use them to recognize his route when he returned to those close to him (Sébillot, *Folk-lore*, IV, 76).

Horse

If a priest comes to visit a patient, one should observe his horse as he approaches; if the horse is walking with his head down, one can despair of the patient's recovery (Estonia; Grimm, *DM*, III, 489).

If the harness of the horses pulling the hearse falls, one can expect a death (Germany).

Horses do not want to pass by a domicile or a place in which there is a corpse, or where a funeral procession is passing by (Germany, Brittany).

Dreaming of a horse is a herald of death (*Vatnsdœla saga*, chap. 42).

In Eastern Prussia it is believed if the horse hitched to a hearse stares fixedly at a person, that person will soon die.[4]

A riderless horse in the retinue of the Wild Hunt is a portent of death.[5]

Leaving

If the patient speaks about leaving, he is going to die; the same is true if he asks after a dead person (Germany).

Leichenbret(t)

When a *Leichenbret(t)** falls, the one who doesn't hear it fall will die within three days (Germany; Grimm, *DM,* III, 473).

Linen

If the linen of the dead individual is not washed quickly, he or she will not be able to rest in peace (Germany).

Lying In and Churching

When a woman dies in labor, the midwife who was with her or another woman should go to the church and be "churched" in her stead, with the thought that the dead woman would not be able to see God or that she could not be brought into the church, or her body could not be buried in consecrated ground without this ceremony (France; Thiers, *Traité*).

Magpie

When a magpie alights on the roof of the house, it is a sign that someone should die there soon (Le Braz, *Légende,* I, 5).

The place where three magpies are hopping up and down in the road is where a funeral procession will pass (Morbihan, Brittany; Rolland, *Faune,* II, 140).

The magpie is called the death bird in Chalonnaise Bresse (France).

A person must make the sign of the cross or take off his hat at the sight of a magpie to dispel the curse, for it is a portent of great misfortune or the death of a close relative (France; Mozzani, *Livre,* 1,380).

Mirror

A mirror that falls is announcing a death (Germany).

Mole, Molehill

If a mole has a litter in the laundry room, the mistress of the house will die (Germany; Grimm, *DM,* III, 466).

---

*[A *Leichenbrett* (literally "corpse board"), also called a *Totenbrett* (death board), is a wooden board painted with memorial inscriptions of the dead, traditionally hung on the walls of hay-sheds, chapels, or cemetery walls in the Austrian Alps and Bavaria. —*Ed.*]

If when weeding in the fall you find a molehill beneath the cabbages, the owner will die (Grimm, *DM*, III, 471).

If a mole gives birth in the house, the grandmother will die (Germany; Grimm, *DM*, III, 455).

Nail

A nail that is bent when being hammered into the coffin announces a death (Germany; Grimm, *DM*, III, 477).

Many families have a custom of sticking a nail in the threshold every time an inhabitant of the house dies (Germany).

Naming

A dead person should not be called a name, otherwise he will come back.

Nettle

A pot filled with nettles should be placed beneath the patient's bed; if they stay green, he will get better; if they dry out, he will die (France, fourteenth century).

If green nettles are soaked in the urine of an ill person and they turn black, he will die (Germany).

Night Bird

When a person is seriously ill, people should take the time to see if some kind of owl or other night bird is flying around the dwelling (France).

Noise

When someone is destined to die, a prolonged, dull noise can be heard, that of the death cart (*carrik ann Ankou*); it stops at the door of the man or woman next to die (Brittany; Kérardven, *Guionvac'h*, 185). In the lower Loire region, this chariot is sometimes pulled by dogs (Sébillot, *Folk-lore*, I, 156).

If the clumps of earth that are thrown into the grave make a dull or very loud sound, a death will occur in the family or in the area (Germany).

If a total silence reigns at church when people are praying for a patient, this person will die, but if anyone coughs or clears their throat, he will live (Germany).

An unexpected noise on the night of the New Year announces the death of an inhabitant of the house (Estonia; Grimm, *DM,* III, 490).

Odor
When the odor of a candle can be smelled in the house, it means that one of its hosts will soon be buried (Brittany; Le Braz, *Légende,* I, 9).

Omens
The last person named by a person on their deathbed will be the next to die (England; Mozzani, *Livre,* 1,156).

If the mouth of the corpse is left open, the dead individual will come back for a relative (Germany).

If one of the cadaver's hands stays warm, or if his shroud stays warm, there will be another death soon in the family (Germany).

If the corpse takes a long time to stiffen, a member of the family or the household will follow him within three months or a year (Germany). It was believed that he could still have been alive this long or that he is going to return.

If a corpse doesn't become stiff after death, it is because there will be another death in the house (Scotland; Gregor, *Notes,* 210. Ireland; Kinahan, "Notes on Irish Folk-Lore," 106).

If the corpse sighs one last time on his straw bed, if he remains flexible, if he takes nearby ribbons or handkerchiefs into his mouth, if he opens his eyes one last time, it means a family member will soon follow him (Brittany. Germany; Grimm, *DM,* III, 463).

If a corpse has a red face, one of his friends will follow him into the grave (Schmidt, *Rockenphilosophie,* V, 4).

If the hands and fingers of the deceased remain soft and their face is faded, or if she lowers her head, the family will experience another death soon (Germany).

If the dead person has a friendly expression, she will soon come for a member of the family or the village (Germany)

If the dead person is smiling, he will take with him someone dear to him (Germany).

If the eyes of the dead person are hard to shut, it means his purgatory will be long (Brittany).

In Ploerden (Finistère), if the left eye of the dead person does not close, one of his close relatives is in danger of dying soon (Brittany; Cambry, *Voyage*, II, 169).

If someone neglects to close the eyes of the deceased, and afterward they cannot be closed but keep opening, even if it is only one eye, and the deceased appears to be staring, he is looking for one of his relatives, who will have to follow him (Germany).

If the fiancée falls after someone has come to get her, it means that her third or fourth child will die (Estonia; Grimm, *DM*, III, 487).

The first of two newlyweds who falls asleep will be the first to die (Estonia; Grimm, *DM*, III, 488).

The half of a couple who is the first to go to sleep on their wedding day will be the first to die (Norway; Liebrecht, *Volkskunde*, 326).

The first of a pair of newlyweds to get out of bed will die first (Chemnitz, Germany; Grimm, *DM*, III, 450).

Of a newly married couple, the one who falls asleep first on the wedding night will die first (Prussia, Austria).

The first person to lose his wedding ring will die first (Germany; Grimm, *DM*, III, 461).

If someone is pale while sitting in church, it is a sign he will die soon (Norway; Liebrecht, *Volkskunde*, 327).

Crickets, dogs, and owls announce death with their cries or calls (Pforzheim, Germany; Grimm, *DM*, III, 455).

The female owl is a witch bird that announces death with her hooting (Tyrol; Heyl, *Volkssage*, 786).

When a person dies, the straw of his bed is burned in the open air and people keep an anxious eye on what direction the smoke takes, for that is where the next death will occur (Tyrol, *Volkssage*, Heyl, 782).

A rooster or a hen that drags a straw behind it in the farmyard announces the imminent presence of a corpse in the house, and its sex (Estonia; Grimm, *DM*, III, 491).

A tile that falls from the roof announces a death in the house (Tyrol; Heyl, *Volkssage*, 782).

When crickets are singing in the house, one of its inhabitants will soon die (Zingerle,[6] *Sitten*, nr. 374).

When will-o'-the-wisps approach a house, someone there will soon die (Zingerle, *Sitten*, nr. 378).

Whoever allows a spoon to fall out of their hands will soon die (Zingerle, *Sitten,* nr. 392).

If the keys jangle by themselves at the sacristan's home, a person will die that night (Zingerle, *Sitten,* nr. 394).

Three knocks at the door herald a death in the next three years (Zingerle, *Sitten,* nr. 406).

If a painting falls off the wall when a person is ill, she has not long left to live (Zingerle, *Sitten,* nr. 408).

If one sees a ghostly burial after the Angelus, the person immediately following the funeral cart will die (Zingerle, *Sitten,* nr. 415).

Ossuary

In the Tréguier region, the souls converse in the ossuaries during All Souls' Night; the person who hears them can learn the names of those who are going to die during the year (Brittany; Sébillot, *Folk-lore,* II, 131).

Owl

The mere presence of the owl is dreaded, for it is a herald of death (Tyrol, Austria; Heyl, *Volkssage,* 785–86).

> *Quand on entend la chou*
> *C'o signe de moue.*

> [When one hears an owl,
> That's a sign of death.] (Franche-Comté)

If an owl rests on a house, then flies over it and hoots, a death will occur (Bielefeld, Germany).

The owl is called "death bird" in the Jura, and *ouhion de lé mô* ["little bird of death"] in the Metz region.

Pall

If the mortuary drape (pall, from Latin *pallium*) is lain carelessly upside down on the bier, a member of the household will die (Germany; Grimm, *DM,* III, 474).

Peas

If the peas placed on a scale start dancing, it is a portent of death for someone in the house (Lower Brittany; Sébillot, *Folk-lore*, III, 514).

Plank

If the carpenter hears the wooden planks stirring in his workshop, he will have a coffin to make the next day (Brittany; Rio, *Voyage*, 26).

Plants

If a fruit tree blossoms out of season, or for a second time, a member of the family will pass away (Germany).

If a furrow is seen in the field in which the seeds are not germinating, the Grim Reaper is on his way to cut down a member of the peasant family (Brittany; Rio, *Voyage*, 28).

When the wheat set out to sprout on December 4, which is intended to be placed in front of the Christmas Day creche, does not germinate or turns yellow, it is a sign of an imminent death in the family (Provence; Sébillot, *Folk-lore*, III, 507).

If the cabbage or other plants have white leaves, someone is going to die (Germany).

Plover

The golden plover that cries at night, or the cuckoo that sings on the top of the roof, announces a death (Scotland; Campbell, *Superstitions*, 256. Ireland; Wilde, *Ancient Legends*, 138).

Precaution

Once a person has died, all shiny and red objects, mirrors, windows, images, and time-keepers are covered with white linen cloths, and the water cask is turned upside down because the soul has bathed in it and anyone who drinks from it will die the same year (Germany).

A popular English expression for dying retains a memory of this: "kick the bucket."

In Wallachia, a specialist is summoned, generally a midwife, to examine the dead individual, no matter their age or sex, in order to provide it with what is necessary to prevent its return to earth as a vampire. A nail is hammered into the skull; its body is rubbed here and there with fat from a pig slaughtered on Saint Ignatius's Day, five days before Christmas, and a wild rose bush is placed on the grave to prevent the dead person from leaving it as its thorns will hold the shroud (Wallachia; Schott, *Walachische Märchen,* 298).

When a person dies, the bladder skin that served as a windowpane is taken from the window so the soul can fly away, and then put back in backward so it cannot return (Iceland; Liebrecht, *Volkskunde,* 371).

At the time of death, all doors and windows must be opened wide so the spirit can leave freely out of fear that evil spirits might intercept its flight to heaven (Scotland; Gregor, *Echo,* 137).

All used combs, knives, and linens should be placed in the coffin and buried with the deceased (Worms, Germany).

The water used to wash the dead person must be tossed onto the cross in front of the door to the house, otherwise the deceased will not find peace and will come back to haunt the living (Lithuania).

The cart used to carry a cadaver should not be returned right away, but left outside for some time, otherwise several family members will die (Estonia; Grimm, *DM,* III, 489).

Barely has the coffin been placed on the "death stone" than all haste is made to return the horse and cart to the farm, but not before taking the time to pick up the *élardes* (movable sticks that are stood up at the four corners of the cart's bed), which had been laid down next to the coffin, when the cart left for the cemetery. This precaution is taken to prevent the soul of the deceased from climbing back in the cart and returning to the home. If, for his part, the cart's driver takes a mind to climb on for going back to the house, he will be sure to die during the year (Laisnel de la Salle, *Croyances,* II, 77–78).

The bed of the deceased is burned right after he dies so he will not have any desire to come back into our world (Portugal; Liebrecht, *Volkskunde,* 374).

When the master of the house dies, all the water that may be in buckets is poured out for fear that his soul may have bathed in it and to prevent others from drinking his sins (France).

No one should leave a knife with its cutting edge facing up or a rake with its teeth in the air, because souls in torment might sit on them (Tyrol; Heyl, *Volkssage,* 783).

Care must be taken to ensure that no corner of the shroud fall into the deceased's mouth when he is on the bier (Württemberg, Germany; Grimm, *DM*, III, 457).

A tablet is placed beneath the chin of the deceased to prevent him from grabbing his death shirt with his teeth and thereby pulling his nearest and dearest ones to him (Ansbach, Germany; Grimm, *DM*, III, 459).

No light should be allowed to go out on Christmas night; otherwise the household will have a death (Germany).

Care must be taken to never let a fiancée leave through a door that a corpse was just carried through (Estonia; Grimm, *DM*, III, 487).

If a woman in labor dies, her bowl must be washed immediately, otherwise she will come back.

As long as a cadaver is in the house, a book of Psalms or an iron object, preferably scissors, should be placed on the coffin (Norway; Liebrecht, *Volkskunde,* 314).

When one cuts the rope used to hang a man, the dead man must be given three slaps to the face, otherwise he will come back (Germany).

People should refrain from "opening the holy earth," which is to say, burying the dead after sunset, otherwise a parishioner will die each day of the week (Laisnel de la Salle, *Croyances,* II, 79).

The comb and razor used to comb and shave the corpse must be placed in the coffin, otherwise those that use them will lose their hair (Germany; Grimm, *DM*, III, 458).

One must not allow tears to fall on the dead person, else she or he will not be able to rest in peace (Germany; Grimm, *DM*, III, 457).

This belief gave birth to the legend of the pitcher of tears:[7] a child is laboring to follow a procession while carrying a pitcher filled with water and asks a living person to tell his parents that they should no longer mourn him because their tears fall into the pitcher and its weight is more than he can bear.[8] This motif is simply a variant of the death shirt soaked in the tears of the living mourning the dead person,[9] which we find in Jacobus Voragine's *Golden Legend* (chap. 27) and in Thomas of Catimpré's *Apiarius* (II, 53).

Punishment

Anyone who has buried money is condemned to wander the earth until someone finds it (Pforzheim, Germany; Grimm, *DM*, III, 455).

The dead person who, while he was alive, lost crumbs of bread through his carelessness, must gather them together after his death (Tyrol).

The texts most often evoke murderers, thieves, and dishonest surveyors.

Raven

When the lord or lady of a house is sick and a raven has just croaked above the chimney or house where the patient lies, it is a certain sign that he will die of this illness (*Distaff Gospels*, §96).

The Bretons believe that two ravens preside over every house and can predict life and death (Finistère; Cambry, *Voyage*, III, 48).

If one raven flies over a dwelling, a woman of the family will die; if there are two ravens, it is a man that will perish (Germany).

If the lord or lady of a house is ill and if a raven crosses over the chimney or roof of the house, it is a good sign that he or she will die from their illness (France).

If a raven knocks at the window of a sick person, that person will die (Germany),

If a raven strikes the roof of a house, there will be a death in that home (France).

A raven croaking above a house is a herald of death there (Owen, *Welsh Folk-Lore*, 304).

When someone is going to a gathering and hears a raven croaking on the left, it means that one of the members of the assembly will be killed (Ireland; Abercromby, "Irish Bird-Lore," 65–66).

Rooster, Hen

When a cock crows three times at night or at an uncustomary time, it is a sign of death (Ireland, Scotland, Brittany).

The rooster that crows at midnight while perched on a wagon is announcing a death (Germany).

The death of a black hen announces a death (Germany).

When a rooster crows before midnight, it is a sign that a family member is going to die (Scotland; Gregor, *Echo*, 133–34).

The crowing of a hen indicates the certain death of a close member of the family (Scotland; Gregor, *Echo*, 134).

Salt

In order to know whether a sick person is going to die, one simply has to put some salt in their hand. If the salt dissolves, this indicates he or she is going to die. If it doesn't dissolve, this is a portent of a long life (Germany; Grimm, *DM,* III, 475).

Place a small pile of salt on the table over Christmas night. If it dissolves during the night, a person will die over the coming year; if it is intact in the morning, he or she will survive (Germany; Grimm, *DM,* III, 475).

When the body is removed from the house, it should be placed on the threshold three times once it has left the farm. Three piles of salt should be made in his room, they should be swept and the sweepings and the broom should then be cast into a field (Germany).

When a poor person dies, a plate full of salt should be placed on his body and a lit candle stuck into the salt to protect him from evil spirits (Wales, Scotland; Chatworth-Musters, "Superstitions," 485).

On the evening of November 12, a thimble should be filled with salt and then turned upside down on a plate. This operation should be repeated as many times as there are people in the house, and a heap of salt is assigned to each of them. The plate is left undisturbed overnight and in the morning people look to see which heap of salt has fallen. The person to which that heap had been assigned will die within the year (Isle of Man; Rhŷs, *Celtic Folklore,* I, 318).

Scratching

If someone scratches their chin, a bearded man will die (Norway; Liebrecht, *Volkskunde,* 327).

Screech Owl

The screech owl announces the death of a person of the house on which it lands (Limousin, France).

When a screech owl lights on a house while calling *"chiou,"* is it a sign of death (Brittany).

Shadow

When sitting at the table on Christmas night, it is possible to see the shadow of the one who will be next to die on the wall, but the shadow has no head (Norway; Liebrecht, *Volkskunde,* 326).

When someone is carrying a candle on Christmas night, the one whose shadow has no head will die that year; if the person sees only half a head, he will die during the second half of the year (Schmidt, *Rockenphilosophie*, I, 56).

When the candles of the Christmas tree are lit, people look at the shadows that are projected on the walls by the persons there; the shadows of those who will die the following year have no head (Germany).

Shoes, Slippers

On Christmas night, the master of the house sits at or on a table, with his back to the door; he then touches his right ear with his left hand, then he slips his right hand, which will throw the shoe or slipper of one of the house's inhabitants, between his chest and his arm, grabs the shoe or slipper from behind and tosses it over his head against the door. If the end of the shoe lands facing the door, its owner will soon die (Norway; Liebrecht, *Volkskunde*, 324).

If, when entering, someone loses a slipper that remains near the door, someone will die in the neighborhood in the near future (Norway; Liebrecht, *Volkskunde*, 327).

If someone tosses a shoe over his head on Saint Matthew's Day and its tip is pointing toward the door, either someone will die or move out during the next year (Germany).

When the tip of a thrown shoe is pointing toward the cemetery or toward the bell tower, this means someone will die (Germany).

Shroud

If a shroud is hanging in the chimney on Christmas night, a member of the household will die (Schmidt, *Rockenphilosophie*, V, 75).

Snake

Anyone who kills a snake around the house will die within the year (Germany).

If a snake crawls over the main road, a corpse will soon travel down it (Norway; Liebrecht, *Volkskunde*, 326).

Sneeze

If someone sneezes when milking a cow, he or she will learn about a death before that milk has been drunk (Norway; Liebrecht, *Volkskunde*, 214).

Spade

The gravedigger's spade will jingle when it is going to dig a grave (Pforzheim, Germany; Grimm, *DM*, III, 455).

Speaking

The person who was addressed or spoken to by a dead person will soon follow him; the same is true for the one who is first to leave the house after the passage of a corpse (Norway; Liebrecht, *Volkskunde*, 327).

Spinning, Working

It is a great sin to believe that one mustn't spin in the room of a patient who has received extreme unction, because he will die if one stops spinning, or if the thread breaks (France).

As long as the dead person has not been buried, it is an offense to him to work (Brittany; Rio, *Voyage*, 84).

Spring

At Coucy castle in Picardy, the so-called Fountain of Death dries up when the lord of the place dies (Bérenger-Féraud, *Superstitions*, III, 302).

In Plougastel-Daoulas, when the spring of Saint Languiz, the patron saint of the dying, is visited and it is found to be dry, it means that the ill person's hour has sounded (Sébillot, *Folk-lore*, II, 239).

If, when leaning over the "Fountain of Death" (*Feunteun an Ankou*), you see a skull instead of you face, it means you are soon to die (Brittany; Rio, *Voyage*, 33).

Star

Someone will die soon in the house near the place where a shooting star fell (Germany; Grimm, *DM*, III, 477).

When a person is about to die, his star will fall in the evening; if one gets up early the next morning, they will see it rising back up into the sky (Germany).

When you see the night sky drop a star, take it as truth that it is a sign that one of your friends has died; because everyone has a star in the sky that falls when he dies (France; *Distaff Gospels*. Germany).

When you see twelve stars above a house, you can be sure that a death is being mourned there that night (Harou, "Météores," 140).

Stone

A stone that falls from the roof announces a death (Germany).

Losing an amethyst stone predicts the death of one's mother (France).

If you transport large stones or blocks of rock on the main road, a corpse will soon be traveling on it; the larger the stones, the more likely is it to be a distinguished figure (Norway; Liebrecht, *Volkskunde*, 327).

Stork

If a stork does not sit on its egg until it hatches, an illustrious figure of the land will die (Germany).

Straw

Blades of straw crossed on a road are a herald of death (Liège and Menton, France; Sébillot, *Folk-lore*, III, 514).

Suicide

A suicide victim is never carried out through the door, but is removed through a hole made between the wall and the thatch of the roof (Scotland; Campbell, *Superstitions*, 242).

Taboo

It is forbidden to make a knot in the thread that sews the shroud, otherwise the dead person will be unable to get out in order to appear before God (Brittany; Rio, *Voyage*, 100).

One must never let tears fall on a corpse; otherwise he will never rest in peace (Schmidt, *Rockenphilosophie*).

Numerous tales illustrate the prohibition of over mourning the dead because it prevents them from finding rest. Three examples can be seen in the work of Anatole Le Braz (II, 106–12): "The Woman Who Mourned Her Son Too Much," "The Young Woman of Coray" (II, 99–103), and "The Drowned Man's Seed" (II, 104–5). The theme entered the international nomenclature under the reference AT 769.

One mustn't stand by the feet of patients receiving extreme unction because it advances their days and they will die sooner; this is a futile observance (France; Thiers, *Traité*).

One should not keep a dead person on a boat more than

twenty-four hours, otherwise the sailing will take three times longer (Pomerania, Germany).

A pregnant woman should not sit upon a cask of water, otherwise her child will drown (Germany).

A pregnant woman should never walk beneath a rope; if she does, her child cannot avoid hanging (Germany).

If a pregnant woman exchanges her belt for a rope, her child will be hung (Germany).

A pregnant woman should refrain from spinning, otherwise she will spin the rope that someone will loop around her child's neck (Germany).

As long as the dead person has not been married, no spinning or laundry should be done (Germany).

Taper
See *candle.*

Tawny Owl
If a tawny owl (*Strix aluco,* Ger. *Habergeis*) hoots close to a house, one of the people living there will soon die (Tyrol, Austria, and Germany).

When a tawny owl flies near the house and knocks at the window, it is announcing a death (Wales; Owen, *Welsh Folk-Lore,* 297).

The tawny owl brings death by perching on a house or by knocking on its window panes (France; Mozzani, *Livre,* 380).

Thirteen
Thirteen at the table means death for the thirteenth person, counting from left to right starting from the lady of the house (France).

Thunder
If it thunders on Sunday, someone in the parish will die during the week (France; Thiers, *Traité,* V, 3).

Tooth
A toothache that lasts three hours in the afternoon is a portent of the death of a close relative; and if you have a toothache when you see an intersign, you are destined to die soon (Brittany; Le Calvez, "Basse-Bretagne," 90).

Losing a tooth in a cemetery at the same time you see a ghost is a sign of certain death (Brittany; Le Calvez, "Basse-Bretagne," 90).

A dream about losing a tooth predicts great misfortune or the death of the dreamer, or a family member (Germany).

Treasure
People who discover a treasure will die a year and a day after their discovery (Brittany; Le Braz, *Légende,* I, 85–86)

Weasel
The person who sees a weasel will die within the year (Le Braz, *Légende,* I, 5).

White-Tailed Eagle
If the white-tailed eagle passes down the street or village, it is bringing death (Carnas, France; Le Rouzic, *Carnac,* 137).

Will-o'-the-Wisp
Fleeing the will-o'-the-wisps in a cemetery predicts your death (Brittany).

Yawning
When one of two people yawns, most often he or she will die soon after (Iceland; Liebrecht, *Volkskunde,* 370).[10]

INDEX OF THE BEYOND

The examples in this index are based on F. C. Tubach's *Index Exemplorum: A Handbook of Medieval Religious Tales,* which shows the Christianization of popular beliefs. The handbook contains 5,400 examples collected from the most popular medieval tales.

29. *Absolution, worth of.* A dead monk returns in a vision to tell his abbot that absolution is of worth even if granted after death.

156. *All Souls' Day.* A vision of heaven and purgatory seen by a monk leads to the institution of All Souls' Day.

505. *Bath in hell and rich man.* A vision of hell shows a rich man in a horrible bath because he loved his riches too much.

784. *Bridge of Dread crossed by knight.* The vision of the knight who crossed the Bridge of Dread.

1190. *Confession saves sinful man.* A sinful man has a vision of hell awaiting him. On the advice of his pious wife he confesses, dies, and goes to paradise. After three days, he appears to tell his wife that she will follow him soon.

1490. *Deathbed vision.*

1790. *Dreams, diversity of.* A monk describes the diversity of dreams and of spiritual visions.

1818. *Dryhthelm, vision of.*

2229. *Fursey, vision of.*

2500. *Heaven and hell shown in vision.*

2517. *Hell, torture in.*

2518. *Hell, various punishments of.*

2772. *Jerome, Saint, reads Virgil.*

2774. *Jerome, Saint, scourged.* In a vision of judgment, Saint Jerome is scourged for being more Ciceronian than Christian.

3239. *Maurilius, Saint, vision of.* Saint Maurilius has a vision of heaven and hell.

4000. *Purgatory shown to soul.* The soul of a monk was taken from his body and shown purgatory and his own tomb.

4998. *Tundalus of Ireland.*

INDEX OF SOME MOTIFS FOUND IN FOLKTALES

This index is based on American folklorist Stith Thompson's *Motif-Index of Folk Literature,* a six-volume catalog. A "motif" is a term used by folklorists to describe individual details within a tale. A motif may refer to a character, action, setting, or object. The examples of motifs found in Thompson's catalog, and included in this appendix, are organized by a motif number and a descriptor, defined as follows:

- The **motif number** is a letter and a series of numbers that are a shorthand way of referring to specific details found in folktales.
- The **descriptor** is a short verbal explanation of what each motif is about.

B151.2.0.2. Birds show the way to otherworld.

    B552. Man carried by bird.

    C211. Taboo: eating in other world.

    C262. Taboo: drinking in other world.

  C331.2. Travelers to other world must not look back.

C423.3. Taboo: revealing experiences in other world.

C712.1. Taboo: staying too long in fairyland.

C950. Person carried to other world for breaking taboo.

C952. Immediate return to other world because of broken taboo.

C953. Person must remain in other world because of broken taboo.

D812.8. Magic object received from lady in dream.

D2011. Years thought days.

D2131. Magical underground journey.

E481. Land of the dead; it is reached by a bridge.

F1. Journey to otherworld as dream or vison.

F2. Transportion to otherworld without dying.

F80. Journey to lower world.

F111. Journey to earthly paradise.

F116. Journey to the land of immortals.

F131. Otherworld in hollow mountain.

F134. Otherworld on island.

F152. Bridge to otherworld.

F159.2. Journey to otherworld on horseback.

F162.2. Rivers in otherworld.

F171. Extraordinary sights in otherworld.

F171.2. Broad and narrow road in otherworld.

F212. Fairyland under water.

F213. Fairyland on island.

APPENDIX 4

INDEX OF SOME STORY TYPES FEATURING THE OTHERWORLD

Based on Antti Aarne and Stith Thompson's *The Types of the Folktale*, this index gives samples of tales on the otherworld. The two authors worked out a numerical system that divides the tales into different classifications. The "AT" stands for Aarne and Thompson.

AT 302: "The ogre's (devil's) heart in the egg."

AT 306 A11: "The pursuit of the heavenly maiden."

AT 306A: "The danced-out shoes."

AT 313* "The magic flight."

AT 400: "The man on a quest for his lost wife."

AT 451: "The maiden who seeks her brothers."

AT 461: "Three hairs from the devil's beard."

AT 462: "The outcast queens and the ogrsess queen."

AT 465C: "Journey to the other world."

AT 468: "The princess of the sky-tree."

AT 470: "Friends in life and death."

NOTES

INTRODUCTION.
"IN THE MIDST OF LIFE WE ARE IN DEATH"

1. Lévinas, *Dieu, la Mort, et le Temps,* 129 and 82.
2. Old Icelandic text in Jónsson and Vilhjálmsson, eds., *Fornaldarsögur Norðurlanda,* vol. I. Translation from the *Nornagests þáttr* excerpts in Anderson, trans., *The Saga of the Völsungs,* 187.
3. Cf. Guiette, "L'Invention étymologique dans les lettres françaises au Moyen Âge."
4. Isidore, *Etymologiae* XI, 2, 31–32.
5. An edition of the original text appears in Schneegans, "*Le Mors de la pomme,* texte du XVe siècle."
6. Wendling, "Le *De hominis miseria, mundi et inferni contemptu* de Hugues de Miramar, une œuvre 'autobiographique' dans la postérité des *Confessions* d'Augustin?"
7. Cf. Bayard, *L'Art du bien mourir au XVe siècle.*
8. Cf. Avenier, "Les Cadrans solaires du Bas-Dauphiné à la période révolutionnaire."
9. Montaigne, *Essais,* I, 20.
10. *Oraison funèbre de Henriette-Anne d'Angleterre, duchesse d'Orléans.*
11. Bechstein, *Le Livre des contes,* 219.
12. Ehrismann, ed., *Der Renner von Hugo von Trimberg,* 277ff.
13. Cambrai, Bibliothèque municipale, ms 351, fol. 174r.
14. London, British Library, ms Sloane 146, fol. 85v.
15. Paris, Bibliothèque nationale, ms Lat. 8654 B. For other examples, cf. Lecouteux, *Traditional Magic Spells for Protection and Healing.*

16. Le Braz, *La Légende de la mort chez les Bretons armoricains*.

17. Rio, *Voyage dans l'au-delà*. See also Bayard, *Bretagne . . . un autre voyage*.

18. Walter, *Croyances populaires au Moyen Âge*, 42.

19. Cf. Vernette, *L'Irrationnel est parmi nous*, 30–34 and 145–175.

20. Petzold, *Märchen, Mythos, Sage*, 110–13.

21. For the full details on the books I mention here, see the bibliography.

22. Motif F1. Journey to otherworld as dream or vision.

23. Donà, *Per le vie dell'altro mondo*.

24. Gaston, *L'Initiation et l'au-delà*.

CHAPTER ONE.
ACCOUNTS OF JOURNEYS INTO THE BEYOND
FROM CLASSICAL ANTIQUITY

1. Homer, *The Odyssey* (trans. Murray), bk. X and XXIV.

2. Plato, *The Republic* (trans. Jowett; punctuation modified), X, 614b ff.

3. Plutarch, *De genio Socratis*, 590b–592e. In *Moralia* (trans. De Lacy and Einarson), vol. VII.

4. Motif F81.1. Orpheus, journey to the land of the dead to bring back a person.

5. Plutarch, *De sera numinis vindicta*, sect. 22–33. In *Moralia* (trans. De Lacy and Einarson; punctuation modified), vol. VII.

6. Proclus, *Commentary on Plato's* Republic, XVI, 114 (trans. Taylor).

7. Johannes de Hauvilla, *Architrenius*, ed. Schmidt. On hell: VI, 6: "De transitu Megere et Mortis ab inferis in potentes."

8. Klaus, "De l'enfer au paradis . . . et retour dans l'*Architrenius* de Jean de Hanville," 33. Note that "Hanville" should be corrected to "Hauville," as the latest research has identified this locale as Hauville-en-Rémois, between Rouen and Pont-Audemer.

9. Johannes de Hauvilla, *Architrenius,* VI, 2: *De transitu Architrenii in Tylon*.

CHAPTER TWO.
THE BEYOND AS SEEN IN
MYTHOLOGIES AND RELIGIONS

1. Hesiod, *The Works and Days* (trans. Lattimore), ll. 169–76.

2. Plato, *Phaedrus* (trans. Jowett, in *The Dialogues of Plato,* vol. I), §249.

3. Origen, *Contra Celsum* (trans. Crombie), bk. 6, chap. 26.

4. Trescases, *La Symbolique de la mort, ou Herméneutique de la résurrection.*

5. Gaster, "Hebrew Visions of Hell and Paradise."

6. Gaster, "Hebrew Visions," 599.

7. Cf. Weber, *Petit Dictionnaire de mythologie arabe.*

8. *Arda-Viraf-Namak*, chap. 5 ("The Chinwad Bridge"), chap. 6 ("Purgatory"), chap. 16ff. ("Hell").

9. Schattner-Rieser, "Les Mandéens ou disciples de Saint Jean."

10. Cf. Lidzbarski, trans. *Ginzā.*

11. Cf. Brock, "The *ruaḥ elōhim* of Gen 1,2," 334.

12. For a complete description, cf. Brandt, *Die mandäische Religion*, 72–82.

13. Motif F93.2. Lake entrance to lower world.

14. Pentikäinen, *Mythologie des Lapons*, 183.

15. *Life and Deeds of Alexander of Macedonia*, II, 23–41, in Meusel, ed., *Pseudo-Callisthenes.*

16. Hugues du Mans, *Actus Pontificum Cenomannis in urbe degentium*, chap. 37; in Mabillon, ed., *Vetera analecta*, III, 326.

CHAPTER THREE.
FROM THE CHRISTIAN BEYOND
TO THE LITERATURE OF REVELATIONS

1. *Gospel (Questions) of Bartholomew* (trans. James, in *The Apocryphal New Testament*), §9.

2. *Actes de Philippe*, in Bovon and Geoltrain, eds., *Écrits apocryphes chrétiens*, 1, 192–201.

3. Bovon and Geoltrain, eds., *Écrits apocryphes chrétiens*, 558–71.

4. Bovon and Geoltrain, eds., *Écrits apocryphes chrétiens*, 788–826.

5. See Brandes, trans., *Visio S. Pauli*, 42–45.

6. Paris and Bos, eds., *Trois Versions rimées de l'"Evangile de Nicodème."*

7. Athanasius, *Leben des Heiligen Antonius* (trans. Mertel), in *Des Heiligen Athanasius Alexandrinus ausgewählte Schriften*, vita 16, 20.

8. Prudentius, *Cathemerimon* (καθημερινῶν ὑμνῶν), IX, 71.

9. Prudentius, *Peristephanon*, V, 125–27; 134–37.

10. This corresponds with an OBE, or out-of-body experience; cf. Hardy, *L'Après-vie à l'épreuve de la science.*

11. Gregory of Tours, *The History of the Franks* (trans. Thorpe), bk. VII, chap. 1.

12. Cf. Tubach, *Index Exemplorum.*

13. Bede, *Historia ecclesiastica gentis Anglorum.*

14. Otloh von St. Emmeram, *Liber visionum,* Visio 20.

15. Bede, *Historia ecclesiastica,* bk. V, chap. 12–14.

16. *Visio Baronti,* in Bruno Krusch and Wilhelm Levison, eds., *MGH, SS rerum Merovingicarum* 5, 368–94.

17. Michael Tangl, ed., *Die Briefe des heiligen Bonifatius und Lullus (S. Bonifatii et Lulli epistolae),* in *MGH, Epistolae selectae* 1, 7–15.

18. Otloh von St. Emmeram, *Liber visionum,* chap. 19.

19. Migne, ed., *Patrologia Latina,* vol. LXXXVII, col. 433d–434a.

20. *Dicta* 17ff., in Migne, ed., *Patrologia Latina,* vol. LXXXVII, col. 433a.

21. *Visio Bernoldi,* in Migne, ed. *Patrologia Latina,* vol. CXXV, col. 115–1119.

22. Motif R121.5. Ariadne-thread.

23. Petrus Damiani, *De variis miraculis narratio,* in Migne, ed., *Patrologia Latina,* vol. CXLV.

24. Farmer, ed., "The Vision of Orm."

25. Cf. Tubach, *Index Exemplorum,* nr. 4998. For an account of the larger vision, see Lecouteux and Lecouteux, eds., *Travels to the Otherworld and Other Fantastic Realms.*

26. *Tondolus der Ritter;* see also Palmer, *"Visio Tnugdali."*

27. Schmidt, ed., *Visio Alberici;* and cf. *Visio Baronti* (note 16 above).

28. Assmann, ed. and trans., *Godeschalcus und Visio Godeschalci.*

29. Heidelberg, Universitätsbibliothek, ms Cpg 401.

30. Ferguson, *The Debate between the Body and the Soul;* Bartholomaeis, "Due testi latini e una versione toscana della *Visio Philiberti.*"

31. Méril, ed., *Poésies populaires latines antérieures au douzième siècle,* 200–217.

32. Cf. Zabughin, "L'Oltretomba classico," 219ff.

33. Cf. Dinzelbacher, *Vision und Visionsliteratur im Mittelalter,* 187.

34. Bede, *Historia ecclesiastica* (trans. Sherley-Price), V, 12.

35. "Ço fu Pol li apostle, li archangle Michael, / Car Deu voleit que Saint Pol veïst les turmenz, / E les peines d'enfer li a tut mustré" (ll. 8–10). Original text in Kastner, "Les Versions françaises inédites de la *Descente de saint Paul en enfer.*"

36. *Legenda aurea,* chap. 140: "Vidit vallem tenebrosam et quatuor ignes in aëre aliquibus spatiis a se distantes; unus est ignis mendacii . . . , secundus supiditatis . . . , tertius est dissensionis . . . , quartus impietatis."

37. Cf. Lecouteux, "Le Rêve et son arrière-plan au Moyen Âge."

38. Cf. Pinon, "Les Prières du soir en Wallonie," 48.

39. Lacuve, "Prières populaires du Poitou," 622.

40. A recollection of this is preserved in the place-name Brünhildenberg in Hesse (Germany).

41. Cf. Rebillard, *"Koimetérion et Coemeterium."*

42. Cf. Augustine, *De Genesi ad litteram,* I, XII, 6, in Migne, ed., *Patrologia Latina,* vol. XXXIV.

43. Le Goff, "Le Christianisme et les rêves (IIe–VIIIe siècle)," in *L'Imaginaire médiéval,* 294.

44. Lactantius, *De opificio Dei* (trans. Fletcher), XVIII, 8.

45. Augustine, *De cura pro mortuis gerenda* (trans. Cornish and Browne), XII, 14–15.

46. *De Miraculis sancti Stephani protomartyris,* in Migne, ed., *Patrologia Latina,* vol. XLI, col. 838.

47. Gregory of Tours, *The History of the Franks* (trans. Thorpe), VII, 1.

48. *Vita Sancti Fursei,* in Heist, ed., *Vitae sanctorum Hiberniae.* Cf. Tubach, *Index Exemplorum,* nr. 229.

49. Knittel, ed., *Heito und Walahfrid Strabo, Visio Wettini.*

50. *Gesta abbatum sancti Bertini Sithiensium,* ed. Oswald Holder-Egger, in *MGH, Scriptores* 13, 607–635.

51. *De miraculis S. Emmerami,* ed. Migne, *Patrologia Latina,* vol. CXLI, col. 1038.

52. Codex n. 2096 (52).

53. Batiouchkof, "Le Débat de l'âme et du corps."

54. Schmidt, ed., *Visio Thurkilli.*

55. Original text in Bugge, ed., *Norrœn fornkvæði,* 357–69. English translation by Michael Moynihan.

56. Motif E481.2. Land of the dead across water.

57. *Acta sanctorum,* Mai, t. 7, 809.

58. "Der æ heitt i helvite, / heitar hell nokon hyggje."

59. Liestøl, *Draumkvæde.*

60. An edition of which appears in Unger, ed., *Heilagra Manna Søgur,* I, 329–62.

61. "Non enim Er ille Platonicus fuco philosophico a simplicite nostra redivivus introdicitur, quem militem officio bello interemptum . . ." (chap. 65).

62. Bede, *Historia ecclesiastica,* II, 6.

63. Cf. Tubach, *Index Exemplorum,* nr. 2772 and 2774.

64. ". . . circa mediam quadragesimam tam subita et ardenti febre corripitur, ut toto

frigescente jam corpore vitalis calor in solo pectore palpitaret" (Jacobus de Voragine, *Legenda Aurea vulgo Historia Lombardica Dicta,* ed. Graesse; English trans. Caxton).

65. "... et ex verberibus, quae ante tribunal susceperat, scapulas terribiliter reperit livientes."

66. Jacobus de Voragine, *The Golden Legend* (trans. Caxton).

67. Nachez, "Le Double dans les ENOCs."

68. Cf. Lecouteux, *Witches, Werewolves, and Fairies.*

69. Cf. Eliade, *Le Chamanisme,* 176ff; Nachez, "Le double dans les ENOCs."

CHAPTER FOUR.
HELL, PURGATORY, AND PARADISE

1. Stephanus de Bourbon, *Tractatus de diversisis materiis predicabilibus, Prima pars* (ed. Berlioz), 69–82.

2. Stephanus de Borbone, *Tractatus de diversisis materiis predicabilibus, Prima pars* (ed. Berlioz), 22–23, 91, 157–58, 245; *Tractatus . . . , Tertia pars* (ed. Berlioz), 231, 553.

3. *Apocalypse of Paul,* in Bovon and Geoltrain, eds., *Écrits apocryphes chrétiens,* I, 816. In the Latin texts it is written: "Nix, glacies, ignis, sanguis, serpens, fulgur, fetor."

4. Vincent of Beauvais, *Speculum historiale,* 1,329.

5. *Etymologiae,* XIV, 8: "Mons aetnae ex igne et sulphure dictus, unde et gehenna."

6. Gottfried of Viterbo, *Pantheon,* ed. G. Waitz, in *MGH, Scriptores* 22, 223.

7. Gregory the Great, *Dialogues* (trans. Zimmerman), IV, 36, and IV, 31. There is a similar legend about King Arthur that says he ended his days *in monte Gyber* ("within Etna"); cf. Caesarius of Heisterbach, *Dialogus miraculorum,* XII, 12.

8. Julien de Vézelay, *Sermons,* II, 450–55.

9. Caesarius of Heisterbach, *Dialogus miraculorum,* XII, 13.

10. Wahlund, ed., *Die altfranzösische Prosaübersetzung von Brendans Meerfahrt,* 76 and 178. In 1976–1977, after he built a *cwrgl,* Tim Séverin recreated the voyage of Saint Brendan and told the story of his expedition in his book *Le Voyage du Brendan.*

11. Benedeit, *Le Voyage de saint Brendan* (ed. and trans. Short and Merrilees), ll. 1131–1148.

12. I have translated from the Middle High German version: Gottschall and

Steer, eds., *Der deutsche Lucidarius, Teil I*; for the Latin text, see Lefèvre, *L'Elucidarium et les Lucidaires*, 447–48.

13. Albertus Magnus, *Opera omnia*, XXX, 603–4. See also Bonaventure, *Opera omnia*, IV, distinctio 45, 923–41, in which Bonaventure responds to the question "Ubi sit infernus?" before listing the "receptacles of souls after death" (distinctio 45: *De diversis animarum receptaculis post mortem*).

14. Cf. Morel, ed., *Offenbarungen der Schwester Mechthild von Magdeburg*, 82–83.

15. Prior, ed., *L'Image du Monde de Maître Gossouin*, 139–41.

16. Thomasset, ed., *Placides et Timéo ou Li secrés as philosophes*, §381, 184.

17. Cf. Lecouteux and Lecouteux, *Contes, diableries et autres merveilles au Moyen Âge*, 48–50.

18. For an edition of the *Visio Lazari*, see Voigt, ed., *Beiträge zur Geschichte der Visionenliteratur im Mittelalter*, 1–118.

19. Schmidt, ed., *Visio Alberici*, 160–207.

20. Regarding these bridges, cf. Dinzelbacher, *Die Jenseitsbrücke im Mittelalter*.

21. Cf. Graf, *Miti, leggende e superstizioni del Medio Evo*, II, 73–126.

22. Regarding this author, cf. Lefèvre, "Regnaud le Queux."

23. Cf. Crane, ed., *The Exempla or Illustrative Stories from the Sermones vulgares of Jacques de Vitry*.

24. Bede, *Historia ecclesiastica* (trans. Sherley-Price), V, 12 and V, 14.

25. Bautz, *Das Fegefeuer*, 187.

26. Le Goff, *The Birth of Purgatory*.

27. Barral, *Légendes carlovingiennes*, chap. 34.

28. Henry de Saltrey, *Tractatus de Purgatorio Sancti Patricii*, in Migne, ed Patrologia Latina CLXXX, col. 975–1004.

29. Pomel, "Les Entre-mondes de l'âme pérégrine," 45.

30. *Liber de introductione loquendi di Filippo da Ferrara* (ed. Silvana Vecchio), V, 21, exemplum no. 305; cited in Polo de Beaulieu, "Les Entre-mondes dans la littérature exemplaire," 81.

31. *Liber de introductione loquendi di Filippo da Ferrara* (ed. Silvana Vecchio), V, 16, exemplum no. 300; cited in Polo de Beaulieu, *Jean Gobi*, 82.

32. Polo de Beaulieu, *Jean Gobi*, 99–100

33. Cf. Lecouteux, *Phantom Armies of the Night*; Ueltschi, *La Mesnie Hellequin en conte et en rime*.

34. *Vita sancti Anscharii*, in Migne, ed., *Patrologia Latina*, vol. CXVIII, col. 959–64.

35. "Muros fulgentes clarissimi splendoris, stupende longitudinis et altitudinis immense" (*Liber visionum*, chap. 20).

36. "Hec est enim illa sancta et inclita celestis Hierusalem" (*Liber visionum*, chap. 20).

37. Constable and Kritzeck, eds., *Petrus Venerabilis*, 95–98.

38. Constable, "The Vision of Gunthelm and Other Visions attributed to Peter the Venerable."

39. Amat, *Songes et Visions*, 399, n. 137; on the palace and gardens, 397–401.

40. Zacher, ed., *Alexandri Magni iter ad paradisum*.

41. English translation from Stoneman, *Legends of Alexander the Great*, 68.

42. Original text edited in Klob, "A vida de Sancto Amaro."

43. *Herzog Ernst* enjoyed enormous popularity and was even translated into Latin several times; editions of it include: Ehlen, ed., *Hystoria ducis Bauarie Ernesti*; Flood, ed., *Die Historie von Herzog Ernst*; Jacobsen and Orth, eds., *Gesta Ernesti Ducis*; Gansweidt, ed., *Der "Ernestus" des Odo von Magdeburg*; and Weber, ed., *Untersuchung und überlieferungskritische Edition des Herzog Ernst B mit einem Abdruck der Fragmente von Fassung A*.

CHAPTER FIVE.
BETWEEN VISIONS, TALES, AND LEGENDS

1. Walter, "Mythologies comparées," 263.

2. Cf. Tiévant and Desideri, *Almanach de la mémoire et des coutumes corses*, 9, IIff.

3. *Lancelot en prose* (ed. Walter), LXVI, 5–6.

4. Walter, *Dictionnaire de mythologie arthurienne*, 191.

5. English translation from Staines, trans., *The Complete Romances of Chrétien de Troyes*, 172–73.

6. Walter, *Dictionnaire de mythologie arthurienne*, 258.

7. English translations from Matarasso, *The Quest of the Holy Grail*, 61–62.

8. *Lancelot, roman en prose du XIIIe siècle* (ed. Micha), vol. 8, XLa, 6–9.

9. *Le Livre du Graal* (ed. Walter), vol. 2, 1350–54.

10. *Perceforest* (ed. Roussineau).

11. Ferlampin-Acher, "Voyager avec le diable Zéphir."

12. "C'est-à-dire, dist l'esprit, que quant une ame yst hors de son corps, elle est icy apportee et jettee en ce trou dont tu vois saillir celle fumee, et puis

elle devale en bas selon ce qu'elle est chargie de pechiez, et de tant que le poix de ses meffais le avale plus parfont, de tant est plus fort tourmentee." *Perceforest*, 4th part, XXXIII, 348–405.

13. Gerbert de Montreuil, *La Continuation de Perceval* (ed. Williams), ll. 9548–633.

14. Original text: Wirnt von Gravenberg, *Wigalois, der Ritter mit dem Rade* (ed. Kapteyn); French edition: *Wigalois, le chevalier à la roue* (trans. Lecouteux and Lévy).

15. Otloh of Sankt Emmeram, *Liber visionum*, chap. 23.

16. Greven, ed., *Die exempla aus den Sermones feriales et communes des Jakob von Vitry*, 3–5.

17. Stephanus de Borbone, *Tractatus de diversis materiis predicabilibus, Liber secundus, De dono pietatis* (ed. Berlioz); *Tractatus de diversis materiis predicabilibus, Liber tertius, De eis que pertinent ad donum scientie et penitentiam* (ed. Berlioz).

18. Gobi, *La Scala coeli* (ed. Polo de Beaulieu), nr. 953.

19. Musäus, "Graf Schwarzenberg."

20. Bechstein, *Le Livres des contes* (trans. Lecouteux and Lecouteux), 51–54.

21. The help one gives to souls in torment in the form of masses, prayers, and alms.

22. Walter, ed. and trans., *Les Lais de Marie de France*, 438, fn. 1.

23. For more on this figure, see Philippe Walter's fine study, "Yonec, fils de l'ogre."

24. The same narrative framework can be seen in an Albanian tale, "The Love of a Dove"; cf. Hahn, *Griechische und Albanesische Märchen*, pt. 2, no. 102 ("Taubenliebe"), 130–34.

25. Afanassiev, *Contes populaires russes*, II, 332–37.

26. The Norse text of the *Ianuals lioð* appears in Rychner and Aebischer, *Le lai de Lanval*, 105–25.

27. Motif C423.3. Taboo: revealing experiences in other world.

28. Cf. Donà, "Les Cantari et la tradition écrite du conte populaire," and, by the same author, "Cantari, fiabe e filologi."

29. Amidei, ed., *Ponzela Gaia*.

30. Chrétien de Troyes, *Œuvres completes* (ed. Poirion), 339–503.

31. Lambert, trans., *Les Quatre Branches du Mabinogi et autres contes gallois du Moyen Âge*, 212–36.

32. Cf. the article by Lutz Röhrich, "Herr der Tiere," in *Enzyklopädie des Märchens*, vol. 6, col. 866–79.

33. This motif can be seen again in Heinrich von dem Türlin's Arthurian romance *Diu Crône* (The Crown), ll. 2194–207 and 24638–651. For the original text, see Heinrich von dem Türlin, *Die Krone* (ed. Knapp, et al.).
34. For more on all this, see Walter, *Canicule*.
35. Hartmann von Aue, *Erec* (ed. Leitzmann and Wolff).
36. Achnitz, ed., *Der Ritter mit dem Bock: Konrads von Stoffeln "Gauriel von Muntabel."*
37. Murray, ed., *The Romance and Prophecies of Thomas of Erceldoune.*
38. La Sale, *Le Paradis de la reine Sibylle d'Antoine* (ed. Desonay).
39. Barbarino, *Guerino detto il Meschino.* Modern adaption in *Travels to the Otherworld and Other Fantastic Realms,* ed. Corinne and Claude Lecouteux.

CHAPTER SIX.
THE OTHERWORLD IN MEDIEVAL
SCANDINAVIAN LITERATURE

1. Sturluson, *Edda* (ed. Jónsson), chap. 49.
2. Saxo Grammaticus, *Saxonis Gesta Danorum* (ed. Olrik and Ræder). All English translations from Saxo Grammaticus, *The History of the Danes* (trans. Fisher; ed. Davidson).
3. "Progressi atrum incultumque oppidum, vaporanti maxime nubi simile, haud procul abesse prospectant. Pali propugnaculis intersiti desecta virorum capita praeferebant. Eximiae ferocitatis canes tuentes aditum prae foribus excubare conspecti."
3. Saxo Grammaticus, *Saxonis Gesta Danorum* (ed. Olrik and Ræder), I, 14. English translations in quotes from Saxo Grammaticus, *The History of the Danes* (trans. Fisher; ed. Davidson), 262–63.
4. English translations in quotes from Saxo Grammaticus, *The History of the Danes* (trans. Fisher; ed. Davidson), 267–69.
5. English translation in quotes from Saxo Grammaticus, *The History of the Danes* (trans. Fisher; ed. Davidson), 30.
6. *Þorsteins þáttr bæjarmagns,* in Jónsson, ed., *Fornaldarsögur Norðurlanda,* IV.
7. Cf. Simek, "Elusive Elysia, or Which Way to Glæsisvellir?"
8. Holthausen, ed., *Beowulf nebst dem Finnsburg-Bruchstück.*
9. Lagerholm, ed., *Drei lygisǫgur,* chaps. 12–13.
10. "Skylda ek þá leysa líf mitt, ok skylda ek fara í undirheima ok sækja þrjá

kostgripi: skikkju þá, sem eigi mætti í eldi brenna, ok horn þat, er aldrigi yrði allt af drukkit, ok tafl þat, sem sjálft léki sér, þegar nokkurr léki annars vegar." From Pálsson and Edwards, *Seven Viking Romances*, 247.

11. "ok er þat með þeiri náttúru, at hverr, sem í þat lítr, má vera þeim líkr, sem ek vil, en ef mik lystir, þá má ek þann verða láta blindan, sem í litr." English translation from Pálsson and Edwards, trans., *Seven Viking Romances*, 248.

12. Wilson, ed., *Samsons saga fagra*, chap. 7.

13. Benediktsson, ed., *Landnámabók, Sturlubók*, chap. 85: "Þat var trúa þeira, at þeir doei allir í fjallit."

14. Benediktsson, ed., *Landnámabók, Sturlubók*, chap. 68 and 197.

15. Sveinsson and Þórdarson, eds., *Eyrbyggja saga*.

16. Sveinsson and Þórdarson, eds., *Eyrbyggja saga*, chap. 11: "Hann sá að fjallið laukst upp norðan. Hann sá inn í fjallið elda stóra og heyrði þangað mikinn glaum og hornaskvöl. Og er hann hlýddi ef hann næmi nokkur orðaskil heyrði hann að þar var heilsað Þorsteini þorskabít og förunautum hans og mælt að hann skal sitja í öndvegi gegnt föður sínum."

17. Sveinsson, ed., *Brennu Njáls saga*, chap. 14: "En fiskimenn þeir er voru í Kaldbak þóttust sjá Svan ganga inn í fjallið Kaldbakshorn og var honum vel þar fagnað en sumir mæltu því í mót og kváðu engu gegna en það vissu allir að hann fannst hvorki lífs né dauður."

18. For more details, see Amilien, *Le Troll et autres créatures surnaturelles*.

19. Cf. Asbjørnsen, *Norske huldreeventyr og folkesagn: Annen samling*, 340–49.

20. For more on all this, cf. Edvardsen, *Huldreland*, 80ff.

21. On the connection between dwarves and the dead, cf. Lecouteux, *The Hidden History of Elves and Dwarfs*.

22. Cf. Granberg, *Skogsrået i yngre nordisk folktradition*.

CHAPTER SEVEN.
THE PATHS TO THE OTHERWORLD

1. Cf. Donà, *Per le vie dell'altro mondo*, 117ff, 175ff, 216ff; and Pschmadt, *Die Sage von der verfolgten Hinde*.

2. See the fine thesis by Storm, *The Hind Game*.

3. *Rochuala cocad n-amra*, edited and translated in Stokes, "The Prose Tales of the Rennes Dindshenchas," 274–75.

4. Motif F377. Supernatural lapse of time in fairyland.

5. Cf. Bonafin, "Relativistic Time and Space in Medieval Journeys to the Other World."

6. Map, *De nugis curialium* (trans. James), I, 11. The story corresponds to the tale type AT 470B, Motif F378.1. Taboo: touching ground on return from fairyland.

7. In *Erzählungen des späten Mittelaters und ihr Weiterleben in Literatur und Volksdichtung bis zur Gegenwart* (vol. 1, 124–45), Röhrich has assembled seventeen texts telling the story of a monk snatched up to paradise and who has spent two or three hundred years there while thinking he has only been there for a moment.

8. "L'Homme qui ne voulait pas mourir," *Revue des Traditions Populaires* XI (1896), 569–71.

9. Luzel, *Contes inédits,* I, 39–43.

10. Translated into French by Christian Guyonvarc'h in *Celticum* 15 (1966). See also Carey, "The Location of the Otherworld in Irish Tradition."

11. Windisch, *Irische Texte,* 113–33.

12. Jellinek, ed. *Friedrich von Schwaben*; French translation by Corinne and Claude Lecouteux in *Contes, Diableries et autres merveilles du Moyen Âge,* 76–94.

13. *La Historia del Liombruno.* Tale type AT 400A* + 518.

14. *Seifrid de Ardemont,* in Füetrer, *Das Buch der Abenteuer* (ed. Thoelen and Bastert), II, 67–168. Tale types AT 400, 401, 425, 313.

15. Cf. Lecouteux, "L'Arrière-plan des sites aventureux dans le roman médiéval."

16. Berthold von Holle, *Demantin* (ed. Bartsch), ll. 2540–678.

17. Wolfenbüttel, Herzog August Bibliothek, ms Cord. 51.2 Aug. 4.

18. Brunel, ed., *Jaufré.*

19. Cf. Walter, *Dictionnaire de mythologie arthurienne,* 159–60.

20. Cf. Graf, *Miti, leggende e superstizioni del Medio Evo,* II, 303–35.

21. Cf. Walter, *Le Bel Inconnu de Renaut de Beaujeu*; Ferlampin-Acher and Léonard, *La Fée et la* Guivre, i–lxvi.

22. Heinrich von Neustadt, *'Apollonius von Tyrland' nach der Gothaer Handschrift* (ed. Singer).

23. Gerbert de Montreuil, *La Continuation de Perceval* (ed. Oswald), III, ll. 14342–556.

24. *Le Chevalier du Papegau* (ed. Heuckenkamp), §51–54, 63–69.

25. Renaut de Beaujeu, *Le Bel Inconnu* (ed. Williams). The plot is close to that of tale type AT 400.

26. *Historia Meriadoci regis Cambriae,* ed. and trans. Jean-Charles Berthet, in

Walter, ed., *Arthur, Gauvain et Mériadoc*, 168–297. English translations in quotations from Day, ed., *Latin Arthurian Literature*.

27. See also Boleslas, ed. *La Damoisele à la mule*, 73–89.

28. Gallais, *La Fée à la fontaine et à l'arbre*.

29. English translation from Tolley, *Shamanism in Norse Myth and Magic*, I, 117.

30. Geoffroy of Auxerre, *Super Apocalypsim* (ed. Gastadelli), sermon XV.

31. Map, *De nugis curialium*, IV, 9.

32. Map, *De nugis curialium*, II, 12.

33. Map, *De nugis curialium*, II, 11.

34. Aimon of Varennes, *Florimont* (ed. Hilka), ll. 2487ff.

35. Johannes de Alta Silva, *Dolopathos* (ed. Hilka), 81.

36. Cf. Lecouteux, "Aspects de la forêt dans les traditions germaniques du Moyen Âge."

37. Walter, *La Mémoire du temps*, 495.

38. Thomas, "Gloses provençales inédites tirées d'un MS. des *Derivationes* d'Ugucio de Pise."

39. Martin of Braga, *De correctione rusticorum*, 8, in *Martini episcopi Bracarensis opera omnia* (ed. Barlow); English translation from Dowden, *European Paganism*, 41–42. Cf. Lecouteux, "Lamia ou les métamorphoses d'un croque-mitaine féminin au Moyen Âge."

40. Cf. Grimm, *Deutsche Mythologie*, II, 882ff.

41. Gervais of Tilbury, *Otia imperialia* (ed. Leibnitz), III, 86.

42. William of Auvergne, *De universo*, II, 3, 24, in *Opera omnia*, vol. 1, 1,066ff.

43. Stokes and Strachan, eds., *Thesaurus Paleohibernicus*, vol. 1, 2; cited in Le Roux and Guyonvarc'h, *Mórrígan, Bodb, Macha*, 35.

44. Walter, *Dictionnaire de mythologie arthurienne*, 278–82.

45. Original text in Best and Bergin, eds., *Lebor na Huidre*, 302–4. For more on the literary genre of adventures, cf. Duignan, *The Echtrae as an Early Irish Literary Genre*.

46. Loth, *Les Mabinogion du Livre Rouge de Hergest avec les variantes du Livre Blanc de Rhydderch*, vol. 2, 95.

47. Afanassiev, "Croyances païennes à propos de l'île Bouïann," in Toporkov, ed., *Proishojdenie mifa: Stat'i po folkloru, etnografii i mifologii* (The Origin of Myth: Articles on Folklore, Ethnography and Mythology), 21ff.

48. Meyer, trans., *The Voyage of Bran Son of Febal to the Land of the Living*. In the same book (101–237) there is an essay by Alfred Nutt on the otherworld of the ancient Irish.

49. Motif C524. Taboo: disembarking from boat on return from other world.

50. Text and English translation in Meyer, ed. and trans., *The Voyage of Bran*, 30–35.

51. *Scéla Ailill & Etaine*, in Müller, ed. and trans., "Two Irish Tales," 350–61.

52. French translation by D'Arbois de Jubainville in *Cours de littérature celtique*, V: *L'Épopée celtique en Irlande*, 174–216, here at 201.

53. Best, ed. and trans., "The Adventures of Art Son of Con, and the Courtship of Delbchæm."

54. *Faghail craoibhe Chormaic mhic Airt*, in O'Grady, ed., *Toruigheacht Dhiarmuda agus Ghrainne*, 212–29.

55. Vries, *La Religion des Celtes*, 265–66.

56. Nitze and Jenkins, eds., *Le Haut Livre du Graal*, II, 152–156; ll. 953ff.

57. Nitze and Jenkins, eds., *Le Haut Livre du Graal*, II, 402, ll. 9988–90.

58. Nitze and Jenkins, eds., *Le Haut Livre du Graal*, II, 109, ll. 2182–84.

59. Cf. Lecouteux, *Mélusine et le Chevalier au Cygne*, 79–85.

60. *La Vengeance Raguidel* (ed. Friedwagner), in Rauol von Houdenc, *Sämtliche Werke*, II; l. 5056–59.

61. Heinrich von dem Türlin, *Diu Crône*, ll. 17361–499.

62. Heinrich von dem Türlin, *Diu Crône*, ll. 15664ff.

CHAPTER EIGHT.
THE OTHERWORLD IN FOLKTALES AND SONGS

1. Siniavski, *Ivan le Simple*, 13–14.

2. Tzetzae, *Historiarum Variarum Chiliades* (ed. Kiessling), "Peri Eurydikēs," ll. 843–57, p. 73.

3. Cf. Hultkrantz, *The North American Indian Orpheus Tradition*; Coman, "Orphée, civilisateur de l'humanité." For more on the influence of Scythian shamanism on Greek spirituality, cf. Dodds, *The Greeks and the Irrational*, 135ff.

4. Bliss, ed., *Sir Orfeo*.

5. Cf. Micha, ed., *Lancelot, roman en prose du XIIIe siècle*, I, 33. Orpheus is also considered to be *l'anchanteor qui le Chastel des Anchantemenz fonda en la marche d'Ecoce* "the enchanter who created the Castle of Enchantments in the borderland Scottish marches" (XCVIII, 39).

6. *Sir Orfeo* (ed. Bliss), ll. 347–56; 383–96; English translation from Weston, *The Chief Middle English Poets*, 137–38.

7. Child, ed., *The English and Scottish Popular Ballads*, I, 217.

8. Boethius, *Philosophiae consolatio* (ed. Bieler).

9. Fulgentius, *Mythologies* (ed. and trans. Wolff and Dain), *Mytologiarum Libri*, III, 10.

10. Thompson, *Contes des Indiens d'Amérique du Nord*, nr. 55.

11. Cf. Wlislocki, *La Rose et le musicien*; Lecouteux, *Dictionary of Gypsy Mythology*.

12. Wlislocki, *La Rose et le musicien*, nr. 84–86.

13. Kreutzwald, *Kalevipoeg*.

14. Thompson, *Motif-Index of Folk-literature*.

15. Aarne and Thompson, *The Types of the Folktale*.

16. Tubach, *Index Exemplorum*.

17. Cf. Luzel, *Légendes chrétiennes de Basse-Bretagne*, II, 187–215. The souls of the damned are plunged into vats of boiling oil and molten lead.

18. Motif F81.2. Journey to hell to recover devil's contract.

19. Gonzenbach, *Sicilianische Märchen aus dem Volksmund gesammelt*, nr. 88.

20. This motif is borrowed from the Bible (Genesis 41:1–4). It appears in the majority of tales of type AT 471.

21. Luzel, *Légendes chrétiennes de Basse-Bretagne*, II, 187–215.

22. Ténèze, "Le Chauffeur du diable."

23. Sébillot, "Légendes chrétiennes de Haute-Bretagne," 484–85.

24. Salvi-Lopez, *Leggende delle Alpi*, 199.

25. Schüle, "Il vaut mieux souffrir du froid maintenant."

26. Belmont, *Poétique du conte*, 230.

27. This motif is borrowed from Genesis 41:1–4. It appears in the majority of the tales of type AT 471; cf. Gaston, *L'Intiation et l'Au-delà*, II, 7–169.

28. Luzel, *Contes populaires de la Basse Bretagne*, I.

29. Luzel, *Les Légendes chrétiennes de Basse-Bretagne*, II, 216–47.

30. Luzel, *Les Légendes chrétiennes de Basse-Bretagne*, II, 216–24.

31. Karlinger and Pögl, eds., *Märchen aus Argentinien und Paraguay*, nr. 45, 163–65.

32. Asbjørnsen and Moe, *Contes de Norvège*, 229–34.

33. Asbjørnsen and Moe, *Contes de Norvège*, 229–34.

34. Cf. *Soria Moria Slott* (The Castle of Soria Moria), *Kari Trestakk* (Kari Wooden-dress), and *De tre kongsdøtre i berget det blå* (The Three Princesses in the Blue Mountain).

35. Gennep, *Les Rites de passage*, 219.

36. Lüthi, "Diesseits- und Jenseitswelt im Märchen."

37. Belmont, "Les Seuils de l'autre monde dans les contes merveilleux français," 74.

38. Andreesco and Bacou, *Mourir à l'ombre des Carpathes.*

39. Cf. Ranke, *Indogermanische Totenverehrung,* I

40. Cf. Lecouteux, "Ramsundsberget."

41. Cf. Conte, "Le Chemin de l'âme vers l'au-delà."

42. See, for example, Dégh, "The Tree That Reached Up to the Sky (type 468)."

43. Afanassiev, *Contes populaires russes,* nr. 260: "The Vampire" (*Upyr'*); nr. 179 and nr. 180: "The Feather of Finist, Light Falcon" (*Përyško Finista jasna sokola*); nr. 229: "The Nocturnal Dances" (*Nočnye pljaski*).

44. Afanassiev, *Contes populaires russes,* nr. 103 and nr. 104: "Ivan of the Birch and the White Woodland Creature" (*Ivan Sučenko i Belyj Poljanin*) and "Dawn, Sunset, and Midnight" (*Zor'ka, Večorka i Polunočka*).

45. Karlinger and Pögl, *Märchen aus der Karibik,* nr. 60, 179–83.

46. Cited in Karlinger, *Zauberschlaf und Entrückung,* 41–42.

47. Wlislocki, *La Rose et le Musicien.*

48. "The Reckless Words" (*Neostorožnoe slovo*), Afanassiev, *Contes populaires russes,* nr. 227. The same events unfold in nr. 174, but the palace is the home of the devil.

49. Motif F92. Pit entrance to lower world. Entrance through pit, hole, spring, or cavern.

50. Ulrich von Zatzickhoven, *Lanzelet* (ed. Hahn), ll. 180–240.

51. Cf. Lecouteux, *Encyclopedia of Norse and Germanic Folklore,* under "Slíðr" and "Geirvimul."

52. Heyl, *Volkssage, Bräuche und Meinungen aus Tirol,* 142.

53. Karlinger and Pögl, eds., *Märchen aus Argentinien und Paraguay,* nr. 50, 179–82.

54. Motif E238. Dinner with the dead. Dead man is invited to dinner. Takes his host to other world.

55. Cited in Karlinger, *Zauberschlaf und Entrückung,* 22–23.

56. Grimm, *Kinder- und Hausmärchen,* I, nr. 25.

57. Gonzenbach, *Sicilianische Märchen,* nr. 64.

58. Obert, *Le Zmeu dupé et autres contes transylvaniens,* nr. 13.

59. Luzel, "Cinquième rapport sur une mission en basse Bretagne," 10.

CHAPTER NINE. IN SEARCH OF THE LOST SPOUSE

1. *Vishṅu-Purāṅa* (trans. Wilson; ed. Hall), IV, 6, 35–94. See also Jamison and Brereton, trans., *Rigveda,* X, 95, written between 1500 and 900 BCE.

2. Brockhaus, *Die Märchensammlung des Somadeva Bhatta aus Kaschmir,* II, 191–211.

3. Apuleius of Madaurus, *Metamorphoses* (ed. Helm), VI, 13: "Videsne insistentem celsissimae rupi puntis ardui verticem, de quo fontis atri fuscae defluunt undae proximaeque conceptaculo vallis inclusae Stygias irrigant paludes et rauca Cocyti fluenta nutriunt? Indidem mihi de summi fontis penita scaturigine rorem rigentem hauritum ista confestim defer urnula."

4. "Nec quicquam ibi rerum nec formonsitas ulla, sed infernus somnus ac vere Stygius, qui statim coperculo relevatus invadit eam crassaque soporis nebula cunctis eius membris perfunditur et in ipso vestigio ipsaque semita conlapsam possidet. Et iacebat immobilis et nihil aliud quam dormiens cadaver."

5. Frobenius, *Volksmärchen der Kabylen,* II, 281–93.

6. Comparetti, *Novelline popolari italiane,* 108–112: "Il palazzo incantato."

7. See the collection of articles edited by Binder and Merkelbach, *Amor und Psyche.*

8. Aeschylus, *Prometheus Bound,* in *Works* (ed. and trans. Smyth), I, 211–318. Quote slightly modernized for style.

CHAPTER TEN.
FOLKTALES AND SHAMANISM

1. Walter, "Conte, légende et mythe," 62–63; cf. Walter, "Du Chamanisme arthurien?"

2. Eliade, *Le Chamanisme.*

3. Cf. Henninger, "Neuere Forschungen zum Verbot des Knochenverbrechens."

4. Vernaleken, *Österreichische Kinder- und Hausmärchen,* nr. 5.

5. Cf. AT 313 and 314.

6. Belmont, "Orphée dans le miroir du conte merveilleux," 76 (quote) and 79 (chart). I would like to thank Nicole Belmont for sending me this article.

7. *Gylfaginning,* chap. 44, in Björnsson, ed., *Snorra Edda.* English translation (slightly modified) from Sturluson, *Edda* (trans. Faulkes), 38.

8. Haltrich, *Deutsche Volksmärchen aus dem Sachsenlande in Siebenbürgen,* nr. 15.

9. *Belmont, "Orphée dans le miroir du conte merveilleux."*

10. Schambach and Müller, *Niedersächsische Sagen und Märchen,* Göttingen, 253–57.

11. Motif D758.1. Disenchantment by three nights' silence under punishment.

12. Zingerle and Zingerle, *Kinder- und Hausmärchen aus Tirol,* nr. 104.

13. Schullerus, *Rumänische Volksmärchen,* nr. 89.

14. Cited in Derungs, *Struktur des Zaubermärchens,* I, 233.

15. Derungs, *Struktur des Zaubermärchens,* I, 237.

16. Cf. Friedman, *Orpheus in the Middle Ages,* 39–55.

17. Cf. Dégh, "The Tree That Reached Up to the Sky"; Kovács, "Das Märchen vom himmelshohen Baum."

18. Motif A652.1. Tree to heaven.

19. Thompson, *Contes des Indiens d'Amérique du Nord,* nr. 51–52.

20. Eliade, *Le Chamanisme,* 154.

21. Zingerle and Zingerle, *Kinder- und Hausmärchen aus Süddeutschland,* nr. 120. Motif F101.3. Return from lower world on eagle.

22. Dozon, *Contes albanais,* nr. 15, 121–34.

23. Karlinger and Pögl, *Märchen aus der Karibik,* nr. 70, 223–29.

24. Thompson, *Contes des Indiens d'Amérique du Nord,* 186–90.

25. Yen, "Shamanism as Reflected in the Folktale."

26. Rasmussen, *Contes du Groenland,* 21–27.

27. Rasmussen, *Contes du Groenland,* 29–33.

28. Rasmussen, *Contes du Groenland,* 35–37.

29. Grundtvig, ed., *Danmarks gamle folkeviser,* II, nr. 90 (A version):

> *For huer en gang du greder for mig,*
> *din hu giøres mod:*
> *da staar min kiste for inden fuld*
> *med leffret blod.*
>
> . . .
>
> *For huer en gang du qveder,*
> *din hu er glad:*
> *da er min graff for inden omhengt*
> *med rosens-blad.* (st. 17 and 19)

CHAPTER ELEVEN.
THE EXPERIENCE OF IMMINENT DEATH (NDE, OBE)

1. Le Maléfan, "La 'Sortie hors du corps' est-elle pensable par nos modèles cliniques et psychopathologiques?"

2. Cf., for example, Knoblauch, "Les Expériences du seuil de la mort en

Allemagne: la fin d'un déni?" which contains an important bibliography.

3. Tyrrell, *Apparitions.*

4. Wallon, *Expliquer le paranormal,* 68.

5. Borjigin, et al., "Surge of Neurophysiological Coherence and Connectivity in the Dying Brain."

6. Vernette, "Stigmates," 752.

7. Hemingway, *A Farewell to Arms,* 55.

8. Cahanin-Caillaud, *Je suis sortie de mon corps.*

9. Moody, *Life After Life,* 21–23.

10. Cf. Dinzelbacher, *Vision und Visionsliteratur im Mittelalter,* 29–33.

11. Otloh of Sankt Emmeram, *Liber visionum,* Visio 4, 55–56.

12. Osis and Haraldsson, "Sterbebettbeobachtungen von Ärzten und Krankenschwestern."

13. Osis and Haraldsson, "Sterbebettbeobachtungen," 57.

14. Osis and Haraldsson, "Sterbebettbeobachtungen," 84.

15. Wilkerson, *Beyond and Back,* 81.

16. Wilkerson, *Beyond and Back,* 7–8.

17. Cf. Moody, *La Vie après la vie,* 32, 36, 53ff, 64, 74, 93ff; Osis and Haraldsson, "Sterbebettbeobachtungen," 197ff, 210.

18. Walker, *The Decline of Hell.*

19. See the 2013 study published in the *Proceedings of the National Academy of Sciences of the USA* referred to in note 5.

20. "Corps et bio-logique du sujet," from the Institut interdisciplinaire d'anthropologie.

21. Nachez, "Le Double dans les ENOCs."

CONCLUSION

1. Gaudé, *La Porte des enfers.*

APPENDIX 1. INDEX OF SIGNS, SYMBOLS, AND OMENS

1. Walter, *Croyances populaires au Moyen Âge,* 42.

2. Lecouteux and Marcq, *Berthold de Ratisbonne,* 154.

3. "Germany" refers to material from Bächtold-Stäubli and Hoffmann-Krayer, eds., *Handwörterbuch des deutschen Aberglaubens,* vol. 8, col. 970–1,010.

4. Negelein, "Das Pferd im Seelenglauben und Totenkult," 414.

5. Grimm, *Deutsche Sagen,* nr. 312.

6. Ignaz Zingerle provides a list of 73 beliefs connected to death and spirits in *Sitten, Bräuche und Meinungen des Tiroler Volkes,* 44–57, nr. 374–446.

7. AT 769; Müller and Röhrich, "Der Tod und die Toten," nr. F41.

8. Tale type AT 769. It can be seen in the work of Thomas de Cantimpré.

9. Motif E324; Müller and Röhrich, "Der Tod und die Toten," nr. F42.

10. Cf. Saintyves, *L'Éternuement et le Baillement dans la magie.*

BIBLIOGRAPHY

Aarne, Antti, and Stith Thompson. *The Types of the Folktale: A Classification and Bibliography.* Second revised edition. Helsinki: Suomalainen Tiedeakatemia, 1964.

Aasen, Ivar. *Norsk Ordbog.* Christiania [Oslo]: Malling, 1873.

Abercromby, J. "Irish Bird-Lore." *The Folk-Lore Journal* 2 (1885): 65–67.

Achnitz, Wolfgang, ed. *Der Ritter mit dem Bock: Konrads von Stoffeln "Gauriel von Muntabel."* Tübingen: Niemeyer, 1997.

Acta sanctorum, Mai, tomus 7. Paris and Rome: Palmé, 1866.

Aeschylus. *Works.* Edited and translated by Herbert Weir Smyth. 2 vols. London: Heinemann, 1922.

[Afanasyev, Alexander] Afanassiev, Alexandre. *Contes populaires russes.* Translated into French by Lise Gruel-Apert. 3 vols. Paris: Imago, 2010.

Aimon of Varennes. *Florimont: Ein altfranzösischer Abenteuerroman.* Edited by Alfons Hilka. Göttingen: Niemeyer, 1933.

Albertus Magnus. *Opera omnia.* Edited by Émile Borgnet. 38 vols. Paris: Vivès, 1890–1899.

Amat, Jacqueline. *Songes et visions: L'au-delà dans la littérature latine tardive.* Paris: Études augustiniennes, 1985.

Amidei, Beatrice Barbiellini, ed. *Ponzela Gaia: Galvano e la donna serpente.* Milan: Luni, 2000.

Amilien, Virginie. *Le Troll et autres créatures surnaturelles.* Paris: Berg International, 1996.

Anderson, George K., trans. *"The Saga of the Völsungs" together with Excerpts from the "Nornageststháttr" and Three Chapters from the "Prose Edda."* Newark: University of Delaware Press, 1982.

Andreesco, Ioanna, and Mihaela Bacou. *Mourir à l'ombre des Carpathes*, Paris: Payot, 1986.

Antoine de la Sale. *Le Paradis de la reine Sibylle*. Edited by Fernand Desonay. Paris: Droz, 1930.

Arda-Viraf-Namak. English and Pahlavi edition. Bombay: Govt. Central Book Depot, 1872.

Árnason, Jon. *Islenzkar þjóðsögur og æfintýri*. Vol. 2. Leipzig: Hinrichs, 1864.

Arnodin, Lionnette, ed. *La Grande Oreille*. Thematic issue on "La Vie des morts: Contes de l'autre monde." Nr. 67–68 (2016–2017).

Asbjørnsen, Peter Christen. *Norske huldreeventyr og folkesagn: Annen samling*. Edited by Knut Liestøl. Oslo: Tanum, 1949.

Asbjørnsen, Peter Christen, and Jørgen Moe. *Contes de Norvège*. Gemenos: Esprit Ouvert, 1995.

Assmann, Erwin, ed. and trans. *Godeschalcus und Visio Godeschalci*. Neumünster: Wachholtz, 1979.

Athanasius. *Des Heiligen Athanasius Alexandrinus ausgewählte Schriften*. Vol. 2. Kempten: Kösel, 1917.

Augustine. *De cura por mortuis gerenda* [On the Care to Be Had for the Dead]. In *Seventeen Short Treatises of S. Augustine, Bishop of Hippo*. Translated by C. L. Cornish and H. Browne. Oxford: Parker, 1847.

Avenier, Cédric. "Les Cadrans solaires du Bas-Dauphiné à la période révolutionnaire." *Le Monde alpin et rhodanien* 27/4 (1999): 7–22.

Amidei, Beatrice Barbiellini, ed. *Ponzela Gaia: Galvano e la donna serpent*. Milan: Luni, 2000.

Apuleius of Madaurus. *Apulei Platonici: Madaurensis Metamorphoseon, libri XI*. Edited by Rudolf Helm. Leipzig: Teubner, 1907.

Bächtold-Stäubli, Hans, and Eduard Hoffmann-Krayer. *Handwörterbuch des deutschen Aberglaubens*. Foreword by Christoph Daxelmüller. 10 vols. Berlin and New York: De Gruyter, 1987.

Barbarino, Andrea de. *Guerino detto il Meschino*. Venice: Baroni, 1689.

Barral, Adrien de. *Légendes carlovingiennes: La Famille de Charlemagne et ses descendants*. Tours: Cattier, 1883.

Barrett, William. *Death-Bed Visions*. London: Methuen, 1926.

Bartholomaeis, Vincenzo de. "Due testi latini e una versione toscana della *Visio Philiberti*." *Studi Medievali* 7 (1928): 288–309.

Batiouchkof, Th. "Le Débat de l'âme et du corps." *Romania* 20 (1891): 1–55.

Bautz, Friedrich Wilhelm. *Das Fegfeuer im Anschluß an die Scholastik, mit*

Bezugnahme auf Mystik und Ascetik dargestellt. Mainz: Kirchheim, 1883.

Bayard, Florence. *L'Art du bien mourir au XVe siècle.* Paris: P.U.P.S., 1999.

———. *Bretagne . . . un autre voyage: Vivants et défunts face au grand passage.* Spézet: Keltia Graphic, 2004.

Bechstein, Ludwig. *Le Livre des contes.* Translated into French by Claude Lecouteux and Corinne Lecouteux. Paris: Corti, 2010.

Bede. *Historia ecclesiastica gentis Anglorum, Historia abbatum, Epistola ad Ecgberctum.* Edited by Charles Plummer. Oxford: Clarendon, 1896.

———. *A History of the English Church and People.* Translated by Leo Sherley-Price; revised by R. E. Latham. New York and London: Penguin, 1988.

Belmont, Nicole. "Orphée dans le miroir du conte merveilleux." *L'Homme* 25, issue 93 (1985): 59–82.

———. *Poétique du conte: Essai sur le conte de tradition orale.* Paris: Gallimard, 1999.

———. "Les Seuils de l'autre monde dans les contes merveilleux français." *Cahiers de Littérature orale* 39–40 (1996): 61–79.

Benedeit. *Le Voyage de saint Brendan.* Bilingual French edition by Ian Short and Brian Merrilees. Paris: Champion, 2006.

Benediktsson, Jakob, ed. *Landnámabók.* 2 vols. Reykjavík: Hið íslenzka fornritafélag, 1968.

Bérenger-Féraud, L.-J.-B. *Superstitions et survivances étudiées au point de vue de leur origine et de leurs transformations.* 5 vols. Paris: Leroux, 1896.

Berthold von Holle. *Demantin.* Edited by Karl Bartsch. Stuttgart: Literarischer Verein, 1875.

Best, R. I., ed. and trans. "The Adventures of Art Son of Con, and the Courtship of Delbchæm." *Ériu* 3 (1907): 149–73.

Best, R. I., and Osborn Bergin, eds. *Lebor na Huidre: Book of the Dun Cow.* Dublin: Royal Irish Academy, 1929.

Binder, Gerhard, and Reinhold Merkelbach, eds. *Amor und Psyche.* Darmstadt: Wissenschaftliche Buchgesellschaft, 1968.

Björnsson, Árni, ed. *Snorra Edda.* Reykjavík: Iðunn, 1975.

Bliss, A. J., ed. *Sir Orfeo.* Oxford: Oxford University Press, 1966.

Boethius. *Philosophiae Consolatio.* Edited by L. Bieler. Turnhout: Brepols, 1957.

Bonafin, Massimo. "Relativistic Time and Space in Medieval Journeys to the Other World." *Cognitive Philology* 2 (2009): [1–7].

Bonaventure, S[aint]. *Opera omnia,* vol. 4. Quarrachi: Collegium S. Bonaventurae, 1889.

Borjigin, Jimo, et al. "Surge of Neurophysiological Coherence and Connectivity in the Dying Brain." *Proceedings of the National Academy of Sciences of the USA* 110 (2013): 14,432–37.

Borst, Arno, et al., eds. *Tod im Mittelalter.* Konstanz: UVK, 1993.

Bosquet, Amélie. *La Normandie romanesque et merveilleuse: Traditions, légendes et superstitions populaires de cette province.* Paris and Rouen: Techener/ Brument, 1845.

Bousset, Wilhelm. "Die Himmelsreise der Seele." *Archiv für Religionswissenschaft* 4 (1901): 139–69, 229–73.

Bovon, François, and Pierre Geoltrain, eds. *Écrits apocryphes chrétiens.* Vol. 1. Paris: Gallimard, 1997.

Brandes, Herman, trans. *Visio S. Pauli: Ein Beitrag zur Visionsliteratur mit einem deutschen und zwei lateinischen Texten.* Halle: Niemeyer, 1885.

Brandt, A. J. H. Wilhelm. *Die mandäische Religion, ihre Entwicklung und geschichtliche Bedeutung.* Leipzig: Hinrichs, 1889.

Brennu Njáls Saga. Edited by Einar Ólafur Sveinsson. Reykjavík: 1954.

Brock, Sebastian P. "The *ruaḥ elōhim* of Gen 1,2 and Its Reception History in the Syriac Tradition." In *Lectures et relectures de la Bible: Festschrift P.-M. Bogaert,* edited by Jean-Marie Auwers, André Wénin, and Pierre-Maurice Bogaert, 327–49. Leuven: Leuven University Press, 1999.

Brockhaus, Hermann. *Die Märchensammlung des Somadeva Bhatta aus Kaschmir.* 2 vols. Leipzig: Brockhaus, 1843.

Brunel, Clovis, ed. *Jaufré: Roman arthurien du XIIIe siècle en vers provençaux.* Paris: Société des anciens textes français, 1943.

Brunel, Pierre, ed. *Le Mythe d'orphée au XIXe et au XXe siècle: Acts du colloque de la Sorbonne.* Paris: Didier, 1999.

Bugge, Sophus, ed. *Norrœn fornkvæði: Islandsk samling af folkelige oldtidsdigte om Nordens guder og heroer almindelig kaldet Sæmundar Edda hins Fróða.* Christiania [Oslo]: Malling, 1867.

Buchholz, Peter. "Schamanistische Züge in der altisländischen Überlieferung." PhD dissertation, University of Münster, 1968.

Caesarius of Heisterbach. *Dialogus miraculorum.* Edited by Joseph Strange. Cologne, Bonn, and Brussels: Herbele, 1851.

Cahanin-Caillaud, Kristelle. *Je suis sortie de mon corps: Témoignage.* Paris: Oh Éditions, 2009.

Campbell, John Gregorson. *Superstitions of the Highlands and Islands of Scotland.* Glasgow: MacLehose & Sons, 1900.

Cambry, Jacques. *Voyage dans le Finistère.* 3 vols. Paris: Cercle social, 1797–1798.

Canavaggio, Pierre. *Dictionnaire des superstitions et des croyances populaires.* Paris: Verviers, 1977.

Carey, John. "The Location of the Otherworld in Irish Tradition." *Eigse* 19/1 (1982): 36–43.

Carozzi, Claude. *Le Voyage de l'âme dans l'au-delà d'après la literature latine (Ve–XIIIe siècle).* Rome: École française de Rome, 1994.

Chatworth-Musters, Lina. "Superstitions du sud du Pays de Galles." *Revue des Traditions Populaires* 6 (1891): 484–85

Chesnel, Louis Pierre François Adolphe de. *Dictionnaire des superstitions, erreurs, préjugés, et traditions populaires, où sont exposées les croyances des temps anciens et modernes.* Paris: Migne, 1856.

Chrétien de Troyes. *Œuvres complètes.* Edited by Daniel Poirion. Paris: Gallimard, 1994.

Child, Francis James, ed. *The English and Scottish Popular Ballads.* 10 vols. Boston: Houghton Mifflin, 1882–1898.

Clade, Jean-Louis. *Médecins, Médecine et Superstitions dans la Franche-Comté d'autrefois et dans le pays de Montbéliard.* Écully: Horvath, 1992.

Coman, Jean. "Orphée, civilisateur de l'humanité." *Zalmoxis* 1 (1938): 130–76.

Comparetti, Domenico. *Novelline popolari italiane.* Rome, Turin, and Florence: Loescher, 1875.

Constable, Giles. "The Vision of Gunthelm and Other Visions Attributed to Peter the Venerable." *Revue Bénédictine* 66 (1956): 92–114.

Constable, Giles, and James Kritzeck, eds. *Petrus Venerabilis: Studies and Texts Commemorating the Eighth Centenary of His Death.* Rome: Herder, 1956.

Conte, Francis. "Le Chemin de l'âme vers l'au-delà." *La Grande Oreille* 67–68 (2016–2017): 88–97.

Couliano, Ioan P. *Out of the World: Otherwordly Journeys from Gilgamesh to Albert Einstein.* Boston and London: Shambala, 1991.

———. *Expériences de l'extase: Extase, ascension et récit visionnaire de l'hellénisme au Moyen Âge.* Paris: Payot, 1984.

Courtney, Margaret Ann. *Cornish Feasts and Folk-Lore.* Penzance: Beare and Son, 1890.

Crane, Thomas Frederick, ed. *The Exempla or Illustrative Stories from the "Sermones vulgares" of Jacques de Vitry.* London: Nutt, 1890.

Crofton Croker, T. *Fairy Legends and Traditions of the South of Ireland.* New and complete edition by Thomas Wright. London: Murray, 1834.

Currie, Ian. *You Cannot Die.* London: Routledge & Kegan Paul, 1979.

Curtin, Jeremiah. *Tales of the Fairies and of the Ghost World Collected from Oral Tradition in South-West Munster*. Boston: Little, Brown & Co., 1895.

Daleau, François. *Notes pour servir à l'étude des traditions, croyances et superstitions de la Gironde*. Bordeaux: Bellier, 1889.

D'Arbois de Jubainville, H., et al., eds. *Cours de littérature celtique*. Vol. 5, *L'Épopée celtique en Irlande*. Paris: Thorin, 1892.

Day, Mildred Leake, ed. and trans. *Latin Arthurian Literature*. Cambridge, U.K., and Rochester, N.Y.: Brewer, 2005.

Dégh, Linda. "The Tree That Reached Up to the Sky (type 468)." In *Studies in East European Folk Narrative*, edited by Linda Dégh, 263–316. Bloomington: Indiana University Press, 1978.

Depiny, Adalbert. *Oberösterreichisches Sagenbuch*. Linz: Pirngruber, 1932.

Derungs, Kurt. *Struktur des Zaubermärchens*. 2 vols. Bern, Stuttgart, and Vienna: Haupt, 1994.

Desaivre, Léo. *Croyances, présages, usages, traditions diverses, et proverbs*. Niort: Clouzot, 1881.

Dinzelbacher, Peter. *Angst im Mittelalter: Teufels-, Todes- und Gotteserfahrung: Mentalitätsgeschichte und Ikonographie*. Paderborn and Munich: Schöningh, 1996.

———. "Die Jenseitsbrücke im Mittelalter." PhD dissertation, University of Vienna, 1973.

———. "Reflexionen irdischer Sozialstrukturen in mittelalterlichen Jenseitsschilderungen." *Archiv für Kulturgeschichte* 61 (1979), 16–34.

———. *Vision und Visionsliteratur im Mittelalter*. Stuttgart: Hirsemann, 1981.

[*Distaff Gospels*] Jeay, Madeleine, ed. *Les Evangiles des quenouilles*. Paris and Montreal: Vrin / Presses de l'Université de Montréal, 1985.

Dodds, Eric R. *The Greeks and the Irrational*. Berkeley and Los Angeles: University of California Press, 1951.

Donà, Carlo. "Les Cantari et la tradition écrite du conte populaire." *Cahiers de Recherche Médiévales et Humanistes* 20 (2010): 225–43.

———. "Cantari, fiabe e filologi." In *Il cantare italian: Fra folklore e letteratura*, edited by Michelangelo Picone and Luisa Rubini. Florence: Olschki, 2007. Pp. 147–70.

———. *Per le vie dell'altro mondo: L'animale guida e il mito del viaggio*. Soveria Mannelli: Rubbettino, 2003.

Dottin, Georges. *Contes et légendes d'Irlande*. Le Havre: Édition de la Province, 1901.

———. *Contes irlandais.* Paris: Welter, 1901.

———. *Manuel pour servir à l'étude de l'Antiquité celtique.* Paris: Champion, 1915.

Dowden, Ken. *European Paganism: The Realities of Cult from Antiquity to the Middle Ages.* London and New York: Routledge, 2000.

Dozon, Auguste. *Contes albanais.* Paris: Leroux, 1881.

Dubost, Francis. *Aspects fantastiques de la littérature narrative médiévale (XIIe–XIIIe siècle): L'autre, l'ailleurs, l'autrefois.* 2 vols. Paris: Champion, 1991.

Duignan, Leonie. "The Echtrae as an Early Irish Literary Genre." PhD thesis, National University of Ireland Maynooth, 2010.

Édelestand du Méril, M. *Poésies populaires latines antérieures au douzième siècle.* Paris: Brockhaus and Avenarius, 1843.

Edvardsen, Erik Henning. *Huldreland: sunkne øyer daget opp av havet, en studie i P. Chr. Asbjørnsens Skarvene fra Udrøst, et eventyrsagen fra Nordlandene.* Oslo: Asbjørnsenselskapet, 2015.

Ehlen, Thomas, ed. *Hystoria ducis Bauarie Ernesti: Kritische Edition des "Herzog Ernst" C und Untersuchungen zu Struktur und Darstellung des Stoffes in den volkssprachlichen und lateinischen Fassungen.* Tübingen: Narr, 1996.

Ehrismann, Gustav, ed. *Der Renner von Hugo von Trimberg.* 4 vols. Tübingen: Literarischer Verein, 1908–1911.

Eliade, Mircea. *Le Chamanisme et les techniques archaïques de l'extase.* 2nd edition. Paris: Payot, 1968.

———. *Shamanism: Archaic Techniques of Ecstasy.* Princeton: Princeton University Press, 2004.

Enzyklopädie des Märchens: Handwörterbuch zur historischen und vergleichenden Erzählforschung. Edited by Kurt Ranke et al. 15 vols. Berlin: De Gruyter, 1975–2015.

Edvardsen, Erik Henning. *Huldreland - sunkne øyer daget opp av havet -. En studie i P. Chr. Asbjørnsens Skarvene fra Udrøst, et Eventyrsagn fra Nordlandene. Juletræet: Asbjørnsenselskapets årsskrift* 8. Oslo: [Asbjørnsenselskapet], 2015.

Farmer, Hugh, ed. "The Vision of Orm." *Analecta Bollandiana* 75 (1957): 72–82.

Ferguson, Mary Heyward. "The Debate between the Body and the Soul: A Study in Relationship between Form and Content." PhD dissertation, Ohio State University, 1965.

Ferlampin-Acher, Christine. "Voyager avec le diable Zéphir dans le *Le Roman de Perceforest* (XVe siècle): La tempête, la *Mesnie Hellequin*, la *translatio imperii* et le souffle de l'inspiration." In *Voyager avec le diable: Voyages réels, voyages imaginaires et discours démonologiques (XVe–XVIIe siècle)*, edited by Grégoire Holtz and Thibaut Maus de Rolley, 45–59. Paris: P.U.P.S., 2008.

Ferlampin-Acher, Christine, and Monique Léonard. *La Fée et la* Guivre: Le Bel Inconnu *de Renaut de Beaujeu, approche littéraire et concordancier (vv. 1237–3252).* Paris: Champion, 1996.

Filippi, Julie. "Légendes, croyances et superstitions de la Corse." *Revue des Traditions Populaires* IX (1894): 457–67.

Fleury, Jean. *Littérature orale de la Basse-Normandie.* Paris: Maisonneuve, 1883.

Folkevennen [periodical]. Christiania [Oslo]: Malling, 1852–1900.

Flood, John L., ed. *Die Historie von Herzog Ernst: Die Frankfurter Prosafassung des 16. Jahrhunderts.* Berlin: Schmidt, 1992.

Ford, Arthur. *Bericht vom Leben nach dem Tod.* Munich: Scherz Verlag, 1975.

Friedman, John Block. *Orpheus in the Middle Ages.* Syracuse, N.Y.: Syracuse University Press, 2000.

Frobenius, Leo. *Volksmärchen der Kabylen.* 3 vols. Jena: Diederichs, 1921–1922.

Füetrer, Ulrich. *Das Buch der Abenteuer.* Edited by Heinz Thoelen with collaboration from Bernd Bastert. 2 vols. Göppingen: Kümmerle, 1997.

Fulgentius. *Mythologies.* Edited and translated into French by Étienne Wolff and Philippe Dain. Bilingual Latin-French edition. Villeneuve-d'Ascq: Presses Universitaires du Septentrion, 2013.

Gaidoz, Henri. "Superstitions de la Basse-Bretagne au XVIIe siècle." *Revue celtique* 2 (1873–1875): 484–86.

Gall, P. Morel, ed. *Offenbarungen der Schwester Mechthild von Magdeburg oder das fliessende Licht der Gottheit.* Regensburg: Manz, 1869.

Gallais, Pierre. *La Fée à la fontaine et à l'arbre: Un archétype du conte merveilleux et du récit courtois.* Amsterdam and Atlanta, Ga.: Rodopi, 1992.

Gansweidt, Birgit, ed. *Der "Ernestus" des Odo von Magdeburg: Kritische Edition mit Kommentar eines lateinischen Epos aus dem 13. Jahrhundert.* Munich: Arbeo-Gesellschaft, 1989.

Gardiner, Eileen. *Visions of Heaven and Hell before Dante.* New York: Italica, 1989.

Gaster, Moses. "Hebrew Visions of Hell and Paradise." *Journal of the Royal Asiatic Society* 25, no. 3 (July 1893): 571–611.

Gaston, Vincent. "L'Intiation et l'Au-delà: Le conte et la découverte de l'autre monde." 2 vols. PhD dissertation, University of Paris VII–Denis Diderot, 2005.

Gaudé, Laurent. *La Porte des enfers*. Paris: Actes Sud, 2008

Gellius, Aulus. *The Attic Nights of Aulus Gellius*. Translated by John C. Rolfe. 3 vols. London: Heinemann, 1927–1928.

Gennep, Arnold van. *Les Rites de passage*. Paris: Mouton, 1981.

Geoffroy of Auxerre, *Super Apocalypsim*. Edited by Ferruccio Gastadelli. Rome: Edizioni di storia e letteratura, 1970.

Gerbert de Montreuil. *La Continuation de Perceval*. Vols. 1–2 edited by Mary Williams; vol. 3 edited by Marguerite Oswald. 3 vols. Paris: Champion, 1922–1925, 1975.

Gervais of Tilbury. *Otia imperialia*. In *Scriptores rerum Brunsvicensium*, vol. I, edited by Gottfried Wilhelm Leibnitz. Hannover: Foerster, 1707.

Gobi, Jean. *La Scala coeli*. Edited by Marie-Anne Polo de Beaulieu. Paris: C.N.R.S., 1991.

Gonzenbach, Laura. *Sicilianische Märchen aus dem Volksmund gesammelt*. Leipzig: Engelmann, 1870.

Gottschall, Dagmar, and Georg Steer, eds. *Der deutsche Lucidarius, Teil I: Kritischer Text nach den Handschriften*. Tübingen: Niemeyer, 1994.

Graf, Arturo. *Miti, leggende e superstizioni del Medio Evo*. 2 vols. Turin: Loescher, 1892–1893.

Grambo, Ronald. "Traces of Shamanism in Norwegian Folktales and Popular Legends: Religious Beliefs Transmuted into Narrative Motifs." *Fabula* 16 (1975): 20–46.

Granberg, Gunnar. *Skogsrået i yngre nordisk folktradition*. Uppsala: Lundequist, 1935.

Gregor, Walter. *An Echo of the Olden Time from the North of Scotland*. Edinburgh & Glasgow: Menzies, 1874.

——. *Notes on the Folk-Lore of the North-East of Scotland*. London: Folk-Lore Society, 1881.

——. "Les Rites de la Construction." *Revue des Traditions Populaires* VI (1891): 172–73.

Gregory the Great. *Dialogues*. Translated by Odo John Zimmerman. Washington, D.C.: Catholic University of America Press, 1959.

Gregory of Tours. *The History of the Franks*. Translated by Lewis Thorpe. London: Penguin, 1974.

Greven, Joseph, ed. *Die Exempla aus den Sermones feriales et communes des Jakob von Vitry.* Heidelberg: Winter, 1914.

Grimm, Jacob. *Deutsche Mythologie* [= *DM*]. 4th edition, edited by Elard Hugo Meyer. 3 vols. Darmstadt: Wissenschaftliche Buchgesellschaft, 1965.

———. *Deutsche Sagen.* Edited by H. Rölleke. Frankfurt: Deutscher Klassiker, 1994.

Grimm, Jacob, and Wilhelm Grimm. *Kinder- und Hausmärchen.* Edited by Heinz Rölleke. 3 vols. Stuttgart: Reclam, 1993.

Grundtvig, Svend, et al., eds. *Danmarks gamle folkeviser.* 5 vols. Copenhagen: Samfundet til den danske literaturs fremme, etc. 1853–1965.

Guiette, Robert. "L'Invention étymologique dans les lettres françaises au Moyen Âge." *Cahiers de l'Association internationale des Études françaises* 11 (1959): 273–85.

Guyénot, Laurent. *La Mort féerique: Anthropologie du merveilleux (XIIe–XVe siècle).* Paris: Gallimard, 2011.

Hahn, Johann Georg von. *Griechische und Albanesische Märchen.* Leipzig: Engelmann, 1864.

Haltrich, Josef. *Deutsche Volksmärchen aus dem Sachsenlande in Siebenbürgen.* Vienna: Graeser, 1882.

Hardy, Christine. *L'Après-vie à l'épreuve de la science.* Monaco: Le Rocher, 1986.

Harou, Alfred. "Les Météores: En Belgique." *Revue des Traditions* 17 (1902): 140–41.

Hartmann von Aue. *Erec.* Edited by Albert Leitzmann and Ludwig Wolff. 6th edition under the supervision of Christoph Cormeau and Kurt Gärtner. Tübingen: Niemeyer, 1985.

Heide, Eldar. "Holy Islands and the Otherworld: Places beyond Water." In *Isolated Islands in Medieval Nature, Culture and Mind,* edited by J. Gerhardt and Thorstein Jørgensen, 57–80. Budapest: Ceu, 2011.

Heinrich von dem Türlin. *Die Krone (Verse 1–12281) nach der Handschrift 2779 der Österreichischen Nationalbibliothek.* Edited by Fritz Peter Knapp and Manuela Niesner, based on preliminary work by Alfred Ebenbauer, Klaus Zatloukal, and H. P. Pütz. Tübingen: Niemeyer, 2000.

———. *Die Krone (Verse 12282–30042) nach der Handschrift Cod. Pal. germ. 374 der Universitätsbibliothek Heidelberg.* Edited by Alfred Ebenbauer und Florian Kragl, based on preliminary work by Fritz Peter Knapp and Klaus Zatloukal. Tübingen: Niemeyer, 2005.

Heinrich von Neustadt. *"Apollonius von Tyrland" nach der Gothaer Handschrift,*

"Gottes Zukunft" und "Visio Philiberti" nach der Heidelberger Handschrift. Edited by Samuel Singer. Berlin: Weidmann, 1906.

Heist, William Watts, ed. *Vitae sanctorum Hiberniae: Ex codice olim Salmanticensi, nunc Bruxellensi.* Brussels: Société Bollandistes, 1965.

Hemingway, Ernest. *A Farewell to Arms.* New York: Scribner, 1997.

Henninger, Joseph. "Neuere Forschungen zum Verbot des Knochenverbrechens." In *Studia Ethnographica et Folkloristica in Honorem Béla Gunda,* edited by József Szabadfalvi and Zoltán Ujváry, 673–702. Debrecen: Kossuth Lajos Tudományegyetem, 1971.

Hesiod. *The Works and Days—Theogony—The Shield of Herakles.* Translated by Richmond Lattimore. Ann Arbor: University of Michigan Press, 1973.

Heuckenkamp, Ferdinand, ed. *Le Chevalier du Papegau.* Halle: Niemeyer, 1896.

Heyl, Johann Adolf. *Volkssage, Bräuche und Meinungen aus Tirol.* Brixen: Katholisch-politischer Pressverein, 1897. Reprint, Bolzano: Athesia, 1989.

La Historia del Liombruno. Rome: Silber, 1485.

Holmes, Annie. *Dictionnaire des superstitions.* Paris: De Vecchi, 1990.

Holthausen, Ferdinand, ed. *Beowulf nebst dem Finnsburg-Bruchstück.* 2 vols. Heidelberg: Winter, 1905–1906.

Homer. *The Odyssey.* With an English translation by A. T. Murray. 2 vols. Cambridge, Mass., and London: Harvard University Press/Heinemann, 1919.

Hultkrantz, Åke. *The North American Indian Orpheus Tradition: A Contribution to Comparative Religion.* Stockholm: Statens Etnografiska Museum, 1957.

Inguanez, Mauro. "La Visione di Alberico." *Miscellanea Cassinese* 11 (1932): 33–103.

Jacobus de Voragine. *Legenda Aurea vulgo Historia Lombardica Dicta.* Edited by T. Graesse. Leipzig: Arnold, 1850.

———. The Golden Legend, or, Lives of the Saints. *Translated by William Caxton.* 7 vols. London: Dent, 1900.

Jacobsen, Peter Christian, and Peter Orth, eds. *Gesta Ernesti ducis: Die Erfurter Prosa-Fassung der Sage von den Kämpfen und Abenteuern des Herzog Ernst.* Erlangen: Universitätsbund Erlangen-Nürnberg, 1997.

James, Montague Rhodes, trans. *The Apocryphal New Testament.* Oxford: Clarendon, 1924.

Jamison, Stephanie W., and Joel P. Brereton, trans. *The Rigveda: The Earliest Religious Poetry of India.* Oxford: Oxford University Press, 2014.

Jankovitch, S. V. "Erfahrungen während des klinisch-toten Zustandes." In

Fortleben nach dem Tode, edited by Andreas Resch, 408–24. Innsbruck: Resch, 1980.

Jellinek, M. H., ed. *Friedrich von Schwaben.* Berlin: Weidmann, 1904.

Johannes de Alta Silva. *Dolopathos, sive De rege et septem sapientibus.* Edited by Alfons Hilka. Heidelberg: Winter, 1913.

Johannes de Hauvilla. *Architrenius.* Edited by P. G. Schmidt. Munich: Fink, 1974.

Jónsson, Guðni ed. *Fornaldarsögur Norðurlanda,* vol. 4. Reykjavik: Íslendingasagnaútgáfan, 1950.

Jónsson, Guðni, and Bjarni Vilhjálmsson, eds. *Fornaldarsögur Norðurlanda.* 3 vols. Reykjavík, 1943–1944.

Jouët, Philippe. "L'Autre monde celtique." In *Mythes et Réalités des Celtes: Actes du colloque de Renac, samedi 10 juin 2000,* 22–41. Fégréac: Ordos, 2000.

Julien de Vézelay. *Sermons.* Edited and translated by Damien Vorreux. 2 vols. Paris: Cerf, 1972.

Karlinger, Felix. *Zauberschlaf und Entrückung: Zur Problematik der Jenseitszeit in der Volkserzählung.* Vienna: Österreichisches Museum für Volkskunde, 1986.

Karlinger, Felix, and Johannes Pögl. *Märchen aus der Karibik.* Cologne: Diederichs, 1983.

———. *Märchen aus Argentinien und Paraguay.* Cologne: Diederichs, 1987.

Kastner, L.-E. "Les Versions françaises inédites de la *Descente de saint Paul en enfer.*" *Revue des langues romanes* 48 (1905): 385–95.

Kérardven, Louis [L. Dufilhol]. *Guionvac'h: Études sur la Bretagne.* Paris: Ébrard, 1835.

Kinahan, G. H. "Notes on Irish Folk-Lore." *The Folk-Lore Record* 4 (1881): 96–125.

Klaus, Catherine. "De l'enfer au paradis … et retour dans l'*Architrenius* de Jean de Hanville." In *Pour une mythologie du Moyen Âge,* edited by Laurence Harf-Lancner and Dominique Boutet, 27–42. Paris: École normale supérieure, 1988.

Klob, Otto. "A vida de Sancto Amaro, texte portugais du XIVe siècle." *Romania* 30 (1901): 504–18.

Knittel, Hermann, ed. *Heito und Walahfrid Strabo, Visio Wetti.* 3rd edition. Heidelberg: Mattes, 2009.

Knoblauch, Hubert. "Les Expériences du seuil de la mort en Allemagne: La fin d'un déni?" *Recherches sociologiques* 32/2 (2001): 49–61

Kovács, Ágnes. "Das Märchen vom himmelshohen Baum." *Veröffentlichungen der europäischen Märchengesellschaft* 7 (1984): 74–84.

Kreutzwald, Friedrich Reinhold. *Kalevipoeg: Épopée nationale estonienne.* Paris: Gallimard, 2004.

La Sale, Antoine de. *Le Paradis de la reine Sibylle.* Edited by Fernand Desonay. Paris: Droz, 1930.

Lactantius. *De opificio Dei* [On the Workmanship of God]. Translated by William Fletcher. In *Ante-Nicene Fathers,* vol. 7, edited by Alexander Roberts, James Donaldson, and A. Cleveland Coxe. Buffalo, N.Y.: Christian Literature Publishing, 1890.

Lacuve, R.-M. "Prières populaires du Poitou." *Revue des Traditions populaires* 4 (1889): 622.

Lagerholm, Åke, ed. *Drei lygisǫgur: Egils saga einhenda ok Ásmundar berserkjabana, Ála flekks saga, Flóres saga konungs ok sona hans.* Halle: Niemeyer, 1927.

Laisnel de la Salle, Germain. *Croyances et légendes du centre de la France. Souvenirs du vieux temps: Coutumes et traditions populaires comparées à celles des peuples anciens et modernes.* 2 vols. Paris: Chaix, 1875.

Lambert, Pierre-Yves, trans. *Les Quatre Branches du Mabinogi et autres contes gallois du Moyen Âge.* Paris: Gallimard, 1993.

Lasne, Sophie, and André Gaultier. *Dictionnaire des superstitions.* Paris: Tchou, 1980.

Laurioz, Hubert. *Dictionnaire des superstitions.* Paris: Albin Michel, 1998.

Le Braz, Anatole. *La Légende de la mort chez les Bretons armoricains.* Definitive edition. 2 vols. [1928]. Paris: Champion, 1990.

Le Brun, Pierre. *Histoire critique des pratiques superstitieuses.* Rouen: Behourt, 1702.

Le Calvez, G. "Basse-Bretagne et environs de Saint-Méen." *Revue des Traditions* 7 (1892): 90–93.

Lecouteux, Claude. "Aspects de la forêt dans les traditions germaniques du Moyen Âge." *Otrante* 27–28 (2010): 33–48.

———. *Encyclopedia of Norse and Germanic Folklore, Mythology, and Magic.* Translated by Jon E. Graham; edited by Michael Moynihan. Rochester, Vt.: Inner Traditions, 2016.

———. *The Hidden History of Elves and Dwarfs: Avatars of Invisible Realms.* Translated by Jon E. Graham. Rochester, Vt.: Inner Traditions, 2018.

———. "Lamia ou les métamorphoses d'un croque-mitaine féminin au Moyen

Âge." In Τίτλος πλήρης, Κανίσκιον φιλίας: τιμητικός τόμος για τον Guy-Michel Saunier, ed. Emmanuelle Moser-Karagiannis, 51–61. Athens: Grafikés téchnes Afoi Tzífa, 2002.

———. "L'Arrière-plan des sites aventureux dans le roman medieval." *Études Germaniques* 46 (1991): 293–304.

———. "Les marches de l'au-delà." In *Par les mots et les textes, mélanges Claude Thomasset*, ed. D. James-Raoul and O. Soutet, 483–92. Paris: P.U.P.S., 2005.

———. *Mélusine et le Chevalier au Cygne.* Paris: Imago, 1997.

———. *Phantom Armies of the Night: The Wild Hunt and the Ghostly Processions of the Undead.* Translated by Jon E. Graham. Rochester, Vt.: Inner Traditions, 2011.

———. "Ramsundsberget: L'arrière-plan mental de l'inscription runique." *Études Germaniques* 53 (1997): 559–61.

———. "Le Rêve et son arrière-plan au Moyen Âge, un apercu." *Cahiers d'études germaniques* 33 (1997): 11–18.

———. *Traditional Magic Spells for Protection and Healing.* Translated by Jon E. Graham. Rochester, Vt.: Inner Traditions, 2017.

———. *Witches, Werewolves, and Fairies: Shapeshifters and Astral Doubles in the Middle Ages.* Translated by Clare Frock. Rochester, Vt.: Inner Traditions, 2003.

———. "Zur anderen Welt." In *Diesseits- und Jenseitsreisen im Mittelalter, Voyages dans l'ici-bas et dans l'au-delà au Moyen Âge.* Edited by Wolf-Dieter Lange, 79–89. Bonn: Bouvier, 1992.

Lecouteux, Claude, and Corinne Lecouteux. *Contes, diableries et autres merveilles au Moyen Âge.* Paris: Imago, 2013.

———, eds. *Travels to the Otherworld and Other Fantastic Realms.* Translated by Jon E. Graham. Rochester, Vt.: Inner Traditions, 2020.

Lecouteux, Claude, and Philippe Marcq. *Berthold de Ratisbonne: Péchés et vertus, scènes de la vie du XIIIe siècle.* Paris: Desjonquères, 1991

———. *Les Esprits et les Morts: Croyances médiévales.* Paris: Champion, 1990.

Lefèvre, Sylvie. "Regnaud le Queux." In *Dictionnaire des lettres françaises: Le Moyen Âge,* edited by Geneviève Hasenohr and Michel Zink, 1,248–50. Paris: Fayard, 1992.

Lefèvre, Yves. *L'Elucidarium et les Lucidaires: Contribution, par l'histoire d'un texte, à l'histoire des croyances religieuses en France au Moyen Âge.* Paris: Boccard, 1954.

Le Goff, Jacques. *L'Imaginaire médiéval: Essais*. Paris: Gallimard, 1985.

————. *The Birth of Purgatory*. Translated by Arthur Goldhammer. Chicago: University of Chicago Press, 1984.

Le Maléfan, Pascal. "La 'sortie hors du corps' est-elle pensable par nos modèles cliniques et psychopathologiques? Essai de clinique d'une marge. À propos d'un cas." *L'Évolution psychiatrique* 70/3 (2005): 513–34.

Le Roux, Françoise, and Christian Guyonvarc'h. *Mórrígan, Bodb, Macha: La souveraineté guerrière de l'Irlande*. Rennes: Ogam-Celticum, 1983.

Le Rouzic, Zacharie. *Carnac: Légendes, traditions, coutumes et contes du pays*. Nantes: Dugas, 1912.

Lévinas, Emmanuel. *Dieu, la Mort et le Temps*. Paris: Grasset, 1993.

Lidzbarski, Mark, trans. *Ginzā: Der Schatz oder das grosse Buch der Mandäer*. Göttingen: Vandenhoeck & Ruprecht, 1925.

Liebrecht, Felix. *Zur Volkskunde: Alte und neue Aufsätze*. Heilbronn: Henninger, 1879.

Liestøl, Knut. *Draumkvæde: A Visionary Poem from the Middle Ages*. Oslo: Aschehoug, 1946.

Loth, Joseph. *Les Mabinogion du "Livre Rouge" de Hergest avec les variantes du "Livre Blanc" de Rhydderch*. 2 vols. Paris: Fontemoing, 1913.

Lüthi, Max. "Diesseits- und Jenseitswelt im Märchen." In *Die Welt im Märchen*, edited by Jürgen Janning and Heino Gehrts, 9–14. Kassel: Roth, 1984.

Luzel, François-Marie. "Cinquième rapport sur une mission en basse Bretagne, ayant pour objet de recueillir les traditions orales des Bretons-Armoricains, contes et récits populaires." *Archives des Missions scientifiques et littéraires*. 3rd series, vol. 1 (1873): 1–49.

————. *Contes inédits*. Edited by Françoise Morvan. 3 vols. Rennes: Presses Universitaires de Rennes, 1994–1996.

————. *Les Légendes chrétiennes de Basse-Bretagne*. 2 vols. Paris: Maisonneuve & Larose, 1881.

Mabillon, Jean, ed. *Vetera analecta, sive collectio veterum aliquot operum atque opusculorum omnis generis . . .* Paris: Montalant, 1723.

MacPhail, Malcolm. "Folklore from the Hebrides." *Folklore* 7, issue 4 (1896): 400–404.

Magnúsdóttir, Ásdís Rósa, and Hélène Tétrel, trans. *La Petite Saga de Tristan et autres sagas islandaises inspirées de la matière de Bretagne*. Brest: Centre de Recherche bretonne et celtique, 2012.

Map, Walter. *De nugis curialium: Courtiers' Trifles*. Edited and translated by

M. R. James; revised by C. N. L Brooke and R. A. B. Mynors. Oxford: Clarendon, 1983.

Martin of Braga. *Martini episcopi Bracarensis opera omnia.* Edited by C. W. Barlow. New Haven, Conn.: Yale University Press, 1950.

Matarasso, Pauline M., trans. *The Quest of the Holy Grail.* London and New York: Penguin, 1969.

Melvin, Perry, and Paul Morse. *Parting Visions: An Exploration of Pre-Death Psychic and Spiritual Experiences.* London: Piatkus, 1995.

Méril, Edelestand du, ed. *Poésies populaires latines antérieures au douzième siècle.* Paris: Brockhaus et Avenarius, 1843.

Meusel, Heinrich, ed. *Pseudo-Callisthenes nach der Leidener Handschrift herausgegeben.* Leipzig: Teubner, 1871.

Meyer, Kuno. "The Vision of St Laisrén." *Otia Merseiana* 1 (1899): 114–19.

———, ed. and trans. *The Voyage of Bran Son of Febal to the Land of the Living.* London: Nutt, 1895.

Meyrac, Albert. *Traditions, Coutumes, Légendes et Contes des Ardennes.* Charleville: Imprimerie du Petit Ardennais, 1890.

[*MGH*] *Monumenta Germaniae Historica.* All volumes online at www.dmgh.de.

Micha, Alexandre, ed. *Lancelot, roman en prose du XIIIe siècle.* 9 vols. Paris and Geneva: Droz, 1978–1983.

Migne, Jacques-Paul, ed. *Patrologia Latina.* 221 vols. Paris: Migne, 1841–1865.

Monseur, Eugène. *Le Folklore wallon.* Brussels: Rozez, 1892.

Montaigne. *Essais.* 2 vols. Lausanne: Rencontre, 1968.

Moody, Raymond A., Jr. *Life After Life: The Investigation of a Phenomenon: Survival of Bodily Death.* Atlanta, Ga.: Mockingird, 1975. French edition: *La Vie après la vie.* Paris: Laffont, 1977. German edition: *Leben nach dem Tod.* Hamburg: Rowohlt, 1977.

Morel, Gall, ed. *Die Offenbarungen der Schwester Mechthilde von Magdeburg oder das fließende Licht der Gottheit.* Regensburg: Manz, 1869.

Mozzani, Éloïse. *Le Livre des superstitions: Mythes, croyances, légendes.* Paris: Laffont, 1995.

Müller, Edward, ed. and trans. "Two Irish Tales: The History of Aillel and Etain." *Revue celtique* 3 (1878): 342–60.

Müller, Georg, and Wilhelm Müller. *Niedersächsische Sagen und Märchen.* Göttingen: 1855.

Müller, Ingeborg, and Lutz Röhrich. "Der Tod und die Toten." *Deutsches Jahrbuch für Volkskunde* 13 (1967): 346–97.

Murray, James A. H., ed. *The Romance and Prophecies of Thomas of Erceldoune: Printed from Five Manuscripts with Illustrations from the Prophetic Literature of the 15th and 16th Centuries.* London: Trübner, 1875.

Musäus, Johann Jacob. "Graf Schwarzenberg." *Jahrbücher des Vereins für Mecklenburgische Geschichte und Altertumskunde* 5 (1840): 80–81.

Nachez, Michel. "Le Double dans les ENOCs." In *Le Corps, son ombre et son double,* edited by Collette Méchin, Isabelle Bianquis-Gasser, and David Le Breton. Paris: Harmattan, 2000.

Negelein, J. von. "Das Pferd im Seelenglauben und Totenkult." *Zeitschrift für Volkskunde* 11 (1901): 406–20.

Nitze, William A., and T. Atkinson Jenkins, eds. *Le Haut Livre du Graal: Perlesvaus.* 2 vols. Chicago: University of Chicago Press, 1932–1937. Reprint, New York: Phaeton Press, 1972.

Obert, Franz. *Le Zmeu dupé et autres contes transylvaniens.* Paris: Corti, 2012.

O'Grady, Standish Hayes, ed. *Toruigheacht Dhiarmuda agus Ghrainne; or, The Pursuit after Diarmuid O'Duibhne, and Grainne the Daughter of Cormac Mac Airt, King of Ireland in the Third Century.* Dublin: O'Daly, 1857.

Origen. *Contra Celsum.* Translated by Frederick Crombie. In *Ante-Nicene Fathers,* vol. 4, ed. Alexander Roberts, James Donaldson, and A. Cleveland Coxe. Buffalo, N.Y.: Christian Literature Publishing, 1885.

Orłowski, Boleslas, ed. *La Damoisele à la mûle (La Mule sanz Frain): Conte en vers du cycle arthurien.* Paris: Champion, 1911.

Osis, Karl, and Erlendur Haraldsson. "Sterbebettbeobachtungen von Ärzten und Krankenschwestern." In *Fortleben nach dem Tode,* edited by Andreas Resch, 425–55. Innsbruck: Resch, 1980.

———. *Der Tod, ein neuer Anfang: Visionen und Erfahrungen an der Schwelle des Seins.* Freiburg: Esotera, 1987.

Otloh von St. Emmeram. *Liber visionum.* Edited by Paul Gerhard Schmidt. Weimar: Böhlau, 1989.

Owen, Elias. *Welsh Folk-Lore: A Collection of the Folk-Tales and Legends of North Wales.* Oswestry and Wrexham: Woodall, Minshall, and Co., 1896.

Palmer, Nigel F. *"Visio Tnugdali": The German and Dutch Translations and Their Circulation in the Later Middle Ages.* Munich and Zurich: Artemis, 1982.

Pálsson, Hermann, and Paul Edwards, trans. *Seven Viking Romances.* London: Penguin, 1985.

Paris, Gaston, and Alphonse Bos, eds. *Trois Versions rimées de l'"Evangile de*

Nicodème" par Chrétien, André de Coutances, et un anonyme. Paris: Didot, 1885.

Passian, Rudolf. *Abschied ohne Wiederkehr: Tod und Jenseits aus parapsychologischer Sicht—Forschung und Erfahrung im Grenzbereich.* Munich: Goldmann, 1989.

Patch, Howard R. *The Other World According to Descriptions in Medieval Literature.* Cambridge, Mass.: Harvard University Press, 1950.

Pedrazzani, Jean-Michel. *Le Dictionnaire des superstitions.* Paris: Contre-Dires, 2011.

Pentikäinen, Juha. *Mythologie des Lapons.* Paris: Imago, 2011.

Perceforest. Edited by Gilles Roussineau. 11 vols. Paris and Geneva: Droz, 1987–2015.

Petzold, Leander. *Märchen, Mythos, Sage: Beiträge zur Literatur und Volksdichtung.* Marburg: Elwert, 1989.

Pinon, E. "Les Prières du soir en Wallonie." In *La Nuit & le Sommeil dans les collections du Musée de la Vie Wallonne,* 47–51. Liège: Musée de la Vie Wallonne, 1987.

Plato. *The Dialogues of Plato.* Translated by Benjamin Jowett. 3rd revised edition. 5 vols. Oxford: Clarendon: 1892.

———. *The Republic.* Translated by Benjamin Jowett. Revised edition. New York and London: Colonial Press, 1901.

Plutarch. *Œuvres complètes de Plutarque, Œuvres morales,* vol. 2. Translated by Victor Bétolaud. Paris: Hachette, 1870.

———. *Moralia.* Translated by Phillip H. De Lacy and Benedict Einarson. 15 vols. Cambridge, Mass.: Loeb Classical Library, 1959.

Polo de Beaulieu, Marie-Anne, ed. *Jean Gobi: Dialogue avec un fantôme.* Paris: Les Belles Lettres, 1994.

———. "Les Entre-mondes dans la littérature exemplaire." In *Les Entre-mondes: Les vivants, les morts,* edited by Karin Ueltschi and Myriam White-Le Goff, 69–86. Paris: Klincksieck, 2009.

Pomel, Fabienne. "Les Entre-mondes de l'âme pérégrine dans 'le Pèlerinage de l'âme' de Guillaume de Digulleville." In *Les Entre-mondes: Les vivants, les morts,* edited by Karin Ueltschi and Myriam White-Le Goff, 39–54. Paris: Klincksieck, 2009.

Prior, O. H., ed. *L'Image du Monde de Maître Gossouin: Rédaction en Prose, Texte du Manuscrit de la Bibliothèque nationale, Fonds Français No. 574.* Lausanne and Paris: Payot, 1913.

Proclus. *Commentaire sur La République*. Translated by A.-J. Festugière. 3 vols. Paris: Vrin, 1970.

———. *The Fragments that Remain of the Lost Writings of Proclus*. Translated by Thomas Taylor. London: Taylor, 1825.

Pschmadt, Carl. *Die Sage von der verfolgten Hinde: Ihre Heimat und Wanderung, Bedeutung und Entwicklung mit besonderer Berücksichtigung ihrer Verwendung in der Literatur des Mittelalters*. Greifswald: Abel, 1911.

Ranke, Kurt. *Indogermanische Totenverehrung*. Vol. 1: *Der dreißigste und vierzigste Tag im Totenkult der Indogermanen*. Helsinki: Suomalainen Tiedeakatemia, 1950.

Raoul von Houdenc. *Sämtliche Werke*. Edited by Mathias Friedwagner. 2 vols. 1897–1909. Reprint, Geneva: Slatkine, 1975.

Rasmussen, Knud. *Contes du Groenland*. Translated by Jacques Privat. Gemenos: Esprit Ouvert, 2000.

Rebillard, Éric. "*Koimetérion* et *Coemeterium:* tombe, tombe sainte, nécropole." *Mélanges de l'École française de Rome* 105/2 (1993): 975–1001.

Reinhard, John R., ed. *Amadas et Ydoine*. Paris: Champion, 1926.

Renaut de Beaujeu. *Le Bel Inconnu, roman d'aventures*. Edited by G. Perrie Williams. Paris: Champion, 1967.

Resch, Andreas, ed. *Fortleben nach dem Tode*. Innsbruck: Resch, 1980.

Rhŷs, John. *Celtic Folklore, Welsh and Manx*. 2 vols. Oxford: Clarendon, 1901.

Rimasson-Fertin, Natacha. *L'Autre Monde et ses figures dans les "Contes de l'enfance et du foyer" des frères Grimm et le "Contes populaires russes" d'A. N. Afanassiev*. PhD dissertation, University of Paris IV & Grenoble II, 2008.

Rio, Bernard. *Voyage dans l'au-delà: Les Bretons et la mort*. Rennes: Ouest-France, 2013.

Rolland, Eugène. *Faune populaire de la France*. 2 vols. Paris: Maisonneuve, 1877–1879.

Röhrich, Lutz. *Erzählungen des späten Mittelaters und ihr Weiterleben in Literatur und Volksdichtung bis zur Gegenwart*, vol. 1. Bern and Munich: Francke, 1962.

Rüegg, August. *Die Jenseitsvorstellungen vor Dante*. Cologne: Benziger, 1945.

Rychner, Jean, and Paul Aebischer. *Le Lai de Lanval*. Paris and Geneva: Droz, 1958.

Saintyves, P. *L'Éternuement et le Baillement dans la magie, l'ethnograhie et la folklore medical*. Paris: Nourry, 1921.

Salvi-Lopez, Maria. *Leggende delle Alpi*. Turin: Lloescher, 1889.

Saxo Grammaticus. *Saxonis Gesta Danorum.* Edited by C. Knabe and Paul Hermann; revised by Jørgen Olrik and Hans H. Ræder. Copenhagen: Levin and Munksgaard, 1931.

———. *The History of the Danes, Books I–IX.* Translated by Peter Fisher; edited by Hilda Ellis Davidson. Woodbridge, U.K.: Boydell and Brewer, 1996.

Sbalchiero, Patrick. *Dictionnaire des miracles et de l'extraordinaire chrétiens.* Paris: Fayard, 2002.

Schäfer, Daniel. *Texte vom Tod: Zur Darstellung und Sinngebung des Todes im Spätmittelalter.* Göppingen: Kümmerle, 1995.

Schambach, Georg, and Wilhelm Müller. *Niedersächsische Sagen und Märchen.* Göttingen: Vandenhoeck and Ruprecht, 1855.

Schattner-Rieser, Ursula. "Les Mandéens ou disciples de Saint Jean." *Mémoires de l'Académie nationale de Metz* (2008): 243–57.

Schmidt, Johann Georg. *Die gestriegelte Rockenphilosophie oder aufrichtige Untersuchung derer von vielent super-klugen Weibern hochgehaltenen Aberglauben.* 2 vols. Chemnitz: Stößeln, 1718–1722.

Schmidt, Paul Gerhardt, ed. *Visio Alberici: Die Jenseitswanderung des neunjährigen Alberich in der vom Visionär um 1127 in Monte Cassino revidierten Fassung.* Stuttgart: Steiner, 1997.

———. *Visio Thurkilli: Relatore, ut Videtur, Radulpho de Coggeshall.* Leipzig: Teubner, 1978.

Schneegans, Frédéric-Édouard. "*Le Mors de la pomme*, texte du XVe siècle." *Romania* 46 (1920): 537–70.

Schott, Arthur, and Albert Schott, eds. *Walachische Märchen.* Stuttgart and Tübingen: Cotta, 1845.

Schüle, Rose-Claire. "Il vaut mieux souffrir du froid maintenant: Le purgatoire dans les glaciers." In *Imaginaires de la Haute Montagne*, edited by Philippe Joutard and Jean-Olivier Majastre, 31–40. Grenoble: Centre alpin et rhodanien d'ethnologie, 1987.

Schullerus, Pauline. *Rumänische Volksmärchen aus dem mittleren Harbachtal.* 1907. New edition edited by Rolf Wilhelm Brednich and Ion Taloş. Hermannstadt: Bucharest: Kriterion, 1977.

Sébillot, Paul. *Le Folk-lore de France.* 4 vols. Paris: Guilmoto, 1904–1907.

———. "Légendes chrétiennes de Haute-Bretagne." *Revue de Bretagne, de Vendée & d'Anjou* 6 (1891): 482–90.

———. *Traditions et Superstitions de la Haute-Bretagne.* 2 vols. Paris: Maisonneuve and Larose, 1882.

Séverin, Tim. *Le Voyage du Brendan*. Paris: Michel, 1978.

Shinoda, Chiwaki. *La Métamorphose des fées: Étude comparative des contes français et japonais autour des contes sur le mariage merveilleux entre humains et non-humains*. Nagoya: Nagoya University, 1994.

Simek, Rudolf. "Elusive Elysia, or Which way to Glæsisvellir? On the Geography of the North in Icelandic Legendary Fiction." In *Sagnaskemmtun: Studies in Honour of Hermann Pálsson*, edited by Hans Bekker-Nielsen and Jónas Kristjánsson. Vienna: Böhlau, 1986.

Siniavski, André. *Ivan le Simple: Paganisme, magie et religion du peuple russe*. Paris: Michel, 1994.

Souché, B. *Croyances, Présages et Superstitions diverses*. Niort: Clouzot, 1880.

Spoerri, Bettina. *Der Tod als Text und Signum: Der literarische Todesdiskurs in geistlich-didaktischen Texten des Mittelalters*. Bern, Berlin, and Frankfurt: Lang, 1999.

Staines, David, trans. *The Complete Romances of Chrétien de Troyes*. Bloomington and Indianapolis: Indiana University Press, 1993.

[Stephen of Bourbon] Stephanus de Borbone. *Anecdotes historiques, légendes et apologues tirés du recueil inédit d'Étienne de Bourbon dominicain du XIIIe siècle*. Edited by Albert Lecoy de la Marche. Paris: Loones, 1877.

———. *Tractatus de diversisis materiis predicabilibus, Prologus, Prima pars: De dono timoris*. Edited by Jacques Berlioz and Jean-Luc Eichenlaub. Turnhout: Brepols, 2002.

———. *Tractatus de diversis materiis predicabilibus, Liber secundus: De dono pietatis*. Edited by Jacques Berlioz, D. Ogilvie-David, and C. Ribaucourt. Turnhout: Brepols, 2015.

———. *Tractatus de diversis materiis predicabilibus, Liber tertius: De eis que pertinent ad donum scientie et penitentiam*. Edited by Jacques Berlioz. Turnhout: Brepols, 2006.

Stöckli, Rainer. *Zeitlos tanzt der Tod: Das Fortleben, Fortschreiben, Fortzeichnen der Totentanztradition im 20. Jahrhundert*. Konstanz: Universitätsverlag, 1996.

Stokes, Whitley. "The Prose Tales of the Rennes Dindshenchas, second supplement: Extracts from the *Book of Leinster*." *Revue Celtique* 19 (1895): 269–312.

Stokes, Whitley, and John Strachan, eds. *Thesaurus Paleohibernicus: A Collection of Old-Irish Glosses, Scholia, Prose, and Verse*, vol. 1. Cambridge: Cambridge University Press, 1901.

Stoneman, Richard. *Legends of Alexander the Great*. London: Tauris, 2012.

Storm, Louise. *The Hind Game: Seen in the Light of European Cervine Tradition*. Bergen: Folkekultur, 1995.

Stumfall, Balthasar. *Das Märchen von Amor und Psyche in seinem Fortleben in der französischen, italienischen und spanischen Literatur bis zum 18. Jahrhundert*. Naumburg: Lippert, 1907.

Sturluson, Snorri. *Edda Snorra Sturlusonar*. Edited by Finnur Jónsson. Copenhagen: Gyldendal, 1931.

———. *Edda*. Translated by Anthony Faulkes. London: Dent, 1995.

Sveinsson, Einar Ólafur, ed. *Brennu Njáls saga*. Reykjavík: Hið íslenzka fornritafélag, 1954.

Sveinsson, Einar Ólafur, and Matthías Þórdarson, eds. *Eyrbyggja saga*. Reykjavík: Hið íslenzka fornritafélag, 1935.

Ténèze, Marie-Louise. "Le Chauffeur du diable: des contextes d'un conte." In *Journées d'études en littérature orale*, edited by Geneviève Calamé-Griaule, 347–76. Paris: C.N.R.S., 1982.

Thiers, Jean-Baptiste. *Traité des superstitions*. 4 vols. Paris: Nully, 1714.

Thomas, Antoine. "Gloses provençales inédites tirées d'un ms. des *Derivationes* d'Ugucio de Pise." *Romania* 134 (1905): 177–205.

Thomasset, Claude Alexandre, ed. *Placides et Timéo ou Li secrés as philosophes*. Paris and Geneva: Droz, 1980.

Thompson, Stith. *Contes des Indiens d'Amérique du Nord*. Translated by Bernard Fillaudeau. Paris: Corti, 2012.

———. *Motif-Index of Folk-Literature: A Classification of Narrative Elements in Folktales, Ballads, Myths, Fables, Medieval Romances, Exempla, Fabliaux, Jest-books, and Local Legends*. Revised and expanded edition. 6 vols. Bloomington: Indiana University Press, 1955–1958.

Tiévant, Claire, and Lucie Desideri. *Almanach de la mémoire et des coutumes: Corse*. Paris: Michel, 1986.

Tolley, Clive. *Shamanism in Norse Myth and Magic*. 2 vols. Helsinki: Suomalainen Tiedeakatemia, 2009.

Tondolus der Ritter. Speyer: Hist, n.d. [ca. 1495].

Toporkov, A. L., ed. *Proishojdenie mifa: Stat'i po folkloru, etnografii i mifologii*. Moscow: Indrik, 1996.

Trescases, Jacques. *La Symbolique de la mort, ou Herméneutique de la resurrection*. Paris: Dervy, 2015.

Tubach, Frederic C. *Index Exemplorum: A Handbook of Medieval Religious Tales.* Helsinki: Suomalainen Tiedeakatemia, 1969.

Tyrrell, G. N. M. *Apparitions.* 2nd edition: New Hyde Park, N.Y.: University, 1953.

Tzetzae, Ioannis. *Historiarum Variarum Chiliades.* Edited by Theophil Kiessling. Leipzig: Vogel, 1826.

Uebel, Michael. *Ecstatic Tranformation: On the Uses of Alterity in the Middle Ages.* Basingstoke: Palgrave Macmillan, 2005.

Ueltschi, Karin. *La Mesnie Hellequin en conte et en rime: Mémoire mythique et poétique de la recomposition.* Paris: Champion 2008.

Ulrich von Zatzickhoven. *Lanzelet.* Edited by K. A. Hahn. Frankfurt: Brönner, 1845.

Unger, C. R., ed. *Heilagra Manna Søgur: Fortællinger og Legender om Hellige Mænd og Kvinder.* 2 vols. Christiania [Oslo]: Bentzen, 1877.

Vaschalde, Henry. *Croyances et Superstitions populaires du midi de la France I: Vivarais.* Montpellier: Coulet, 1876.

[*Vatnsdœla saga*] *The Saga of the People of Vatnsdal.* Translated by Andrew Wawn. In *The Sagas of Icelanders*, 185–269. New York: Viking, 2000.

Vendryès, J., ed. "Aislingthi Adhamnáin." *Revue Celtique* 30 (1909): 356–83.

Vernaleken, Theodor. *Österreichische Kinder- und Hausmärchen.* Vienna: Braumüller, 1864.

Vernette, Jean. *L'Irrationnel est parmi nous. Magie, divination, envoûtements, paranormal.* Paris: Salvator, 2000.

———. "Stigmates." In *Dictionnaire des miracles et de l'extraordinaire chrétiens,* edited by Patrick Sbalchiero. Paris: Fayard, 2002.

Vincent of Beauvais. *Speculum historiale.* Douai: Belleri, 1624.

Virgil. *The Bucolics, Æneid, and Georgics.* Edited by J. B. Greenough. Boston: Ginn, 1883.

The Vishńu-Puráńa: A System of Hindu Mythology and Tradition. Translated by Horace Hayman Wilson; edited by Fitzedward Hall. 5 vols. London: Trübner, 1864–1870.

Voigt, Max, ed. *Beiträge zur Geschichte der Visionenliteratur im Mittelalter I. II.* Leipzig: Mayer & Müller, 1924.

Vries, Jan de. *La Religion des Celtes.* Paris: Payot, 1963.

Wagner, Albrecht. *Visio Tnugdali.* Erlangen: Deichert, 1882.

Wahlund, Carl, ed. *Die altfranzösische Prosaübersetzung von Brendans Meerfahrt nach der Pariser Hdschr. Nat.-Bibl. fr. 1553.* Uppsala: Almqvist & Wiksell, 1900.

Walker, D. P. *The Decline of Hell: Seventeenth-Century Discussion of Eternal Torment.* London: Routledge and Kegan Paul, 1964.

Wallon, Philippe. *Expliquer le paranormal.* Paris: P.U.F., 1999.

Walter, Philippe, ed. *Arthur, Gauvain et Mériadoc, récits arthuriens latins du XIIIe siècle.* Grenoble: ELLUG, 2007.

———. *Le Bel Inconnu de Renaut de Beaujeu: Rite, mythe et roman.* Paris: P.U.F., 1996.

———. *Canicule: Essai de mythologie sur "Yvain" de Chrétien de Troyes.* Paris: Sedes, 1988.

———. "Du chamanisme arthurien? Strates culturelles et réflexes cognitifs." In *Lo Sciamanismo come artefatto culturale e sinopia letteraria,* edited by Alvaro Barbieri, 121–38. Verona: Fiorni, 2017.

———. "Conte, légende et mythe." In *Questions de mythocritique,* edited by Danièle Chauvin, André Siganos, and Philippe Walter, 59–68. Paris: Imago, 2005.

———. *Croyances populaires au Moyen Âge.* Paris: Gisserot, 2017.

———. *Dictionnaire de mythologie arthurienne.* Paris: Imago, 2014.

———. "Les Îles mythiques de l'autre monde dans la navigation de la barque de maelduin, texte irlandais du XIIe siècle." In *Insula: Despre izolare și limite în spațiul imaginar,* edited by Lucian Boia, Anca Oroveanu, and Simona Corlan-Ioan, 41–56. Bucharest: Colegiul noua europă, 1999.

———, ed. and trans. *Les Lais de Marie de France.* Bilingual French edition. Paris: Gallimard, 2000.

———, ed. *Le Livre du Graal.* 3 vols. Paris: Gallimard, 2001–2009.

———. *La Mémoire du temps: Fêtes et calendriers de Chrétien de Troyes à La Mort Artu.* Paris: Champion, 1989.

———. "Mythologies comparées." In *Questions de mythocritique,* edited by Danièle Chauvin, André Siganos, and Phillippe Walter, 261–70. Paris: Imago, 2005.

———. "Yonec, fils de l'ogre: Recherches sur les origines mythiques d'un lai de marie de France." In *Plaist vos oïr bone cançon vallant? Mélanges de langue et de littérature médiévale offerts à François Suard,* vol. 2, ed. Dominique Boutet et al, 993–1000. Lille: Septentrion, 1999.

Waring, Philippa. *Dictionnaire des présages et des superstitions.* Monaco: Le Rocher, 1990.

Weber, Cornelia, ed. *Untersuchung und überlieferungskritische Edition des Herzog Ernst B mit einem Abdruck der Fragmente von Fassung A.* Göppingen: Kümmerle, 1994.

Weber, Edgar. *Petit Dictionnaire de mythologie arabe et des croyances musulmanes.* Paris: Entente, 1996.

Wendling, Fabrice. "Le *De hominis miseria, mundi et inferni contemptu* de Hugues de Miramar, une œuvre 'autobiographique' dans la postérité des *Confessions* d'Augustin?" *Rursus* 6 (2011): 2–16.

Weston, Jessie L. *The Chief Middle English Poets: Selected Poems.* Boston: Houghton Mifflin, 1914.

Wilde, Francesca Speranza. *Ancient Legends, Mystic Charms and Superstitions of Ireland.* Boston: Ticknor, 1888.

Wilhelm-Schaffer, Irmgard. *Gottes Beamter und Spielmann des Teufels. Der Tod in Spätmittelalter und früher Neuzeit.* Cologne, Weimar, and Vienna: Böhlau, 1999.

Wilkerson, Ralph. *Beyond and Back: Those Who Died and Lived to Tell It.* New York: Bantam, 1978.

William of Auvergne. *Opera omnia.* 2 vols. Paris, 1674.

Wilson, John, ed. *Samsons saga fagra.* Copenhagen: Jorgensen, 1953.

Windisch, Ernst. *Irische Texte.* Leipzig: Hirzel, 1880.

Wirnt von Gravenberg. *Wigalois, le chevalier à la roue.* Translated by Claude Lecouteux and Véronique Lévy. Grenoble: ELLUG, 2001.

———. *Wigalois, der Ritter mit dem Rade.* Edited by J. M. N. Kapteyn. Bonn: Klopp, 1926.

Wlislocki, Heinrich von. *La Rose et le musicien: Contes tziganes.* Translated and annotated by Corinne and Claude Lecouteux. Paris: Corti, 2016.

Woledge, Brian, ed. *L'Atre périlleux, roman de la Table Ronde.* Paris: Champion, 1936.

Wuttke, Adolf. *Der deutsche Volksaberglaube der Gegenwart.* 3rd edition revised by Elard Hugo Meyer. Leipzig: Ruhl, 1925.

Yen, Alsace. "Shamanism as Reflected in the Folktale." *Asian Folklore Studies* 39/2 (1980): 105–121.

Zabughin, Vladimiro. "L'Oltretomba classico e medievale dantesco nel rinascimento." *L'Arcadia, Atti dell'Accademia* 4 (1919): 85–253.

Zacher, Julius, ed. *Alexandri Magni iter ad paradisum.* Königsberg: Thiele, 1859.

Zingerle, Ignaz Vinzenz. *Sitten, Bräuche und Meinungen des Tiroler Volkes.* Innsbruck: Wagner, 1871.

Zingerle, Ignaz Vinzenz, and Josef Zingerle. *Kinder- und Hausmärchen aus Süddeutschland.* Regensburg: Pustet, 1854.

———. *Kinder- und Hausmärchen aus Tirol.* Innsbruck: Schwick, 1911.

INDEX